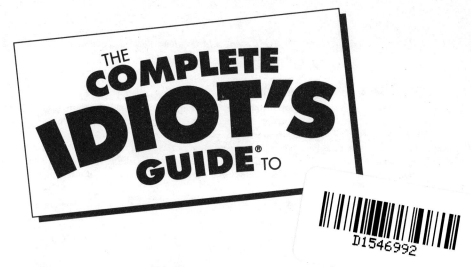

THE COMPLETE IDIOT'S GUIDE® TO

Spells and Spellcraft

by Aurora Greenbough and Cathy Jewell

ALPHA

A member of Penguin Group (USA) Inc.

To all honest seekers everywhere: May you find the door that opens you up to the gift that you are. —Aurora Greenbough

Publisher: *Marie Butler-Knight*
Product Manager: *Phil Kitchel*
Senior Managing Editor: *Jennifer Chisholm*
Senior Acquisitions Editor: *Randy Ladenheim-Gil*
Book Producer: *Lee Ann Chearney/Amaranth Illuminare*
Development Editor: *Lynn Northrup*
Production Editor: *Janette Lynn*
Copy Editor: *Molly Schaller*
Illustrator: *Chris Eliopoulos*
Cover/Book Designer: *Trina Wurst*
Indexer: *Angie Bess*
Layout/Proofreading: *Ayanna Lacey, Donna Martin*

Contents at a Glance

Contents

Foreword

In the tradition I come from, the Dagara people of West Africa, ritual is the lifeblood of every human being, something that no one can live without. I find Wiccan spell-craft to be a similar way of relating to the world as if all of life is sacred and alive, where ritual is a language for interacting with the universe and the divine.

From time immemorial, human beings have sought to understand their world, to give meaning to their life, to make sense of the universe. They have explored the created philosophies and doctrines, used science or religion to prove the presence or lack thereof of higher forces. And still, when it comes to our everyday life—our luck, health, love life, profession, and future—we crave for ways to make them better, holy, and attuned to the divine.

People from all over have traveled the world to find prayers, rituals, and masters from among the world's cultures and traditions to light their way and unveil the mystery of their life. These people are never satisfied with the way life is, with the status quo, they want more: Their curiosity, stubbornness, and general dissatisfaction drag them out to seek truth and wisdom. Such people, perhaps *you* among them, are often the catalysts, enriching their own people and culture by seeding new ideas and insights. They deepen the roots of their own tribal tree, allowing it to bear more and tastier fruit.

In reading this book, this is how I have felt about these two authors—full of excite-ment, determination, and thirsty for wisdom. Actually, I have known Aurora for some years now, and know her to be a deeply rooted, extraordinary woman. I have no doubt that her co-author, Cathy, is also endowed with great wisdom, for I see that together they are digging their cultural roots to find meaning and rituals through spellcrafting in the Wiccan tradition to nourish the soul of the world. Their two wisdoms converge to create a way of life that allows one to dance in unity.

I see hope in this book. I have found in this book a respectful attitude toward other people, spirit, nature, and oneself—a refreshing change from the attitudes and values so common in the popular culture of the West. This book is not about abuse of power; it's not about how you can control others or take revenge on people you are dissatisfied with. This book is a chalice of wisdom on the positive power of spellcraft, a wealth of valuable insights and customs to savor.

My prayer is that by the time you finish reading this book, you, too, will have a better sense of spellcrafting and the Wiccan tradition, and you can begin to use ritual to cre-ate balance and harmony in your life.

—Sobonfu Somé

Sacramento, CA

Recognized by the village elders as possessing special gifts from birth, Sobonfu's destiny was foretold before her birth, as is the custom of the Dagara Tribe of Burkina Faso and was fostered by early education in ritual and initiation in preparation for her life's work. One of the first and most widely respected voices of African spirituality to come to the West, Sobonfu tours the United States and Europe often, offering training programs, lectures, and workshops on spirituality, ritual, the sacred, and intimacy. Sobonfu is the author of three books: *The Spirit of Intimacy: Ancient African Teachings in the Ways of Relationships; Welcoming Spirit Home;* and *Falling Out of Grace: Meditations on Loss, Healing, and Wisdom.* Sobonfu's message about the importance of spirit and ritual in our lives rings with an intuitive power and truth that Alice Walker, author of *The Color Purple*, writes "can help us put together so many things that our modern Western World has broken." Sobonfu's writing has also appeared in a number of anthologies. She is the founder of Ancestors Wisdom Spring, an organization dedicated to the preservation and sharing of indigenous wisdom, and is involved with Wisdom Spring, Inc., a nonprofit whose ongoing project is to provide water to the villages of West Africa. For more information about her work, visit: www.sobonfu.com or write to:

Ancestors Wisdom Spring,
5960 South Land Park Drive #200
Sacramento, California 95822
Sobonfu@sobonfu.com
Walkingforwater.org

Introduction

You may have thought of magick in the abstract, but we're here to make it real, and to show you how magick and spellcasting can become part of your everyday life. And once it does, magick will *change* your life. You'll feel your own power and your connection with the creative energy of the universe.

Sounds like a bit much, we're sure, but it's true. Once you've committed to the study of spellcraft, and you've begun working spells yourself, you'll find that it's easier to see how everything is interconnected, and how the energy of the world can be seen and felt everywhere.

If this sounds like where you want your life to go, then get ready to see the magick in your life. We have certainly found spellwork to be life-changing, each in our own way. Once you open yourself to the magickal flow of energy that works for spellcraft, you will begin to see that flow manifest in many amazing ways in your life. You might just find out exactly where you need to be!

Aurora is a practicing Wiccan with 18 years of experience with spellcraft, while Cathy is not Wiccan—she's drawn to spellwork for its natural power and simplicity. Our experiences illustrate the range—there is a magickal path for you, too, and we're ready to help you find it.

How to Use This Book

Please don't expect to read a few chapters of this book and start working fabulous, powerful spells—read the whole book, and think about what it means to work magick. Then use this book as a resource to guide you in your spellwork and on your magickal path. As we'll say often, it's all about intent: If you have good intentions for learning about and working spells, you're ready to get started.

The five parts of the book are as follows:

Part 1, "Spellcasting Basics," introduces you to spellcasting and Wicca, and will show you how to craft a spell and work magick, from raising a magick circle to writing and timing spells to keeping a Book of Shadows.

Part 2, "Spells for Ritual," will show you how to prepare for working magick, discussing the tools you will need, and how to prepare your altar and dedicate yourself to magick. You'll also learn about celebrating Esbats and Sabbats.

Part 3, "Spells Manifesting Magickal Correspondences," is filled with information on the magickal correspondences of colors, incense, stones, herbs, oils, astrology, and magickal alphabets. Spells using such correspondences are also included.

Part 4, "Practical Magick," is filled with spells! Spells for love, romance, prosperity, success, and health are included, along with tips for working them.

Part 5, "For All Occasions," includes useful information and spells for blessings and ritual baths, as well as a final chapter on ways to break spells and bind negative energy.

At the end of this book, you'll find a glossary of terms and a useful resource list, as well as a simple pattern for making a poppet.

Extras

To highlight certain information, we've included the following boxed tips, anecdotes, definitions, and cautions throughout the book:

Making Magick

These boxes contain anecdotes from our magickal lives.

Spellcasting

These are helpful tips for working magick.

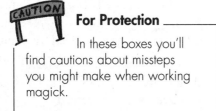

For Protection

In these boxes you'll find cautions about missteps you might make when working magick.

Words of Power

Here we include useful terms and their definitions, which you'll also find cross-listed in the glossary.

Acknowledgments

From Aurora:

Thanks to Dennis for telling me to "go for it!" and to Kim and Matt for always being there for me. My deepest gratitude to Liguana for always answering my crazy phone calls, even when she had to balance halfway out of her car to do so. Also, thanks to Sobonfu for always challenging me to move out of my comfort zone! To my three muses: Jade, Kirian, and Kat—your elders learn as much from you as you do from them! And, of course, to my family, for putting up with me while I took on this project.

From Cathy:

Thanks to Aurora and to Liguana for all of their magickal help, and to Lee Ann Chearney at Amaranth Illuminare, whose vision and energy kept us all going. Most of all, I'm indebted to my family, who gave me the space to write this book, and told me I *could*. Through them I truly see the power of the universe at work.

A Special Thanks to Our Spell Consultant

To help ensure a variety and liveliness in our presentation of spells and spellcraft, we enlisted the vivacious and fun-loving energy of Miria Liguana, who contributed to Part 4 of this book with her extensive knowledge of spellcraft, her deep practice of Wicca, and her grimoire of terrific and creative spells. For more from Liguana, look for *The Complete Idiot's Guide to Wicca Craft* (Alpha Books, 2004) by Miria Liguana and Nina Metzner, which weaves a web of wonderful Wicca projects to enhance your practice of the craft. Liguana practices and teaches Wicca in the Pacific Northwest. Thanks also to writer Katherine Gleason, co-author with Denise Zimmermann of the best-selling *The Complete Idiot's Guide to Wicca and Witchcraft, Second Edition* (Alpha Books, 2003) for her invaluable contributions to the spells in Part 4 of this book.

A Very Special Thanks to Alpha Books

We also want to take the time to thank Alpha Books for its excellence and commitment to publishing New Age and esoteric titles for its *Complete Idiot's Guide* series. The vision of publisher Marie Butler-Knight and senior acquisitions editor Randy Ladenheim-Gil penetrates with a light of warm encouragement for readers seeking self-awareness and personal empowerment. This positive energy helps to raise the vibration of magickal energy for us all!

Trademarks

All terms mentioned in this book that are known to be or are suspected of being trademarks or service marks have been appropriately capitalized. Alpha Books and Penguin Group (USA) Inc. cannot attest to the accuracy of this information. Use of a term in this book should not be regarded as affecting the validity of any trademark or service.

Part 1

Spellcasting Basics

Wicca is a nature-based religion practiced by Wiccans. You can learn about spellcraft and cast spells without being a *witch* or a *Wiccan*. Wiccans follow the Wiccan Rede: *"An it harm none, do what ye will."* We'll follow this tenet as we learn about creating a sacred space in which to work magick, and about the ethics and basics of spellcasting. We'll also talk about the timing of magick, and the importance of creating a Book of Shadows to record your magickal life.

Chapter 1

"An It Harm None"

In This Chapter

- The Wiccan Rede
- What is spellcraft?
- Wicca and spellcasting
- Wicca: Is it Goddess worship?
- Covens and solitaires
- Everyone has the potential to do magick

Who hasn't heard the saying "under a spell?" For Wiccans, doing spells—whether you call it spellcasting, spellworking, or spellcrafting—is a way harnessing and directing natural energy. Perhaps you're eager to find out how doing spells is connected to observing Wiccan ritual. Or maybe you're looking for some new ideas to personalize and inspire your spell-working. Whatever your reason for coming to this book, we hope it will give you what you need—to protect, inspire, and nurture you on the spiritual path.

And so here's a spell from Aurora, put to work for you, dear readers:

> *When in these pages you do look*
>
> *May your path become clear as a book.*
>
> *May inspiration flow through your being*
>
> *Seeing is believing and believing is seeing.*

Now, let's start on the pathworking journey of spells and spellcraft by taking a look at Wicca's most fundamental spellworking principle. Without it, no spell you cast works true to the sacred practice of Wicca.

"An It Harm None, Do What Ye Will"

"An it harm none, do what ye will ...." This is known as the Wiccan Rede, and it governs the ethics of Wicca and spellworking. The Wiccan Rede is the most basic tenet of Wicca. As you learn in this book what spells are and how to work with them, you will find yourself returning to the Wiccan Rede as the underlying principle of the Wiccan religion, and the foundation of all spellcraft. When you explore the meaning and application of the Wiccan Rede, you come to understand the shared ethics of the Wiccan community and responsibility inherent in using spells as a part of your practice of the Wiccan craft.

Witches believe that everything in the universe (seen and unseen) is connected by a complex web of energy. So everything you do affects the universe in a very real way. This means that we are all powerful beyond our wildest imaginings. It also means we all have a responsibility to take great care when we set about to change things.

"An it harm none, do what ye will" doesn't mean do whatever you like, it means you can do what you will, provided no one is harmed in the process—including yourself. Come to think of it, this is a good guideline for life, not just spellcasting, isn't it? The Wiccan Rede is the one rule that practitioners of Wicca generally agree on and try to live by.

Wicca and Witchcraft

Wicca and *witchcraft* are often used interchangeably, but this can be confusing. It is relatively safe to say that all Wiccans are witches, but not all witches are Wiccans. Wicca is a religion practiced by Wiccans. Wiccans usually identify themselves as witches, although a few may not. Wicca refers to a modern, Western form of worship based on nature and our human connection with it. Wiccans like to think they are reconnecting with ancient European indigenous religions (although most Wiccans will add elements from their personal cultural heritage, or those that call to them, such as African, Hindu, or Egyptian) that worship goddesses (and gods) and saw everyone as empowered to make connections with deities. Most Wiccans do include *magick* as part of their practice. Witchcraft refers to anyone working with energy, magick, healing, and ritual in any culture or religion around the world, and as such it is not necessarily Wiccan. Witchcraft, then, has a broader application and is a more generic term, while Wicca refers to the practice of a specific Western, nature-based religion.

Words of Power

Wicca is a Western, nature-based spiritual practice. This differs from **witchcraft**, which includes a variety of practitioners from any culture. **Magick** (note the *k* at the end—Wiccans spell it this way to distinguish it from the stage magic performed by people like David Copperfield) is the word for the Wiccan practice in which the power of nature is harnessed toward a particular goal.

When you hear the word *witch*, some stereotypical images may come to mind: You may think of the Halloween witch, with her broom and her pointed black hat, or perhaps Samantha Stevens, the character played by Elizabeth Montgomery in the TV series *Bewitched*. Maybe you think of the Salem, Massachusetts, witch trials of the seventeenth century. These trials were examined as a metaphor for persecution and prejudice by Arthur Miller in his 1953 play *The Crucible*, which you may have studied in high school. During the trials, a number of people (mostly women) were accused of practicing witchcraft (actually, of bewitching a number of young girls and women). Those who were tried and convicted were hanged. The "witch hunt" spread to other towns in Massachusetts, where a number of innocent people were similarly persecuted.

This last image may be the most realistic: Witches don't look a particular way, and there's a great deal of prejudice against them in society, perhaps because of the misapprehensions that surround the practice of witchcraft. Because modern witches look like everyone else, chances are you know one or two, even if you don't *know* you do. While Wiccans practice magick, they don't worship Satan; they don't even believe in Satan. Some people (Wiccans included) may be (mis)guided by personal or selfish interests, and base their actions on this, but Wiccans don't believe an evil force causes people to behave in such ways. We'll talk more about Wicca a little later in this chapter.

Why Do Spellwork?

Spellcasting is often misunderstood as simply an attempt to change things to suit our needs, which brings up serious ethical questions, such as—who are we, spellworkers, to mess around with such things, and who says we know best? These are legitimate concerns, and part of why we, when we cast spells, have to be very, very careful with spellcraft. Most witches use spellcraft to change themselves, not to alter those around them. Spellcraft can be used to give one more self-confidence, or strength in facing a difficult situation, as well as being a meditative method to bring harmony to your family, your work environment, or other relationships. Spellcraft can be a tool to help you deal with your everyday life, and is a valuable way to help you understand and own your power as a person. Wiccans believe in the Wiccan Rede, and will not promote spellcraft that might be of harm to others. Wiccans do not practice magick with a desire for negative (or even controlling) effects—only positive ones. If you're looking for revenge, you're on the wrong path—and reading the wrong book!

What Is Spellcraft?

Spellcraft is a form of magick practiced by Wiccans. Casting a spell is a way of creating or focusing natural energy toward a particular goal. Spells are at the center of many Wiccan rituals. A spell is like a prayer, but when casting a spell, you may call on a variety of forces—gods, goddesses, Elementals, stones, herbs, helper spirits—to help achieve your goal. In casting a spell, you will use the interconnection of all things (the All) to harness natural power directed to affect a particular outcome. In addition to spellcasting, there are many other types of magick, which use colors, crystals and gems, binding, and poppets. You might use some combination of these and other forms of magick, as well as various tools, in casting a spell. All of these elements together make up a sort of energy package, or recipe, that is your spell.

> **Making Magick**
>
> As you clean your house, you may be thinking about how calming it will be, having the floor clean, things put away, etc. While cleaning, you are creating a spell for harmony in your home.

Types of Spells

There are spells for just about every imaginable purpose, and spells that use all sorts of magickal correspondences. You can create sympathetic spells: leaping high in the fields to show the crops how high to grow, having sex in the garden to bless it with fertility, ritually sprinkling your plants with water to call in needed rain, or drawing an animal being hunted successfully by the tribe that you want to call to your area. You can create spells for particular rituals: for a dedication, or of practical magick (for abundance or well-being, perhaps). And you can create spells of divination; Aurora likes to cast a sacred circle, calling in the balancing influences of all the Elements, and ask for the guidance of ancestors and spirits of place. The spell sets up the atmosphere in which you can tune in to what the divination is trying to tell you.

You might use an amulet or incense or a poppet to create your spell, and you might also look to astrology or the runes for your spell. There are limitless possible combinations; later in this book we'll show you some of the tools of spellcasting as well as how to combine them and make them work for you.

Successful Spells

When crafting your own spells, and especially to create successful spells, you must first have your intention firmly in mind. What is it you want to accomplish? Think about what you want the spell to do, and what you do not want it to do. Consider how the outcome will affect you and others—remember that everything is connected through the web of life. Notice how thinking about carrying out the spell makes you feel. This is the best way to tune in to whether or not you are acting in accordance with spirit. Does casting the spell make you feel powerful (like you will have power *over* others)? Devious? A little naughty? Then look out! You may be doing the spell for the wrong reason. Or does casting the spell make you feel calm, with inner strength? If you are unsure, it is probably best to check with someone you trust, someone in the magickal community, or perhaps just someone whose ethics you hold in high esteem. You might also use divination (such as doing a Tarot card reading) to see if a spell is the correct course of action. And when others are involved—perhaps you want to create a healing spell for a sick friend—always ask permission before casting a spell. Try not to proceed with any act of magick until you're sure you're following the Wiccan Rede, and you aren't acting only in your own self-interest.

> **CAUTION**
>
> **For Protection**
>
> When considering whether to do a spell, be sure to plan it out—consider all your options before you turn to magick. Also be sure you are following the Wiccan Rede, and that you aren't acting with purely selfish motivation before you proceed.

We'll get more specific about spellcrafting in Chapter 3, and you'll learn how to craft spells for specific purposes in Parts 2 through 5 of this book. For now, we want you to understand what a spell is, and how it fits into the Wiccan practice.

Wicca and Spellcasting

How much do you *really* need to know about Wicca to cast spells? Will the spells really *work* if you aren't a practicing Wiccan? These are good questions. Let's learn more about Wicca and how it relates to doing spells and spellcraft. We'll start on the path for answers by taking a closer look at Wicca.

The Natural Religion

Wicca is a modern spiritual practice based on ancient pagan religions. You may already know a lot about Wicca from reading *The Complete Idiot's Guide to Wicca and Witchcraft, Second Edition* (see Appendix B) or similar books; you might even be a longtime practitioner. If so, this will be familiar information for you, a refresher. If you're new to the topic, a little background might be helpful. First, let's dispel some myths: Wiccans don't perform human or animal sacrifices, and the pentagram—a five-pointed star—is not a satanic symbol. Wiccans do not proselytize, and they generally believe that each person is the best judge of their own path. Wiccans don't have anything personal against Christianity or other religions—they generally share the morals of other faiths. Wiccans don't believe in one true faith, though, nor do they believe in hell. They prefer to live in the now and believe in the universal law of karma, through which we learn from our past, and try not to repeat past mistakes, because our every action determines our future path. Wicca looks back to pre-Christian religions for inspiration. It's a nature-based, Earth-centered spirituality.

Gerald Gardner and Modern Wicca

Though its roots are pre-Christian, what we know as modern Wicca is a recent phenomenon, and only came to public awareness in the 1950s. Gerald Gardner and his high priestess, Doreen Valiente, are considered by many to be the founders of modern Wicca; so while Gardner didn't invent this religion on his own, he certainly popularized it and contributed greatly to putting Wicca in a contemporary context for modern practitioners. Gardner published *High Magic's Aid* as a novel in 1949 under the pseudonym Scire, because the witchcraft laws of England hadn't been repealed at that time. After their repeal in 1951, Gardner published *Witchcraft Today* (1954), in which he established himself as a witch, and claimed the flourishing state of Wicca in the United Kingdom. British anthropologist Margaret A. Murray, who believed witchcraft to be a remnant of pre-Christian pagan religions, wrote the introduction to *Witchcraft Today*. It's not difficult to see where much of Gardner's material came from. Gardner lived and traveled in the Far East as a British civil servant for a number of years, and was a member of many organizations, including the Freemasons, the

Rosicrucians, the Folk-Lore Society, and the Order of Woodcraft Chivalry. He was also a great admirer of Aleister Crowley. Gardner's final book was *The Meaning of Witchcraft*, published in 1959.

Though Gardner's writings are very important to Wicca, and his followers practice what is called Gardnerian Wicca, these writings are not the "bible" of the religion, for in fact, there isn't one. Wicca, like nature, is an ever-evolving practice, and it's different for everyone who practices it. If the personal experience of practicing Wicca is different for everyone, how will you know if *your* practice and your approach to spell-casting are in harmony with the tenets of the Wiccan religion? Read on!

Is Wicca Goddess Worship?

In Wicca, the All, the original source of the universe, is a female spirit (Goddess); she created the male spirit (God). Wicca is practiced in homage to the All, honoring deity as represented through goddesses and gods. Many Wiccans sum up the unknowable (deity) as a single, dualistic pair, Goddess and God, Lord and Lady. Though they have much in common, Wicca is not simply Goddess worship. To begin with, Wicca generally doesn't just consult the Goddess, or Lady, but also the God, or Lord. Dianic Wicca, discussed later in this chapter, is more specifically tied to Goddess worship. The concept of deity, the All, is divided into female and male spirituality (the Lady and Lord), but these are simply two complementary parts of the All. Many Wiccans choose to relate personally to the Lady, which is the more creative and inclusive side of the All.

If you practice Wicca, you might choose a particular goddess and create an altar to her (the Venus of Willendorf, prehistoric symbol of the Great Mother Goddess, is a popular choice; as is Athena, Greek Goddess of wisdom), or you might want to keep her in the abstract. The Lady is often thought of as having three aspects: Maiden, Mother, and Crone. These aspects represent the different stages in a woman's life, aspects or personas that we all have within us, which manifest or we can call on at different times.

The Lord represents a more active and playful side of the All. As with the Lady, you can choose to pay homage to the Lord in the abstract, or you can choose a particular god to represent him—perhaps Cernunnos, the Celtic Stag God; or Pan, the Greek woodland God. Even if you choose to relate to the All through the Lady, you

> **Spellcasting**
>
> For some background on goddess worship, you might want to read *The Witches' Goddess: The Feminine Principle of Divinity* by Janet and Stewart Farrar (see Appendix B for details).

might turn to the Lord when you have need for action or protection. The Lord's three life phases are Nature's Royal Prince, King, and Elder.

However you choose to see them, the Lady and the Lord represent the All, the power of nature inherent in everything, animate and inanimate. Today's Wiccans are deeply concerned about the environment and the future of the earth—views that have become popular among many groups in recent decades.

Popular Witchcraft: Covens and Solitaires

If you're like us, you love *Buffy the Vampire Slayer*'s resident witch, Willow, but you may also wonder what she has to do with witchcraft and Wicca. She doesn't belong to a *coven*, does she? And what about those witches on *Charmed?* Are they a coven of three? Practicing witches can be part of a coven or they can be solitary—or they can be somewhere in between, creating their own more eclectic path. (The term *eclectic* is used to describe a modern, personally defined approach to the practice of Wicca.) A coven is usually led by a high priestess, referred to as "first among equals." This means that everyone who is a witch is a priest or priestess; there is no gulf between priesthood and laity. But the high priestess, and sometimes high priest, organize, coordinate, and lead the group. A coven has its leaders and follows its chosen tradition, but doesn't report to a higher organization within Wicca. The coven structure came out of the need for secrecy, and today many witches no longer feel the need to hide their practice.

Words of Power

A **coven** is a group of witches who choose to practice their religion together, while a **solitaire** is a witch who practices alone.

Aurora has been in covens and does some workings *solitary*, but prefers to have a community of friends to work with, who don't necessarily organize themselves into a formalized coven. They network at pagan gatherings, Sabbat rituals, classes, metaphysical bookstores, food co-ops—everywhere. When one of them feels the need for a ritual or wants to schedule one to celebrate an event, they know a lot of witches (and pagans) they can call on to participate. This kind of practice doesn't provide the committed, cohesive feeling of a coven, but it certainly requires less maintenance. Covens can be a lot like families. They are great to have for support, but also can be a lot of work. If your family already provides the support you need, maybe you don't need another one. This is a very personal choice.

A solitary witch, or solitaire, can create her own form of Wicca, pulling from any number of traditions. Though some traditions indicate that one must be initiated by a coven to be a witch, others are fine with self-initiation, believing it to be an individual choice to dedicate oneself to the Goddess's work. Many of us learn on our own and practice Wicca on our own as well. This book is one of many out there that can help you in this quest. While you might find that you'd like the companionship and support afforded by other people, you might also find the structure and tradition of a coven stifling or confining. Aurora was initiated by a Gardnerian coven, but she currently finds it simpler to work with other like-minded witches when the need arises, without the formal structure of a coven. If you feel called to work with other witches, ask around at your local metaphysical bookstore for classes or groups that have rituals that are open to the public. Most places have Sabbat rituals that are open to the public, and this is a good time to network.

Solitary witches are more free to create their own traditions, though, of course, as a solitaire, you have only yourself (and the resources you find) to rely upon, and you have to go looking for other witches—you can find them at festivals, and even through many online sources these days. Solitaires sometimes feel prejudice from coven witches, who believe their initiation and heritage is a necessary part of becoming a witch. Of course, you may choose to be a solitaire, or you may become one out of necessity—perhaps you can't find a coven in your geographical area. Whatever your situation, remember that there are pros and cons to all forms of practice, and you have to both work within your situation and do what feels right for you.

Spellcasting

Before deciding to join a coven, be sure to check out a few, sit in on a few meetings, attend a ritual (or several, if possible), and get some background on the coven's tradition. Be particularly attentive to the power dynamics between the people involved. Do the leader or leaders insist on being addressed in a formal manner, or does the group have an egalitarian feel? Do all coveners take turns leading and planning? Is the power structure clearly laid out, and how do you feel about it? Once you've done the research, you can make an informed choice about your Wicca family.

The Different Traditions of Wicca

If you practice spellcraft, are you a witch? Ah, if only it were as simple as that. The answer is no; in fact, you can learn about spellcraft and cast spells without being a witch or a Wiccan. Wicca is a spiritual practice and a lifestyle; it's not just about casting spells. You may choose to study Wicca, and we'll keep referencing it in this book, because it's the basis for the spellcasting we'll study and perform here.

When Wicca first came to public attention, there were few books on the subject, and you had to know someone to learn about Wicca. These days, your local library or bookstore—perhaps there's even a metaphysical bookstore in your town—will likely have an entire section of books on Wicca, and you can learn about and follow your own solitary spiritual practice without being initiated into a coven. You may find classes on Wicca at a local college, and can also get information at festivals and on the Internet. (Be sure to check out Appendix B for some resources we recommend.)

This easy accessibility strays from the traditional Gardnerian practice of Wicca, which is fairly hierarchical, and utilizes Ceremonial Magick—you have to go through certain training and rituals before you become initiated into the coven, and then there are three degrees of initiation.

Other traditions include the Dianic tradition, which evolved from the feminist move-ment of the 1970s and could be called a more feminist version of the practice. As such, it is mainly a for-women-only tradition and is much more a Goddess-centered worship than other Wiccan traditions.

The Reclaiming tradition was popularized by Starhawk, whose book *The Spiral Dance* (see Appendix B) introduced thousands of people to Wicca. Reclaiming emphasizes egalitarian control, environmental and feminist values, and political awareness. Georgian Wicca was founded by George Patterson in California, in 1970; Seax-Wica was founded by Gardner protégé Ray-mond Buckland in 1973; and Celtic Wicca follows Celtic and Druid traditions. There are numerous other witchcraft traditions; see Appendix B for more information.

> **Spellcasting**
>
> The Reclaiming tradition high-lights the difference between *power over* and *power with*. Wanting to exercise power *over* someone else would not be ethical spellwork (or magick or anything). We can all be empowered by understanding power *with*: In groups we can share leadership roles, use con-sensus decision-making, take turns, and acknowledge that we are all powerful.

Where does Aurora place her practice of Wicca among these traditions? Like most who practice modern Wicca, Aurora has her own eclectic form of spiritual practice. There are Wiccans of all colors and stripes practicing today—Wiccans are everywhere!—and you can add *your* particular style of practice to the mix.

Spellcasting Is Only One Kind of Magick

Spellcasting is just one aspect of manifesting Wiccan magick—one that it's best not to jump into without a little forethought. Not all Wiccans practice magick (although most do), and they may not choose spellcasting as a form of magick they practice.

Everyone has the potential to do magick and many people do so without even realizing it: singing a repetitive song that raises energy, improves the moods of children, or focuses your mind on the task at hand; all gardening is magick, as are cooking, child-birth, childrearing, sex, and small connections with other humans. Spellcasting is a particular form of magick, and it will take some preparation and practice, but with these, you can learn to cast spells for yourself.

If you're looking for superpowers, power over others, or would like to be able to turn your cheating spouse into a toad, you're looking in the wrong place. Wicca is power-ful, but there's nothing unnatural about it—Wiccans learn to harness their own power and the power inherent in nature toward positive ends. One of the ways they do this is through casting spells. Some people are quite frightened by the power of nature, and some believe spellcasting is inherently wrong, but we think Wicca can help you understand and strengthen the power you already possess within yourself. So, as we begin, focus your meditation on the Wiccan Rede, *"An it harm none, do what ye will …."* Remember, this basic Wiccan principle lies at the heart of all spellcraft. If you take it to heart and make it a part of your life, you are well launched on the Wiccan path and ready to explore the positive energy of doing spells and spellcraft.

The Least You Need to Know

◆ Practice spellcraft following the Wiccan Rede: *"An it harm none, do what ye will."*

◆ Wicca is a modern nature-based religion inspired by ancient wisdom.

◆ Spellcraft is a method of creating or focusing natural energy toward a particular goal.

◆ Don't cast first and think later—be aware of your intentions, follow the Wiccan Rede, use ethical judgment, and, if necessary, get a second opinion.

◆ Learn about coven and solitary witches before you decide which (if either) is right for you.

◆ You can practice spellcraft without becoming a witch.

Raising Magickal Energy for Spellcrafting: Creating Sacred Space

In This Chapter

- ◆ Grounding yourself before raising magickal energy
- ◆ How to cleanse and consecrate your sacred space
- ◆ Raising and lowering a magick circle
- ◆ Aiming your cone of power
- ◆ Connect to your natural power

Magickal energy, the fuel that powers the work of spellcrafting, waits within each of us. Instead of fearing it, embrace the energy or power you have. You control it. And once you learn how to reach within to use your power, you will have *better* control over it, and you'll come to rely on it, not just for magick, but for everything you do. Because magickal energy comes from *within you*, you'll have better access to it if you're well and take care of yourself—your body, mind, *and* spirit. You will also be better able to raise your magickal energy more successfully if you practice doing so.

In this chapter, you'll learn how to raise magickal energy by preparing not only your self, but also your environment—by grounding yourself and then cleansing and con-secrating the space you choose to make sacred for magick. Sometimes you will want to raise a formal magick circle for this purpose, and we'll show you how. The magick circle is a sacred space you create in which you can feel safe when working magick, a protected place. Nothing uninvited can enter, and the energy you raise will be kept inside the circle until you release it. But before putting up a magick circle (if indeed you *really* need one!), let's start at the beginning: grounding.

Grounding Yourself for Raising Magickal Energy

The first step in preparation for working magick is to be completely clear on your intention (say it out loud or write it down if you need to); make sure you have every-thing you are going to need, and then *ground* yourself. Grounding can be done in any way that works for you. Many witches use a tree visualization, seeing the earth energy flowing up your roots and your own energy flowing freely down to the earth; you might visualize a harpoon going down into the earth from your center, anchoring you to the earth; you can imagine your chakras (the centers of energy in your body) all aligned and a shaft of clear white light going through you up to the universe and down to the earth. There are many ways to ground, and whatever method you choose, always make sure you do this first.

Energy flows through the body's chakra centers. Each chakra is associated with the energy of a planet, color, and musical tone, among other correspondences.

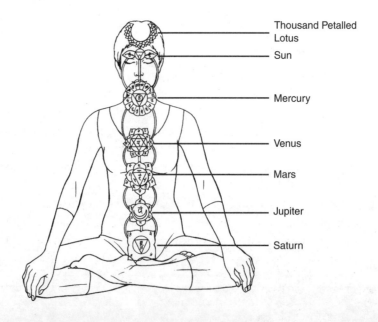

Thousand Petalled Lotus

Sun

Mercury

Venus

Mars

Jupiter

Saturn

Does the Energy Feel Right?

The energies you draw on when working magick are very real powers and you need to remember this when making preparations for doing magick by casting spells. Remember to check in with your stomach and your heart: Make sure your intent feels pure and that you are not only clear on your intention, but ready to state it clearly, out loud, to the spirit world.

Be aware of the natural power of magick, and be respectful of that power. Don't enter into spellcasting lightly, and be very aware of your own motives and mindset when preparing to work magick. If you're overly tired, sick, in a hurry, or just in a bad mood, this may not be the right time to proceed. Check in with yourself: Does this spellworking need to be done now? If the working is time-sensitive—perhaps a spell to heal the very situation that is making you sick— then you may have to proceed (more on this in Chapter 18). But if you can, work your magick when you are prepared and have the time, energy, and focus for the work ahead.

Words of Power

Grounding is the vital process of connecting your energy with the earth's energy. This enables your mind, body, and spirit to raise magickal energy. When you are grounded you are relaxed and calm; energy can flow freely and fully through you from the source of the All and into the earth without hurting you, to be used for the specific purpose of your spell.

For Protection

Don't do magick when your mind isn't clear and focused on the task at hand. Do what you need to do to get yourself focused and clear, perhaps a ritual bath first, or a grounding meditation, or a ritual cleansing with smudge. The power for magick comes from within you, and your energy will be sent out into the world. Don't send unfocused energy and don't attempt to harness your energy when you're tired or sick or not in a good frame of mind. Things likely won't turn out as you plan.

Magick Circle or No Magick Circle?

Once you are grounded and connected to your magickal power, you'll need to decide whether you want the formal protection of a magick circle or whether you feel comfortable doing your spell without casting a circle. If you feel the need to contain the magickal energy you raise with your spell until you are ready to send it off—this is a cone of power, which we'll talk about later in this chapter—or create some protection for yourself while working, then you will probably want to cast a formal magick circle. Aurora pretty much always casts a circle if she's working with other people or calling up any serious magick, but she doesn't always feel the need to cast a formal magick circle for doing simple spells. If she's leaving the house on a road trip, she might go to her altar for a safe-travel spell, calling on the four directions for their blessings and doing a quick spell without pulling up a formal circle.

Making Magick

Sometimes casting the magick circle is the spell in itself. Once, when Aurora had just received a phone call (from someone she didn't know personally, asking for specific spellcraft advice), she felt the need for additional protection for her home and family, so she walked around the house three times: once with incense, once sprinkling saltwater, and once with her athame (a special knife used to direct magickal energy; read more about it in Chapter 5), all the while asking for protection and strengthening the circle around her. After this she went inside, feeling that her "fortress" had been reinvigorated.

If you do decide that a magick circle is desired for working your spell, you'll need to consider where the circle should be cast. Magick is a form of ritual and worship, so choose the space for your magick circle carefully. There are practical and personal aspects to choosing a sacred space—if you're working alone you will need less space than if you are working with others, for instance, and you will want the space to be someplace you feel comfortable, positive, and confident. Outside is best, if possible. This is where you will feel most connected to all your relations: the earth, sky, animals, and the spirit world. But if you need to be inside, that's fine, too. You can make an inside space a place of connection to the universe. If you're inside, find a place where you won't be distracted: Turn off the phone and the computer, for instance, and don't be right next to a noisy entryway or window. Think about it before you decide, and ask yourself what's important to you in this space: privacy, comfort, serenity? Choose the space that works for you, and in which you feel powerful.

Cleansing and Consecrating Your Sacred Space for Magick

After you decide where you will raise your magick circle (where you want to work magick), you should first cleanse the space, ridding it of any negative energy. If you are inside (or on a deck), it can be a great meditation (or spell!) to use a broom. Aurora has a beautiful ritual broom that she bought from the man who handmade it, with a tree-spirit face carved into it. It is especially magickal because it is the one she and her husband jumped over, as is traditional, at their wedding (for more on Wiccan wedding ceremonies, or handfastings, see Chapter 15). She sweeps out the space in the house that she will be using for the ritual, envisioning any negative energy or unwanted thoughts and intrusions being swept out as well. Sweeping is a wonderful way of connecting with our ancestors; it is something humans have been doing for a very long time; it is in our bones! You can sweep while singing or chanting:

Out with negative,

I banish negativity.

Only pure stays in,

Clean is my circle,

Pure is my magick.

If actual sweeping isn't practical, you can envision a broom, and go through the motions. If you envision that you are sweeping out negativity or unwanted energy, which is the purpose of the activity, it will work.

You can also cleanse ritual space with a smudge stick or incense, or by sprinkling (called *asperging*) the area with saltwater or any water you may have. We have been at rituals where people have had special water that they brought back from a trip to some sacred site or from their last beach walk. If you are going to use regular tap water, you may want to bless it first. This is traditionally done by placing the dish of water on your pentacle and dipping your athame into it, saying "I purify thee, creature of water, be pure unto my intent." You could cleanse a space by wafting a bundle of herbs that feels right for the occasion (like lavender for healing, or mugwort for a dream spell; more on herbs in Chapter 12).

As part of creating a sacred space, you will want to consecrate the space, dedicating it to your magick. Putting down some kind of offering is a good way to do this. You can offer anything

> **Making Magick**
>
> Aurora's handfasting, her wedding, took place outside, and she had the bridesmaids "sweep" the circle before she and her husband entered it, by going through the motions with their brooms, though not actually touching the ground with them. They swept from the center out to the circle's edge, going around in a deosil (clockwise) motion.

For Protection

When you use tobacco ritually or burn a smudge stick to cleanse yourself or your spaces, be aware that you are using things learned from the native people of this land. If you use African-based drums in your rituals, or cowrie shells, know that you are taking these things from indigenous African peoples. Always give thanks and be respectful of cultures that your practices come from, and don't use elements from a culture you know nothing about.

you value, perhaps a sacred herb or stone. You might place it on the ground (or on a plate, if you're indoors and prefer this; leave the offering in the space overnight, and then place it outside the next day) and say "I consecrate this place for magickal work." Or call on helping spirits:

> *Lord and Lady consecrate this space,*
>
> *Be it prepared for magick to take place.*

When working outdoors, Aurora always puts down a bit of tobacco as an offering to the spirits of place, as a tribute to the fact that she is living and working on this continent. Native American friends have taught her that this is the way of "opening the door" to spirits. You don't get anywhere if the door isn't opened first, so this is a good first step for the space you will be working in.

Creating a Magick Circle

Okay, so you are grounded, you've chosen your sacred space, and you've cleansed and consecrated it. Now you're ready to put up a magick circle to protect yourself and give yourself a secure and relaxed environment so you can relax and concentrate on the magickal energy you will need to focus. Remember, if you're tired, sick, angry, or just not in a good frame of mind, you should not raise a magick circle—*you should not work magick!* Wait for the optimal conditions to give your spell the best chance of success; don't take any unwarranted risks.

If Wicca and magick circles and spellcraft is all new to you, you'll want to do a lot of study before you attempt to work *any* magick. *Don't read just this section of this book and then try raising a magick circle.* You need to have thought through your entire plan, and your spell, and be clearly aware of the steps you need to take. A magick circle is a dynamic and powerful place; create it only when you are ready for the magick you intend to perform through doing your spells within it.

The magick circle forms a boundary that you create on the ground, by visualizing or pointing directly at the ground (with your finger, athame, or a feather—whatever works for you). While you do this you are mentally visualizing (creating) an energy *sphere*. It is like a safety bubble that you are now inside. You should visualize yourself standing on a plane in the center of this sphere, with the sphere projecting into the ground as well as above you, in three dimensions.

You can delineate your circle with chalk or rope, or just envision it and trace the path of the circle in a clockwise, or *deosil*, direction with your tool of choice. (We'll discuss ritual tools in Chapter 5.) At festivals and workshops, sometimes the protective circle is cast large enough to encompass an entire building or camp. For intense working, or for working alone, you will likely want a smaller circle so you don't spread out your energy too far. But make your circle the size you need to work your magick comfortably—don't box yourself in. You can point several feet (or yards for that matter) out from where you are walking.

Making Magick

Aurora has a yurt (a circular, domed structure) set up as a temple for ritual and classes. As she casts, she simply walks around the inside of the space, pointing the edge of the circle to the edge of the building. If you are working in a square space, don't fret. Just define the edge of the working space that you will need. Make sure to include any altars you are using inside the circle.

Casting and Raising the Circle

Many witches like to cast a circle by walking it three times, because three is an important number in the craft, as you'll find out later in this chapter. This could be done once with your athame or some incense, once with a candle, and once with saltwater. This way the circle is blessed with each Element, because the athame or incense represents Air, the candle represents Fire, and saltwater represents Earth and Water mixed together.

The ritual you choose depends on how strongly you are concerned with protection, as well as what it takes to make the circle real and physical in your own mind, body, and spirit. While tracing the circle, concentrate on it, and visualize the sacred and protected space you are delineating.

While you are casting the boundaries of your circle, you need to concentrate and visualize your circle actually going up around you; you must imagine the circle being formed from you or from the tool you use to trace the circle. Perhaps you will envision a white light emanating from the tool, tracing the shape of the circle and going up from the outline over your head to create a protective dome over you and the circle. You can create whatever imagery works for you, but you will need to work on this until you find imagery that you feel comfortable with, and that lets you see and feel the protected space of the circle.

Why a circle? The circle and sphere are sacred shapes in most cultures. The sphere is the shape of the earth, the circle is the shape of a group of people standing together as equals. Can you imagine a group of people getting together and holding hands in a square? That would have to be carefully orchestrated because it would be so unnatural. Circles are sacred because they mimic the curved nature of the universe.

See the sphere of your magick circle coming up around you. Aurora tends to visualize it as glowing, light-blue light, but you should use whatever works for you. You can also chant while casting your circle. Here's a chant Aurora often uses:

> *I conjure thee, O magick circle: protect, contain, create a sacred space where only love may enter, only love may leave. So mote it be.*

Working Magick Within the Circle

After you have cast and raised your circle, you will call in the four Elements in this order: East, South, West, and North (because this is going around the circle clockwise, or deosil). If you are not familiar with what the directions and their corresponding Elements represent, read Chapter 7 before you invoke these spirits. You go to each quarter in turn (so before you begin you must know where you stand in relationship to the directions), asking for that direction's presence and blessing on your circle/ritual/working. Just ask whatever you feel is appropriate for that direction; don't spend time worrying over whether or not you are saying the "right" thing. Only practice will make this flow easily for you. You could ask the East for a fresh breeze of new knowledge to enlighten your endeavor, the South for the warmth of summer, the West for the never-ending flow of the rivers of intuition, and the North for the stability and nurturing of the earth. Now you are ready to do your spellwork within the circle's protective and nurturing influence.

Spellcasting _____

We use the most widespread, Northern-hemisphere correspondences in this book: East-Air, South-Fire, West-Water, North-Earth. These are certainly not universal. In the Southern hemisphere it would make much more sense to put Fire to the North because that is where the sun is hottest. And there are those who feel the rest of the Elements should be aligned depending on where your nearest large body of water is, where your nearest large land mass is, and so on. See Chapter 7 for more on this.

The Cone of Power

Once your circle is up, you create a cone of power to direct the magickal energy of the spell you want to do. Think of the energy you will raise within your magick circle and envision it in the shape of a cone. The cone will start at the outlined circle, and will rise, pointing upward to the center of your circle and toward your goal; you should visualize it this way as you raise the cone of power. If you are alone, the cone will come from your energy; if you are working with others, the cone will be a combination of the energy of everyone in the circle, who all direct and release their energy toward the same purpose.

At a group ritual where they were all strengthening their feeling of connection with the Goddess and God and with each other (a community of witches), Aurora and her friends wanted to feel that they could take this magick home with them, to strengthen them every day in their daily practice. They raised a cone of power and shot off the energy at each of their home altars. Envision this beautiful energy raining down like fireworks into each person's home, directly to their altars. They then each had some of that energy to draw upon when the others in the group wouldn't be around physically to share their energy.

Entering and Leaving the Circle

If you cast the magick circle around you, then you're already inside it, but if you want to enter a circle created by someone else, you will need someone inside the circle to cut a door in the energy of the circle to let you in—ideally, this won't happen, as you'll be inside when the circle is raised. That person then closes it off again once you're inside. This is often done with the same tool that did the original casting, but once again, anything will do. If you need to leave the circle and don't have a tool in your hand, cut yourself a door with your finger. Often, if the person casting knows he or she is going to welcome others into the circle, he or she will cast it leaving a door, allowing the others to enter, and then closing the door with the tool. But usually the circle is cast with all participants inside.

Likewise for leaving a magick circle: If for some reason you need to depart before the circle is lowered, you or someone else must cut a door through the energy. Don't just walk through the circle, because this will break the focus of energy that you and the others have worked hard to create. This could dissipate the energy before its time has come and weaken the defenses of the circle. Once you have left the

Spellcasting

Children and animals can enter and leave a magick circle at will without disturbing the energy because they are energetically and magickally in-tune creatures. They are loved by spirit and are not caught up in the rules of human adults. So what happens if a child enters the circle and starts talking? This is exactly what spirit *wants* to have happen and is a message from the spirit world.

circle, close the door behind you with the tool you are using (perhaps your finger). In some covens someone else would open and close a door behind you.

Lowering the Magick Circle

Once you have finished working your spell within the magick circle, you will need to lower the circle. Before you do this, it is good if you can spend some time relaxing in the circle, regrounding yourself and the energy you have raised. One way to do this is to partake in some food and drink. This portion of the ritual is traditionally called "cakes and wine," referring to British cookies or shortbread. Use whatever works for you. Bread and vegetables are good for grounding, but there are also those who swear by the magickal qualities of chocolate!

We have some concerns about eating sugar when you are trying to ground and relax, but if you have worked really hard, perhaps your blood sugar is low and you need it boosted. As for the beverage, it can be water or juice—whatever feels right. It is traditional to use red wine (representing the blood of the Goddess), and some traditions use whiskey or vodka. If you choose to use alcohol, please be careful. If you are working with other people, you may alienate those who abstain from alcohol. Also, the energy in the circle will dissipate very quickly if people start partying. Make sure you take down the magick circle and dismiss any energies you have called before that happens. Practically speaking, when everyone drinks from a chalice of wine, germs spread, and we may all share one another's colds, too. Aurora found it very refreshing when she began working with Reclaiming tradition witches, who simply don't allow alcohol into the magick circle. Finally, as with any potentially addictive substance, make sure you have an honest relationship with it before it enters your circle or your life.

Whatever you choose to partake in within your magick circle, make an offering of some of it to the spirit, or to the Lord and Lady, however you choose to look at this. If you're working with others inside the circle, you can consider this the cool-down part of your ritual. Relax, have a snack, and chat a bit; refresh yourself after working magick.

Once you're ready, you can bid farewell to the Lord and Lady, or whomever you have called upon for help with your magick, and then bid farewell to the Elements of the four quarters. This is usually done counterclockwise, or *widdershins*: North, West, South, East. Go to each quarter in turn, thank that Element for its presence and blessings and bid it "hail and farewell"—or whatever rolls off your tongue. Then, using the tool you used to trace your circle when raising it, trace the circle walking widdershins, all the while envisioning the circle, and its energy, receding back into the earth.

Words of Power

Deosil means sunwise, and in the Northern hemisphere, is the clockwise direction; widdershins means anti-sunwise, and in the Northern hemisphere, is the counterclockwise direction. Deosil action draws positive energy, and widdershins action dispels negative energy. In the Southern hemisphere, many witches work the other way around, honoring the idea that we should go the same direction as we see the Sun going. But some don't, being perhaps in the habit from the Northern hemisphere. Some witches believe you should do everything deosil, considering widdershins to be the left-hand path, or evil. This is not a widely held opinion, though.

Use Your Power Wisely

When doing spells by raising magickal energy, whether within a formal magick circle or not, remember the Wiccan Rede and always, *always* use your power wisely. Once you've cast a magick circle and raised a cone of power, you will be able to direct it toward your goal, working your spell. The energy you raise in your magick circle is very powerful, and you don't want it to go astray, nor do you want to use it for a negative purpose.

The Law of Three

The Law of Three says that whatever you do will return to you threefold. This is very similar to the concept of karma. It ties in to the Wiccan Rede and acts as another balance, and ethical code, to keep those practicing spellcraft from doing harm to others. Simply put: When you hurt others, you hurt yourself. We are all connected.

When we say that whatever you do will come back to you three times over, we mean that if you do a lot of good with your magick, you'll find it comes back to you threefold. Of course, if you use magick for negative purposes, you'll get that energy back threefold, instead. This doesn't translate literally—if you wish someone to be heartbroken, you won't necessarily have your heart broken three times, but you will have three times that negative energy come back your way. It's like the Golden Rule: Do unto others as you would have them do unto you. If you're kind to your neighbor, he or she will likely return the favor. And if you curse your neighbor ... well, you get the picture.

Connecting to Your Natural Power

There are any number of ways you might try to better connect yourself with your own magickal power. You might use meditation to center or focus yourself, and there are also some simple rituals and spells that will help you with this work. It's important that you recognize and be able to focus this natural energy, because you will need it in spell work, and once you are in better touch with this flow, we hope you will also develop a healthy respect for your own power.

Drumming, playing music, singing, and dancing—especially outdoors—are wonderful ways to help you connect to your power. You might want to cast a magick circle and call on the spirits of place or the local Earth energies (the energies of the place where you live) to help you. Some people see these as fairy people. Bring an offering (food, tobacco, pretty stones, anything you like) and ask them to help you connect to your own magick. Sit quietly, clearing your mind and opening it for inspiration. Maybe you'll want to play them some music instead, or dance. Perhaps ask these beings to imbue some magickal item you have brought (such as a stone or feather), and dance around it for added power! Here's a chant you might try:

> *Fairy powers, powers of place,*
>
> *Help me see my inner face.*

There are also many scents (available as essential oils or incense) that can help you connect with your magickal abilities: sandalwood, patchouli, frankincense, or myrrh, to name a few. You could burn incense as part of this ritual or place a few drops of oil on something you can smell (it could go into a candle you are burning) while again chanting or meditating on your purpose.

Divining Your Power

Divination is a way of opening a door of communication with the spirit world or your higher self or your inner knowing—call this whatever you feel comfortable with. That communication wants to take place, and allowing it to do so opens you up to seeing what you have probably needed to see. Perhaps this is a clear solution to a problem, or a next step in a certain realm of your life.

You can think of divination as getting in touch with your intuition and learning to recognize and listen to it. Have you ever had a feeling about something, and either trusted or not trusted your instincts, only to realize later that they were right on? This could be something as simple as knowing that your mom is on the phone, or feeling that something just isn't "right" in a particular situation. If you have this feeling, you should trust it, because it's probably meaningful. If you're planning to work magick and you get this feeling, put off the magick until you can find out what the problem is!

You can test your own intuition in simple ways, like trying to guess who is calling when the phone rings or who the latest e-mail is from. You can also do this in a more mindful way, using meditation of focused practice to get in touch with your psychic energy. And you can also use simple spells to help you connect with your psychic mind. You could burn incense to help you to open your psychic centers, and you could do the following Tarot practice in a sacred circle after asking the fairy folk to help you get in touch with your psychic energy.

Try this divination practice with a deck of Tarot cards (you can use any Tarot deck where the images resonate with meaning for you): Hold a card facedown and try to *feel* what that card has to tell you before you turn it over. Tarot cards are so rich in imagery that there is a lot of opportunity to get hits of some of the archetypes on the card you are holding. You don't have to try to determine that the next card is the Page of Swords, but perhaps the energy of a young man might come to you.

Once you recognize it, divination can be useful to you in your everyday life. You can think of divination as a way of connecting with deity, the spirit world, or just connecting with your subconscious mind and your own psychic energy. There are a number of techniques used for divination and you may be familiar with a few of them: Tarot cards, pendulum, shells, bones, the I Ching, astrology, and runes, for example. We'll discuss runes in detail in Chapter 14. Right now, we want to help you connect with your intuition and listen to it so you can make it work for you in your spellworking.

The Least You Need to Know

- Grounding yourself is the first step in doing any kind of magick.

- Most of the time you will want to create a magick circle before doing your spell-work, but sometimes you won't need the formality a circle provides.

- A cone of power is the focus of magickal energy you create or channel in working your spells.

- The Law of Three says that whatever energy you send out into the world will come back to you three times over—so practice positive magick!

- You can practice rituals and spells to help you connect with your natural power.

Chapter **3**

Writing and Casting Spells

In This Chapter

- How to create a spell
- When should you cast your spell?
- Where to work your spell
- Types of spells: cords, poppets, candles, and kitchen magick

There is a lot involved in writing and casting spells, which is why we've written an entire book on the subject. In this chapter, we'll talk about what's involved in creating a spell, as well as some of the aspects of timing for spellcasting and some of the types of spells you might want to cast.

If this is your first foray into the realm of magick, you may find spellcasting overwhelming at first, but once you've made it through this book and tried your hand at it a couple of times, we hope you'll have a grasp on what it takes to compose and cast spells of all kinds. Let's get started!

Creating Spells

Spellcraft is a very creative process: After you decide to work magick, there are a lot of variables open to you. The content can include a chant or song, the timing of the spell, and the type of spell you will use, to name a few. Every spell you use merits serious consideration, but because spellcasting is a creative, intuitive art, there are also great rewards: a feeling of accomplishment, connection, and creativity can flow from your spellwork. Let your creative mind open up as you plan to work magick, always remembering the purpose and intent behind your magick.

Spell Content

We'll give some examples of spells for different kinds of magick throughout this book and you can always use these, and adapt them to your needs, or you can create your own spells, composing chants or songs to go with them. You may want to read through the rest of this book to see what your options are—candles, amulets, colors, herbs, etc.—so that you can choose the components of your spell with knowledge and information. The more you know about all of the possibilities, the more powerful your magick will be.

> **Spellcasting**
>
> For some people it's easy to come up with chants; others have to work hard at it. Composing chants is something you can learn and become better at with practice, so if it's difficult at first, give yourself some time. Don't worry if the wording sounds silly or trite—you're not trying to impress anyone, you're just finding something to get your energy flowing. Even repeating one phrase can work well to put your conscious mind out of the way so your intuitive and magickal power can go to work. Try repeating *"I come with love and trust"* to open up your psychic abilities as you go about creating a spell.

Chants

In addition to the physical ingredients of your spell, you may want to use visualization or meditation, and you'll likely want to create a chant or song to help you complete the spell. Maybe you have a poet lurking within who is longing for expression—now's the time! Chants don't have to rhyme or have a consistent meter, though, when working magick, these things can help you to get into a frame of mind to build your cone of power. The rhyming can also be fun to do. The rhyme and meter of a good chant can distract your conscious mind enough to let your subconscious mind work on the magickal task at hand. Try this one:

Spirits hearken unto me,

As I will so mote it be;

By Earth, by Air, by Water, by Fire.

If you are drawn to rhyming chants, try thinking up rhymes while driving or waiting in line at the bank; come up with rhyming foods at the grocery store; and if you have kids, make rhyming into a game, and you all might have fun! It's often easier to come up with rhymes by saying words aloud (so maybe you'll feel less self-conscious if you work on this with the kids!): Try naming something you see, and then go through the alphabet, trying to find words for each letter that rhyme with the object you named. For example, if you're taking a walk and see a rock, try to come up with words that rhyme with "rock" (clock, dock, lock, mock, sock, tock).

If this exercise is easy for you, move on to longer phrases, with rhymes at the end: *"I saw a little girl / dancing in a whirl."* Once you're comfortable with this, you can move on to another couplet and another, until you're well on your way to writing your own rhyming chants! You can do some of the same kinds of practice with meter, giving each line the same number of syllables, perhaps, or having them both end on a stressed word. You really don't have to make your chants with consideration of rhyme and meter, but if this is something you're interested in, it can truly become a creative outlet, one you can practice by creating chants for a lot of future spells.

Timing Your Spell

Another element of successful spellcasting is timing. How do you know if it's the right time to cast your spell? Well, we can start with what we've already discussed: How do you feel? If you feel like it's a good time, you aren't rushed or angry, or sick or tired, then you're in a good place personally to work magick.

Once you are more tuned in to your inner voice, you will know if a bit of magick working needs to be done. Often if something needs to be done, the best time to do it is *now!* Things to do with spirit work tend to get put off in our busy world, relegated to a better time that may never come. Don't worry too much about perfecting the timing of your spell: If you know in your heart that a particular bit of magick needs to be done, just do it! On the other hand, if you have a big, important magickal working to do and you want it to be especially powerful, plan to do it at an especially powerful time (for example, magick for getting into graduate school could be important to you, so you might want to save it for a New Moon: new endeavors = New Moon; see "Lunar Cycles" later in the chapter).

Though you can certainly decide to do magick based on your own feelings alone, there are optimal times for everything, and particular seasons, lunar cycles, and times or day of the week, for example, have different energies. You don't have to consider all of these elements in your planning—we aren't trying to make the issue of timing burdensome. But we do want you to consider your options, or at least know what

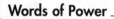

Words of Power _____

Sabbats are Wiccan holidays, based on the annual cycle of the Sun. The eight Sabbats are: Samhain (Halloween), Yule, Imbolc (Candlemas), Eostara, Beltane, Litha, Lughnasadh (Lammas), and Mabon.

they are, before you plan on working magick. While not necessary (you may find your magick to be quite effective without considering timing), researching the most opportune time to practice magick may give your spell the extra boost it needs to be very successful. And if you know you're going to work magick during a certain week, why not look into the timing and see if a particular day might have a better energy for your spell than others? Aligning your purpose with a perfect time (a _Sabbat_ or important lunar day, for example) gives your work that extra boost of power from the alignment.

Time of Day

Some people are early birds and some are night owls. Whichever you are, know that there are different energies inherent in the different periods of a day. If you're a morning person, you know how energetic you feel each morning, and for this reason alone, morning may be a good time for you to work magick. Mornings are when many people start work and school, and it's generally a good time to work magick related to these areas. It's good to start the day with a fresh outlook, so if there are negative issues you want to deal with, morning is a good time to work magick to release negative energy, or to rid yourself of destructive habits or addictions.

Midday is a good time to utilize the power of the Sun—when it's at its height. You might have time off for lunch, and you could use this time to refocus or reenergize yourself. In the evening, as the day winds down and the sun sets, you may find yourself tired and relaxed or tired and frazzled. This is a good time to look at issues of willpower, and to work magick to help yourself kick bad habits, as well as relax and release stress.

If you're a night owl, you might be a person who responds to the energy of the Moon. The Moon is linked to the Goddess, and night is a good time to work magick dealing with issues of love, as well as divination. Magick traditionally has been seen as a "hidden art" and therefore is associated with night and the reflected light of the Moon. Some people will only feel "magickal" working spells at night. If this is how you feel, that's great—follow your instincts. There is certainly a beautiful energy in a sacred space lit in candlelight. Since having children, Aurora's favorite time to do magick is whenever she has a few minutes to herself! Don't feel restricted by time or place; do what works for you and your magick.

> **Making Magick**
>
> "Hidden" or "secret" is one meaning of the word *occult*. Magick deals with hidden energies, and we use chants, incense, and other tools to distract our linear minds and access this energy. Those who worked magick once had to do so in secret—which is why magick began to be called occult. Many people use the word *occult* as a synonym for *satanic*, which is incorrect as well as an undeserved affront to the occult arts.

Day of the Week

The day of the week is also an important factor in deciding when to work magick. The days of the week are associated with planets and deities, which are associated with masculine or feminine energy. The following table shows you which planet is associated with each day of the week, as well as what kind of magick might work especially well on that day.

Day	Planet	Energy	Magick
Sunday	Sun	Masculine	Power, health, prosperity
Monday	Moon	Feminine	Divination, fertility, dreams
Tuesday	Mars	Masculine	Conflict, leadership
Wednesday	Mercury	Masculine	Communication, arts, fears
Thursday	Jupiter	Masculine	Success, abundance, desires
Friday	Venus	Feminine	Romance, loyalty, trust, friendship
Saturday	Saturn	Feminine	Divination, illness, binding

If you're planning to work a spell for your own abundance and you can manage it, why not choose Sunday or Thursday, to help your spell along?

Lunar Cycles

The Moon, which is associated with the Goddess, is very important in Wiccan ritual. On the Full Moon many witches celebrate an Esbat, during which the power of the Goddess is honored and also drawn upon to work magick. Esbats are the subject of

Chapter 8. For now, let's look at the phases of the Moon, and what they indicate for you in working magick.

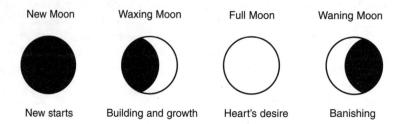

New Moon	Waxing Moon	Full Moon	Waning Moon
New starts	Building and growth	Heart's desire	Banishing

- The *New Moon* is a great time to start new projects: Get a new job, start a new relationship, start a family—and work magick related to these things.

- The *Waxing Moon* is a time for working toward your goals: Construct plans and work magick for fulfilling goals or for prosperity. While the Moon is increasing, you can best work magick to increase (your prosperity, health, etc.).

- During the *Full Moon*, the Goddess is at the height of her powers. This is a very powerful time for working magick, when you can utilize the power of the Goddess for just about anything, but particularly for divination, love, and psychic energy. You can use the energy of the Full Moon for three days before and after the date of the Full Moon.

- The *Waning Moon* is a good time for banishing magick. This kind of magick helps you get rid of things—generally negative things: energy, habits, illness, stress. While the Moon decreases, work magick to decrease (your bad habits, negative relationships, etc.).

Words of Power

The **Waxing Moon** is the Moon as it grows toward Full; the **Waning Moon** is the Moon as it decreases in size toward the New Moon. You can tell them apart because as it waxes, the Moon will begin to look like a backward letter C, moving to the O of the Full Moon, and then, as it wanes, the Moon will look like the letter C.

The phases of the Moon are visible in the sky, though it's sometimes difficult to tell if the Moon is waxing or waning—and sometimes it's too cloudy to see what phase the Moon is in. If you want to be sure what phase the Moon is in or you want to be able to plan your magick ritual ahead of time, we suggest you find a good lunar almanac, which will provide this information for every day of the year. The *Lunar Calendar* (see Appendix B) is a good source for lunar information because it is a calendar of lunations, instead of months. Each page is flipped with the New Moon and shows the phases in a circle. It tells a bit about that lunation and releases the user from the linear sense of time, bringing the Moon into central focus. Most pagan or New Age calendars or day planners include the Moon phases.

Seasons

The four seasons also have different associations and energies. We'll give some general ones here; to get more specific about this, you'll want to consider the astrological signs within each season and the energies of each sign. We'll go into this in Chapter 13.

◆ As you might expect, spring is a good time to start new projects of all kinds. We plant our gardens in spring and it's a time symbolizing fertility. You might also want to try divination in the spring, to see what the rest of the year holds for you.

◆ Summer is the hot season; it's the time of the strongest energies of the Sun and a good time for magick related to health, relationships of any kind, fulfillment, beauty, and strength.

◆ Fall is the season of harvest and also a time when the natural world is preparing for winter. It's a good time to work magick related to prosperity and work, the intuitive arts, reconciliation, as well as family. In fall it's also beneficial to assess your year so far and to finish up projects you've been working on.

◆ Winter, the natural time of hibernation, is a great time for introspection. You can work on divination now, going within, and you might also want to meditate or work magick related to your own and others' prosperity.

If you keep track of the planning you do for working magick, along with the results, you may find patterns regarding your success related to the season or the astrological or lunar cycle. Pay special attention to how you feel during these different times, as this will give you the best clues about when to work what kinds of magick.

Where to Work Magick

We talked about casting a magick circle, which is the safest place to work magick, in Chapter 2. If you have the time, cast a circle and call the Elements of each direction, facing East, South, West, and North and asking the energy of each Element to enter your circle and assist with your magick. You can practice simple rituals without a magick circle, but if you are taking the time to plan a ritual or spell, choose a place you feel is magickal and set up sacred space there. The only time you are likely to work without a circle is if you're working on the fly: You're on your way out the door and you remember that you should step up to your altar and ask for protection on your trip, or a blessing for your child's big day at school, or some similar thing you just learned about but don't have the time to set up an elaborate ritual for.

The ritual or spellworking space is one you will have chosen carefully, based on its location and your feelings about it. You should feel safe and secure there, comfortable and confident, and it should be a place where your work won't be interrupted. It will be a good place to relax and meditate, as well as a place for working magick. Because we covered this in depth in the section on magick circles, we won't go into it here. Just remember that it's important to think about where you'll practice magick, and to choose that space thoughtfully, just as you will the time for your magick and the type of magick you work.

> **Making Magick**
>
> While traveling in Germany, Aurora found herself entering a chapel under a castle. She realized it was a tomb and had some undealt-with energy floating around. She mentally cast a circle of protection around herself, discreetly using a finger. This action was recognized by a man in the chapel, who turned out also to be a practitioner of magick. It began a wonderful friendship.

Types of Spells

As I'm sure you can imagine, there are spells for just about anything, from losing weight to finding your soul mate. You can work a spell using a variety of materials, and in the following sections, we'll give you some information on a few of these.

Cords

Cord magick is worked with a length of string or cord. Your string can be of any length, but you will be tying knots into it, so be sure it's long enough for this purpose. You should choose your string in a color that corresponds with the magick you are trying to work. Cathy, the co-author of this book, knits and always has a selection of colored yarns lying around that work great for this purpose. Traditionally, a witch will keep three silk cords, each 9 feet long, in his or her ritual "kit." One cord is red, one white, and one blue, for use in different kinds of spells. In general, natural materials are better than synthetic for working magick, unless there is a reason that mitigates your choice (like "this is the gold ribbon that I used on the Maypole so I want to use it for this year's prosperity spell"). We'll talk about the significance and use of color in magick in Chapter 10, so you can look there before choosing your cord.

You'll say your spell as you tie knots into the string, and you'll tie nine knots total. For every two lines of your chant, tie one knot. Here's one Aurora learned. The "it" in the chant is your spell, and you hold it in your concentration as you chant:

> *By knot of one,*
>
> *it is begun,*
>
> *By knot of two,*
>
> *it cometh true,*
>
> *By knot of three,*
>
> *so mote it be,*
>
> *By knot of four,*
>
> *I open the door,*
>
> *By knot of five,*
>
> *it comes alive,*
>
> *By knot of six,*
>
> *I see it fixed,*
>
> *By knot of seven,*
>
> *it's seen in heaven,*
>
> *By knot of eight,*
>
> *It's through the gate,*
>
> *By knot of nine,*
>
> *The spell is mine.*

(So your chant will have 18 lines.) You can start by tying a knot in one end of the string and then another one right next to it, and so on down the cord. Some witches begin with one knot at either end. And then tie a knot between the first and third knots, then the second and third knots. Anything you wish to bring to pass could be worked as a cord spell. For example, if you want to do a cord spell for getting a job, getting into school, getting pregnant, or stopping smoking, concentrate on that outcome while knotting, and as you say each line of "By knot of one, it is begun ..." visualize that outcome. You can also work magick with cords by braiding them together while chanting and concentrating on your goal.

Making Magick

Before her handfasting (in which a cord was used to represent each Element to bless the union with each Element's gifts), Aurora braided silk cords for the ceremony. For Air, she braided strands of white, yellow, and light blue and braided in a feather at the end. For Fire, she used red, yellow, and orange. For Water: blue, green, and purple, with a shell at the end. For Earth: brown, green, and dark orange. After the ceremony, these cords must be stored where both partners know where they are, so that each has equal power to burn or dispose of them. It is in *choosing not to do so* that a union has magick.

Cord magick is very useful in bringing energy to you or for banishing it. It's also a kind of magick that's easy to undo. Once you've finished the spell and tied all of your knots, put the cord away in a safe place while your magick is working.

Some spells come to a finite end: You got your new job or got into school, so now you can release the cord from its job so that it can be used another time. Simply untie the knots while chanting:

> *As I untie my knotted cord,*
>
> *My magick is done, Lady and Lord,*
>
> *Release the energy, and do no ill,*
>
> *As I untie, this is my will.*

Now your cord is free to go back to being just a cord. You could bury or burn the cord, if you don't want to use it for anything else, but be sure you first make it clear in ritual that you are releasing the magick.

Words of Power

Poppets are dolls created to represent someone with a magickal purpose in mind. They are very useful in healing spells and in bringing about change in yourself.

Poppets

Poppets are dolls used in doing magick. You may have heard of voodoo dolls—the ones stereotypically used with pins in old episodes of, say, *Gilligan's Island*. In the TV shows and movies, the dolls are stuck with pins to cause pain or injury to the person represented by the doll. This is simply a case of the media focusing on only the negative aspects of magick, because they are more sensational. Poppets can be used for many healing spells and are powerful ways of bringing about change. The key to successful magick is focusing your mind, and creating something visible and substantial is often the most powerful way to do this.

Poppets are somewhat labor-intensive, because as part of the magick, you make the doll, cutting and sewing it out of material (you'll select a color to represent your intent with the spell—see Chapter 10), and then stuffing it with wool, cloth, or fiber-fill, as well as other materials that will help with your spell: herbs, crystals, messages, and perhaps something representative of the person your magick is about—the person you're trying to heal—such as a snip of their hair or a photo of them. (See Appendix C for a simple poppet pattern.) Keep the intention of the poppet in mind as you make it—concentrate on its healing purpose.

Once the poppet is ready, you will need to consecrate it in a magick circle by "showing" it to each Elemental energy and asking the energy to be involved with the magick. If you're not familiar with the magickal Elements and their correspondences, see Chapter 7. For example, you might wave the poppet over the candle, saying: "Fire, bless this work"; over the bowl of water: "Water, bless this work"; over the Earth representation (pentacle, plant, dish of salt): "Earth, bless this work"; over the incense: "Air, bless this work."

The consecration might also be the spell itself. Each Element is associated with one of the four directions, so holding the poppet up to the East, you might say: "Elementals of Air, bring Sally your blessings of clear knowledge in this situation." (Now, we're assuming you've asked Sally's permission for this!) Then, facing South: "Elementals of Fire, bring Sally your warm intensity, and a desire to dance!" Facing West: "Elementals of Water, bring Sally your healing waters and the ability to flow with the situation." Facing North: "Elementals of Earth, bring Sally your strength and abundance, healing her body and soul."

Making Magick

Aurora recently got into grad school and decided she needed a "new Aurora"—one who would succeed at grad school. She envisioned what she would want this new Aurora to be like: earthy, grounded, studious. She made a poppet out of green and brown fabric, then made the poppet some accessories to represent the blessings of each Element and the ancestors standing with her. She took the poppet, unaccessorized, to the Earth altar during a transformation ritual, with her accessories on the Air altar. During the ritual, the poppet acquired the accessories and is now blessed and ready to help Aurora buckle down! She might continue to add things to her—perhaps a mortarboard as graduation nears?

Another thing that makes poppets a bit more complicated is that they continue to represent the persons you intend them to represent when you make the dolls, so you have to be careful with poppets even after you've worked your magick—don't lose track of them, or let a poppet wind up your dog's chew toy! This also brings us to an advantage of working with poppets: Using the poppet, you can pretty easily undo or stop your spell. Store the poppet safely, and once your magick has worked, ritually discharge the energy. Then you will need to take the poppet apart and bury or burn the pieces. You can give yourself a rhyme or chant to conclude the magick:

> *I discharge this poppet from its work,*
>
> *Constituent parts are returned to Earth,*
>
> *No longer magick, you are free,*
>
> *As I will, so mote it be.*

We hope you never work a spell that you later come to regret. By carefully thinking through all the consequences of your actions (as the Wiccan Rede requires) you can reduce the number of spells you cast that you want to undo. This happens to most spellcasters now and again; we all make mistakes.

Should you wish to undo the magick you have started, you'll need to use a different chant, and again, afterward, take the poppet apart and bury or burn the pieces:

> *Undo the spell that I did start,*
>
> *I reverse it now with all my heart.*
>
> *No ill shall come from what's been done,*
>
> *Here now ends what was begun.*

Candle Spells

Candle spells are very popular because they are relatively easy, and a burning flame is a wonderful focal point for your magickal energy. Begin by imbuing a candle or stick of incense with your intention and then lighting it. Candles come in all colors and shapes, and you should choose one that represents, for you, the magick you are trying to work (again, we'll talk about color and magick in Chapter 10). You can use a candle of any kind, or you can go to a metaphysical shop or a botanica and purchase one for a specific purpose (these tend to be more expensive, and there is no reason to assume that they are any better than one you imbue with meaning yourself). You might want to dress the candle with essential oils or herbs related to your magick, as well, but be careful if adding plant material to a candle, as it may burn by flaring up and you may suddenly have a burning leaf floating around on your altar. We'll talk a lot more about candle and incense magick in Chapter 10 as well. For now, here is a simple candle spell you might use for strengthening your position in a job interview.

Choose a green candle for prosperity and perhaps carve a rune for success into it, and burn it, while chanting:

>*As you burn, the tides shall turn,*

>*Strengthen my hand, this job I shall land.*

You can first take the candle and write into it what you want to achieve (prosperity, patience, time off, or something more specific—be careful what you wish for though, because you might get it!), using a crystal or knife (not your athame, of course, as it should never be used to cut anything—see Chapter 5 for information on the correct use of the athame) or other magickal tool to write into the candle. You can write in English, or choose a rune or other symbol that represents what you are trying to achieve with the spell. You may want to consecrate your candle by, again, introducing it to all four Elements on your altar (or by facing each direction in turn) and chanting, as you do so:

>*By Earth, by Air, by Water, by Fire;*

>*Burn and let my spell transpire.*

For Protection

Never leave a burning candle unattended in your home! If you have to go out or leave the room, snuff out the candle and relight it later to complete your spell.

Then repeat your chant until you can feel the energy building within you, and when you're ready to release it, light the candle, and send the energy into it.

If you don't want to burn the candle completely for this one spell, you can draw a line on it, making it clear that burning to that point will conclude the spell. You can also drive a sewing needle through the candle (especially if it is beeswax and you warm the needle first) and specify that burning to the needle will conclude the spell.

For Protection

Once you have lit a candle and are working a spell with it, don't blow it out! If you must put the candle out, snuff or pinch it out (and relight it later to complete the spell). Blowing the candle out disperses your magickal energy.

Then allow the candle to burn down to the point you have decided will complete your spell, sending the energy for your spell out into the world. When the candle is spent, your spell is complete. If you must extinguish the candle before it has burnt to the point of completing your spell (and this isn't unlikely, because it can take many hours for a candle to burn down), do so by pinching or snuffing it out, so you can relight it later. When you relight the candle, concentrate on your intent, and sit with the candle for a few minutes after you first relight it, meditating on the flame and the intent of your magick.

Kitchen Spells

We mentioned earlier that a spell can be thought of as a recipe, made with a combination of different ingredients. Well, kitchen magick takes us a step closer to that idea of recipe: It's magick you work with things you find in your kitchen: herbs and spices, fruits and vegetables. To work magick with spices and foods, you might want to see what their magickal correspondences are, and create your recipe based on this. We discuss some of these correspondences in Chapter 12. If you are a good cook, you probably have an intuitive feel for this!

You can work on imbuing the ingredients in your recipe with energy before you prepare your meal, and you can also concentrate your energy into the food as it cooks. Here's a chant you might use while cooking your magickal meal, concentrating on the health or harmony or whatever it is you are trying to create:

> *I imbue this meal with my power and intent,*
>
> *Working my powerful spell to its end.*
>
> *As I prepare this magickal feast,*
>
> *My magickal energy be released.*

Once it's ready, relax and enjoy!

If you're planning some kitchen magick, be sure your intent is consistent with the consensus of your family. Don't make a meal for fertility if you and your spouse are not in agreement on whether or not this is a good time for reproducing! And if someone other than a family member is going to eat the meal, make sure the magickal intent is not specific to something that may not agree with all your guests. For example, if you want all your friends to agree on going on a certain outing, and you put that magickal intent into the meal, aren't you really just trying to manipulate your friends? Keep your goal nonspecific, such as asking for harmony.

The Least You Need to Know

◆ Spellcraft is creative and involves many choices, from the type of spell to timing and chant.

◆ While rhyme and meter aren't necessary to spellcraft, they can help free your subconscious mind for working magick, and you can easily practice making rhymes.

◆ Elements of timing for your spell can include the time of day, day of the week, lunar cycle, and season.

◆ Cords, poppets, and candles are some of the ingredients you might choose from when working your magick.

◆ Kitchen magick is worked using food and everyday items found in your kitchen.

Chapter 4

Magickal Records and Your Book of Shadows

In This Chapter

- ◆ Creating your own Book of Shadows
- ◆ How to track the success of your spells
- ◆ Organizing your Book of Shadows
- ◆ Worksheet: Book of Shadows magickal record
- ◆ What if your spell doesn't work?
- ◆ Passing on your Book of Shadows

Most witches keep a Book of Shadows, a notebook in which they copy down rituals, spells, chants, and other useful information. Traditionally, a newly initiated witch would be allowed to copy this information from the High Priestess or High Priest of the coven that initiated him or her. Lore such as the direction of invoking and banishing pentagrams, Elemental correspondences, and Sabbat ritual outlines would be copied here. Aurora's High Priest held that this all had to be done inside a magickal circle (which, for Gardnerians, means skyclad—that's naked!—for hours of cold, difficult work). The idea was that each witch had their own book, and it would be destroyed upon their death.

Nowadays, so much is published that you need only record special spells and rituals that you found helpful, interesting, or that you create yourself. You (fortunately) don't need to handwrite the whole of Wiccan lore, because it's available in many good books, such as this one.

We think you'll find your Book of Shadows to be an important tool for enhancing your magickal life. But while your Book of Shadows encompasses your magickal learning and practice, always remember that *you* are the living record of your magickal knowledge and the *real* source of magickal power and inspiration. Use your written Book of Shadows as a resource in which you keep records of your magickal activities.

Words of Power

A **Book of Shadows** is where you record magickal information, from spells cast to chants, research, and your dream diary. A **grimoire** can be part of your Book of Shadows or a separate book. It includes spells, chants, and facts on herbs, oils, and crystals. (The word *grimoire* is derived from the French *grammaire*, meaning grammar, a work that includes the basic elements of an art or science.)

Your Book of Shadows

We've suggested that you keep track of when you do magick and what the results are, and your *Book of Shadows* is a good place to do this. Some witches keep all sorts of information in their Book of Shadows, from the specifics on spells cast to dream diaries to personal reactions to rituals. Some witches prefer to keep the personal stuff separate, and will keep this kind of information in their Book of Shadows. Less personal material—the recipes for spells, say, or research into herbs—can go into a separate notebook called a *grimoire*. You can decide to use one or two books (or more); do what feels right for you.

Do I Need a Book of Shadows?

The simple answer is that you don't need anything to do magick but you. In many indigenous societies, where magick is much more a part of everyday life than it is for us in the Western world, writing things down is seen as very *unmagickal*.

But for most of us, writing things down is a good way to learn. If you want to collect spells and rituals that work for you, it's a good idea to keep a Book of Shadows. When you write your own spells, you'll likely find it best to keep them all in one place so that it is easy to refer to them later. Your Book of Shadows is also a good place to record the thoughts and feelings you have around magick and ritual. (Perhaps you'll want to take notes as you read this book!) If you plan to work magick, you will probably want to keep track of your plans, record your chants, take notes on what you learn about the elements of your spell, and, when you work a spell, take specific notes on the spellwork and its outcome.

Making Magick

While in London, Aurora was browsing the witchcraft section of an occult bookshop when she saw a book with "Book of Shadows" on its spine. She wondered, who would publish something and simply call it "Book of Shadows"? She pulled the book off the shelf to see what it contained, surprised to leaf through its blank pages. An elderly British gentleman standing next to her smiled and said, "You have to fill it in yourself!" "All for the best!" Aurora answered.

You can choose whatever kind of notebook you like; a loose-leaf binder will allow you to take out pages with specific spells on them, but you may prefer a hardbound journal for your Book of Shadows, or you might want to use your computer. If you're using one book, it should be a pretty big book, and if you're using two, the one you'll want to be able to remove pages from is the grimoire, because this is where all of your recipes for spells and rituals will go. In this case, your Book of Shadows will be more like a diary of magick: It will contain all of your magickal records for spells and rituals performed, as well as personal responses to your spells, your personal notes, dreamwork, and anything else you might want kept private.

When you have a journal or binder that you are going to start using as your Book of Shadows, you will want to consecrate it for magickal use. Cast a magick circle, and when you call in the Elements, make a special mention to the Air Element that you will be consecrating a tool under its domain. You might say something like:

> *Element of Air, you who rule over the Eastern skies, I call you here today to guard my circle, and witness a consecration of a tool sacred to you. Come, witness my rite.*

Light incense associated with Air and thought, such as lavender, sage, or pine.

If you have a special writing implement that you wish to consecrate at this time, have it laying on top of the book.

Invoke deities (or a deity) that you associate with books, knowledge, and writing—maybe Athena and Thoth, if you don't mind mixing pantheons. You could say something like this:

Great goddess Athena, as you are known for your wisdom and your owl, come and bless this new endeavor of mine. This Book of Shadows shall hold my thoughts and gained knowledge as I move along this path. Bless it with your wisdom, and see that I ever use these pages for the highest good.

With the book in the center (or on your altar), chant:

As I will so mote it be,

This book shall be sacred to me.

All spells and knowledge it shall hold,

Shall be for good as they are told.

Hold the book over the incense, then the candle, the bowl or cup of water, and pentacle or plant on the altar, as you bless it with each Element (see Chapter 7 for more on Elemental correspondences). Chant:

May this book be infused with the knowledge of Air.

Then change the chant for each Element: "the connection of Fire," "the intuition of Water," and "the grounding of Earth."

Hold your new Book of Shadows up over your head facing the East and say: *"Behold, the sacred Book of Shadows, may it aid and guide me!"*

If you wish, this might be a good time to start writing in your Book of Shadows. You could start by inscribing your magickal name in it, if you have one. Aurora's says "The Book of Aurora."

When you are done, thank and dismiss each deity and Element that you invoked. You now have a magickal book—use it well and store it wisely!

Protecting Your Book of Shadows

Some witches are very guarded about their Book of Shadows and like to keep it hidden away, while others keep it displayed prominently in their home as the sacred object it really is. Your Book of Shadows is a very personal record of your magickal life, and you may wish to protect it from damage or theft. If you're in a coven, you may be given instructions on the caretaking of your Book of Shadows.

Think of your Book of Shadows as your personal thoughts on your Wiccan path-working. Like a journal or diary, it should be kept only in safe places where everyone is trustworthy, such as your home or altar. When you take it with you somewhere you may want to wrap it in a silk cloth; some people consider red to be very protective, but you could use whatever seems right to you. Writing and books are associated with the Element of Air, which governs rational thought, so your Book of Shadows could also go in your Air medicine bag, which is where you'll keep your Air Element–related supplies for working magick (see Chapter 7 for more on Elemental correspondences). You might want to work a spell to protect your Book of Shadows.

Once you have your Book of Shadows wrapped in the cloth or bag you intend to keep or transport it in, you may want to strengthen the magickal protection around it. The following spell will help keep it protected from physical or spiritual harm.

Set up your sacred space with the book uncovered (not wrapped). Burn incense associated with protection, such as rosemary or sage, or burn one of these herbs on activated charcoal: bay, vervain, angelica, sage, or rosemary.

You may want to sew (or draw with a fabric marker) a protective sigil onto the cloth or bag that will cover the book, or you can sew a protective stone onto it, such as obsidian or malachite. (See more about magick sigils and runes in Chapter 14.)

As you ritually "clothe" the book, by wrapping it or tucking it into its bag, chant:

> *As this book in cloth is wrapped*
>
> *Power of the Earth is tapped*
>
> *To keep from harm, it safe and sound*
>
> *Ne'er in wrong hands it will be found*
>
> *Lord and Lady keep this book*
>
> *Away from any prying look*
>
> *Always let its good intent*
>
> *Travel to where it is meant.*

Once again, hold the book (now covered) over incense, candle, water, and pentacle or plant, saying:

> *By Air, by Fire, by Water, by Earth, protect this Book of Shadows.*

Now you can dismiss your circle. If you ever need to replace the cloth or bag that you keep your Book of Shadows in, simply repeat this spell.

For Protection

Your Book of Shadows is a personal record of your magickal life, and whether you feel the need to keep it hidden away or displayed, you should take care to handle it well and always know where it is—back up those computer files! Losing your Book of Shadows can be a devastating event.

Tracking Your Spells

Your Book of Shadows can be a very useful tool in helping you to track your spells and record their results. Perhaps you once did a spell to create prosperity in your life, but you can't remember what you used and how it went. Aside from noting how prosperous you feel right now, the best place to find this information is in your Book of Shadows. If your spell doesn't work, you can go back and review your magickal record for the spell, and see if you can pinpoint where your spell might have gone astray. What was the lunar phase? The day of the week? What color candle or cord did you use? What was your frame of mind? There are many variables to casting even a simple spell, and your Book of Shadows will help you keep track of all the details as you develop and refine your spellcasting skills.

What to Record in Your Book of Shadows

It will be of greatest use to you to keep a magickal record of each of your magickal works, from beginning to end, in your Book of Shadows. You might also want to have a section for your research notes, perhaps notes from readings or classes, records of any festivals or ceremonies you've attended, dream journals, and perhaps a journal of your experiences and responses to the magickal world. If you're keeping one book, you'll also have a section of recipes for spells and magickal correspondences in your Book of Shadows. This is a lot of information, and you'll want it to be accessible, which means it has to be *organized*.

Organizing Your Book of Shadows

This may be an obvious step for some of you, but for those of us who are organizationally challenged, organizational tips are more than welcome. Whether you use an actual book or you keep all of your magick notes on the computer, you really have to keep them organized. Your Book of Shadows will be of nearly no use to you if it's a jumble of notes in no order with papers and napkins and all kinds of other note-collecting paraphernalia peeking out of it. You should create a Book of Shadows that will truly *work* for you. We suggest dividing it into sections: Keep your magickal records in one section; have another section for information on gems and herbs and other research and magickal correspondences, perhaps including chants you are working on; and keep personal information (if it's all in one book), such as notes on dreams or a personal journal, in another section.

Another part of making your Book of Shadows a useful tool is to keep it up-to-date: Try not to work magick and fill in a magickal record a week later. To be sure all the information is accurate (it's of little use if it's not), you have to do the record for your spell as close as possible to when you do the spell. Work out the details beforehand,

and then add in your responses and how the spell worked out afterward. You might want to keep fliers from festivals and metaphysical bookstores or even photos in your Book of Shadows. We suggest that you fasten such materials into your Book in some way (use a hole punch and binder or pockets for fliers, glue photos in) so they don't fall out. If you tend to collect a pile of such information, make one day each month the day when you file everything where it goes, updating your Book of Shadows so it's ready for future spellwork.

We know one computer-savvy witch who keeps a "Disk of Shadows" instead of a Book of Shadows. You can do this as well, if you're more comfortable with the keyboard than with a pen. Choose the record-keeping method that works for you, so that your Book of Shadows becomes a useful tool for your magick. If you decide to keep your records on your computer, you may also want a hard copy for portability, and you'll still need a place to keep loose papers, photos, and other information. Perhaps a loose-leaf binder will be useful. Computer files can be great when you're looking for that one thing you researched—you can do a word search! Just as it's important to keep your Book of Shadows safe if it's an actual book, you must take care with your computer files. Organize them as you would a paper Book of Shadows. You may want to keep them accessible only to you (with a password), and you'll certainly want to regularly back up your Book of Shadows files and keep your backup disks in a safe place, perhaps even in a safety deposit box.

Organization can be hard work (we know!), but once you have a system in place and your Book of Shadows is divided into sections according to the material you decide to keep there, you'll find it's really quite easy to maintain. When thinking about putting the organization of your Book off for a rainy day, remember: Your Book of Shadows will only be useful if you can find what you need within it.

> **Spellcasting**
>
> For your Book of Shadows, any blank book will do, even a spiral-bound notebook or three-ring binder—whatever feels right to you. We have seen beautiful, leather-bound ones for sale with crystals and pentagrams/pentacles decorating them—you can find whatever you fancy. What matters is that your Book of Shadows feels magickal to you. Aurora likes to write in hers with ink and a quill pen.

Magickal Record Worksheet

Following is a worksheet we've made for making a magickal record in your Book of Shadows. A magickal record is a record of any ritual or magick you practice, and it includes details such as the day, date, time, and place of the event, as well as the lunar phase and the elements of the ritual, and personal information on the emotional and physical health of the practitioner of the ritual or magick. You may not want to track all of the information this worksheet calls for, but do remember that the more detailed your records, the better able you will be to track reasons for the success or failure of the magick you work.

Spellcrafting Ritual Worksheet

Type of ritual, spell, or magick: _____

Day, date, and time of magick: _____

Astrological information

    Moon phase: _____

    Planetary positions consulted: _____

    _____

Weather: _____

Personal physical/mental/emotional health: _____

_____

Location of magick: _____

Purpose/intent of magick: _____

Ingredients/supplies (candles/herbs/oils/stones/crystals) used:

_____

_____

Deities invoked: _____

Chants/music used: _____

Persons taking part in ritual/magick: _____

Step-by-step process of ritual/magick: _____

_____

_____

Results of magick, if any, and length of time before manifestation of results:

_____

_____

Personal response to and feelings about ritual/magick performed:

_____

_____

Troubleshooting: What If My Spell Doesn't Work?

This is where your Book of Shadows will really come in handy. With an accurate record of your spell, you can look back at all of the variables and take the spell apart, looking for the areas that need work. Because you have a written record to go back to, you don't have to worry about how accurate your recall of the spell is, and you can look back at the record without the emotions you might have had when casting the spell. Let's take a look at a sample magickal record and see what we can learn about why this spell didn't work as well as it could have.

Sample Spellcrafting Ritual Worksheet

Type of ritual, spell, or magick: *Earth spell for prosperity/abundance*

Day, date, and time of magick: *Monday morning, 10 A.M.—squeezed in between dropping kids off and going grocery shopping*

Astrological information

    Moon phase: *Waning*

    Planetary positions consulted: *Didn't notice*

Weather: *Pouring rain*

Personal physical/mental/emotional health: *Harried, rushed, tired, sniffling, feeling anxious*

Location of magick: *In the hallway*

Purpose/intent of magick: *Gain in prosperity/end financial woes/obtain new job*

Ingredients/supplies (herbs/oils/stones/crystals) used: *Leftover votive candle, unknown incense*

Deities invoked: *Hestia for home and hearth*

Chants/music used: *Throat hurt too much to chant*

Persons taking part in ritual/magick: *Just me*

Step-by-step process of ritual/magick: *Shoved laundry aside, lit votive, visualized green fields of money raining down on me*

Results of magick, if any, and length of time before manifestation of results: *None*

Personal response to and feelings about ritual/magick performed: *Rushed off to grocery store right afterward*

What Went Wrong?

Let's look at this sample magickal record to see where the spell may have failed. It's not too difficult to see some trouble spots here—we've made the problems obvious on purpose. This spell would have benefited from forethought—the timing wasn't considered, nor was the place for the ritual. The spell was worked in a rush, the person working magick was harried and under-the-weather, and the votive and incense used weren't selected with abundance in mind. As a result of this sloppy and haphazard work, the spell wasn't successful.

How to Revise This Spell for Success in the Future

Using what we know about how the spell worked and what the spell entailed (because we kept such an accurate magickal record!), we can make better choices for more successful spellcasting in the future. To better the chances of success for this spell, we would have to reconsider the timing: Most important here is that the spell not be rushed, and that the person working magick feel well, rested, and ready to work magick. Also regarding timing, Sunday or Thursday are better days for working on issues of abundance, and during the Waxing Moon is a great time for work on prosperity (the Waning Moon is good for banishing magick). Green is a color associated with prosperity and would be a good choice for this spell. Finally, a simple chant would help relax and focus the mind on the spellwork at hand. Something like this, perhaps:

CAUTION

For Protection _____

Be careful not to get so caught up in your record-keeping that it distracts you from the ritual. When you are working spells, do what comes naturally, don't worry about being a reporter. Do your recording after your mind has come back from ritual space.

Goddess and God, empower me,

Bring me wealth and prosperity.

Keep notes in your Book of Shadows on any revisions to your original spell, and of course, if you cast the spell a second time with revisions, complete a new magickal record so you can again track the success of your work. Now that we've revised our spell, here's a new magickal record for it:

Revised Sample Spellcrafting Ritual Worksheet

Type of ritual, spell, or magick: *Earth spell for prosperity/abundance*

Day, date, and time of magick: *Thursday morning, sunrise, after a grounding meditation*

Astrological information

     Moon phase: *Waxing*

     Planetary positions consulted: *Planetary hour of Jupiter*

Weather: *Clear and cool*

Personal physical/mental/emotional health: *Relaxed and focused, feeling awake and well*

Location of magick: *In my backyard, where I could watch the sunrise*

Purpose/intent of magick: *Gain in prosperity/end financial woes/obtain new job*

Ingredients/supplies (herbs/oils/stones/crystals) used: *A green candle dressed in cinnamon oil, frankincense incense*

Deities invoked: *None*

Chants/music used: *Goddess and God, empower me,*

                      Bring me wealth and prosperity.

Persons taking part in ritual/magick: *Just me*

Step-by-step process of ritual/magick: *Lit incense and did a grounding meditation, then lit candle and chanted in the light of the rising sun. After 10 minutes, snuffed candle and began my day.*

Results of magick, if any, and length of time before manifestation of results: *I'm feeling more abundant already (48 hours later), and just asked for (and got) a raise at my job!*

Personal response to and feelings about ritual/magick performed: *Feeling strong and positive*

What Happens to Your Book of Shadows?

Because your Book of Shadows is such an important personal record of your magickal life, you should consider it a sacred and valuable piece of property. You may want to determine where it will go when you die—will you pass it on to a friend or to another witch, be buried with it, or have it burned; or perhaps you'll leave it to your coven to dispose of as they see fit? If you've kept track of your spells carefully and have an organized Book of Shadows, it can become a great resource for others when you no longer have a use for it.

Burying a Book of Shadows with its owner is a powerful way to underscore a magickal connection: the connection of the book with its owner. If the family situation allows for this, it is very fitting, and allows for other Wiccans to grieve in an open and empowering way. Place the book with its owner, perhaps under the arm or under the head, whatever seems right. It might be best to do this ritual privately, while the book is being placed in the coffin, or during the funeral itself. Allow any members of the community to place herbs or stones with the book: Some lavender or rowan or an obsidian or clear quartz are good choices. Now chant: *"Your Book of Shadows with you go, to the ancestors you now flow."*

If there is a worthy inheritor of someone's Book of Shadows, this allows for creating a powerful connection between the past and the future. Wouldn't it be wonderful if we had all inherited a Book of Shadows from our own great-great-grandmothers? Think how powerful it would feel to hold in your hands such a venerable object passed down from blood or spiritual ancestors. The book can be bestowed on another person with this ritual.

Cast the magick circle and call the Elements. Burn incense such as frankincense, myrrh, or cedar—something with an ancient connection. Call on the personal deities (or helper spirits) of the person who wrote the book, as well as those of the person inheriting it:

> *From past to future this book flows,*
>
> *With* [person's name] *to a new home now it goes.*
>
> *May the thoughts and knowledge contained here*
>
> *Be brought forward without any fear.*
>
> *May it bring her [him] wisdom and delight*
>
> *Always for the highest spiritual might.*

Devoke and take down the circle as usual.

Destroying the Book of Shadows of a person who no longer has any need for it is by far the most traditional method of disposal. The conventional way to do this is by burning. Burning sends the thoughts and wisdom of the person who wrote the book up into the spirit realm by way of the smoke. In this way the writer is both immortalized and honored. (Burning also neutralizes any possible harmful information in the book, if there is any.) Gather people who knew the person and his or her magickal working and wish to honor the person in this way. This can be a helpful part of the grieving process.

Light a fire in a safe, outdoor fire pit. This could be done indoors in a fireplace or wood stove as well. Assemble around the fire. Cast a magick circle and invoke the Elements to witness the rite. Allow each person to say something about the departed. If people have stories about this person's magick or specifically the connection with his or her Book of Shadows, so much the better. When all have spoken, place the book into the flames, chanting:

> *Ashes to ashes and dust to dust,*
>
> *Pages of this book are bust.*
>
> *No longer here needed, we put you to pyre,*
>
> *And send you with love and the kiss of fire.*

Now the herbs that people brought can be tossed into the fire (lavender and rowan are good choices), and if people feel like continuing to tell stories they can do so. After this ritual it would be important to ground by sharing food and drink, because people have done a fair bit of grieving. Then dismiss the circle by the usual method.

We think you'll find keeping a Book of Shadows a very rewarding part of spellcasting. It's not only a record of the magick you work, but also of the progress you make in spellcasting and magick. You will be amazed as you see it grow, and proud of your own growth as well. You might want to choose a date each year (or several times each year) for sitting down with your Book of Shadows and reviewing the year—or years— of work, writing, and other information within it. This is a great way to gain insight into what magick means in your life and to reevaluate where you want to go in your magickal life. Winter, the time of introspection, is a good time for this, but you should plan a date that feels good to you.

If you've ever kept a journal, you'll understand the kind of self-awareness that comes from exploring your feelings and intentions, and how heightened this becomes when you write these feelings down. Even if all you do is keep accurate magickal record sheets in your Book of Shadows, you'll learn a lot about your own feelings, and if you decide to keep a journal or a dream diary, you will find yourself coming more in tune with yourself, developing an understanding of your emotional and thought processes—all of which will bring you closer to the center of your personal power, the source of your magick.

The Least You Need to Know

- ◆ You can create your own Book of Shadows, a record of your magickal life.

- ◆ Your Book of Shadows must be organized for it to be useful.

- ◆ Use your Book of Shadows to track the success of your spells over time.

- ◆ If your spell doesn't work, go back to your Book of Shadows and see where your spell may have gone astray.

- ◆ Your Book of Shadows is a sacred and valuable piece of property; as such, you may want to determine where it will go when you die.

Part 2

Spells for Ritual

Rituals with spells can be created and performed for any number of occasions, and most witches perform rituals to dedicate themselves to the craft, as well as for cleansing and consecrating their tools and altar. The Elements—Air, Fire, Water, and Earth, as well as spirit, or Akasha—are very important in spellcasting and ritual, and we'll talk about their uses and meanings, and give you a lot of simple spells and chants you can use. We'll also give you spells that are perfect to celebrate the Esbats (lunar rituals) and Sabbats (the solar-calendar Wiccan holidays).

Cleansing and Consecrating Your Tools and Altar

In This Chapter

- Athames, cups, wands, and other magickal tools
- Cleansing and consecrating your tools
- Charging your tools
- Creating a sacred altar
- Where should you create your sacred space?

There are limitless tools and other items available for working magick, and while you may find some of these essential to you, you may not have a use for all (or any!) of them. What do you really need to cast spells? Just your own energy, of course, and your good intentions. If you feel drawn to a particular tool, look into its lore and associations more closely, and make your purchase when you're ready.

In this chapter, we'll talk about some magickal tools, and we'll also provide spells and rituals for their cleansing and consecration. It's important that you store and care for your tools mindfully, which is another consideration in owning them. There are many tools to consider—let's get started.

Tools for Spellcasting

How do you know which tools you'll need to work magick? Well, you don't, until you start to work magick. If you belong to a coven, you may be directed to purchase specific tools and accessories, but you may be left to decide this yourself, and if you're working on your own, it's really up to you. We describe some of the tools used for magick in the following sections. Which tools to own is largely a matter of personal preference, however, and you will have to decide what you really need and what you can do without. Many people practice magick without any of these tools, and some people have a house full of tools and other accessories.

The main purpose of any magickal tool is to help our rational mind relax and focus on the task at hand and to channel our natural energy in the direction we intend. Some tools help us to get into that spiritual frame of mind where it becomes easier to focus and relax or visualize the outcome we are trying for. The closer you live your life to the magickal frame of mind, the less you need tools to help you get there.

You can find most of the tools we describe at your local metaphysical bookstore or occult shop. Once you know what you want to buy, spend some time considering your options before you make a purchase—unless you feel in your heart without a doubt that a specific item is calling to you. If you are not sure whether this is a true spiritual connection or sneaky materialism, you can pull out a pendulum (or other quickie divination device) and ask this simple yes-or-no question: Am I drawn by truth to this magickal tool? Flip a coin, for example. The tools you own will be used a great deal in spellcasting, and it's very important that you feel comfortable and confident with them.

The Athame

Perhaps the most obvious tool used in magick is the *athame* (pronounced ath-*am*-ay), or ritual knife. In a coven, this is really the only tool that each witch would be required to own, as all the other tools would be shared by the coven. The reason it is called a *ritual* knife, and not just a knife, is that it is *never* used to cut anything (with the exception of a handfasting cake). It is part of the discipline of magick to own something and keep it exclusively for one use: ritual. In a magick circle the athame is used to ritually cut and direct energy, but never for cutting a material object.

Words of Power

An **athame** is one of the essential tools used in Wiccan rituals, including spellcasting. It is a ritual knife used not for physical cutting, but to direct magickal energy.

The athame represents the Element of Air. (Some traditions actually link the athame with the Element of Fire, and the Wand with Air—there are no hard-and-fast rules in magick!) The athame is associated with knowledge (because it is traditionally double-edged and cuts both ways, as does knowledge), energy, and ambition, as well as the God (the knife is a phallic symbol). Athames are traditionally double-edged, with a blade of 6 inches or longer. The handle may be made of anything, but most are wood, bone, antler, or leather. They all feel different, so hold a few before you decide to purchase one and choose one that feels good to you. Some witches believe that a handle made of natural material is best, but it's most important that you be comfortable with how the handle feels, as well as with the weight of the knife, and also that you are able to afford the athame. Some people make their own athames, though this isn't so common these days. You can certainly look for one at a local cutlery or hunting shop, or better yet, at a craft fair, where you may have the opportunity to buy one directly from the craftsperson who made it.

The athame is a tool for magick and is never to be used as a weapon. It, along with the other tools mentioned here, is a very personal possession, and you should never touch another person's athame or other tools without his or her permission. Likewise, try not to let others touch or use your magickal tools, unless they are someone you completely trust and love, because that person's energy will be left on the tool. You will use your athame to direct the energy created in your magick working, cast the magick circle, and invoke the Elements (and anyone else—deities, spirits, etc.—you may invoke). You would also use it to cut a door in your magick circle if you or someone else needed to go through temporarily.

Spellcasting

The athame is the most personal tool a witch has, so if you feel the need for one, make sure you find one that calls to you; don't get caught up too much in what you read or hear it *should* be like. You can also do a small spell to help you find the perfect one: Before you go out, find the Queen or King of Swords in your Tarot deck and place that card on your altar. Light a yellow candle (for Air) and some incense and chant, *"Athame that has been mine for all time, find me today, come back and be mine."*

If you're not comfortable with the idea of owning an athame, you don't have to. We know witches who have used a small Swiss army knife for ritual purposes, and you can also learn to use the first two fingers of your right hand as you would an athame, which can be just as effective as the knife.

Swords are used for basically the same purposes as the athame. The sword is also the symbolic tool of Air. (Just as in most Tarot decks, the suit of swords is the suit of Air and heady knowledge.) Swords are larger and more visible and dramatic than athames, and are good for large outdoor gatherings where you may need to be seen by a circle of hundreds of people. Swords are fine for coven work, provided there is adequate space (don't try to do kitchen magick in a small kitchen, casting with a sword!). A sword is certainly not a necessity, but, again, it is all about what enables you to focus your mind and energy. Just make sure you are not purchasing one (and they are not cheap!) to feel that surge of power *over* others. Are you a person who can be trusted to be peaceful with a large weapon in your lap?

Keep in mind that, while you will not use your athame or sword as a weapon, they will look like one to—and can be used as one by—others. You will need to keep these tools in a safe place in your home, one not accessible to others, and, especially if you have children, they should be locked away where they cannot be reached. When traveling, you will need to pack your athame safely away and generally should not carry it on your person. Note that even small knives are no longer allowed on airplanes, so don't carry one with you for working magick. If you need a magick circle during your flight, use your finger to cast it. It's a good idea to check on your local ordinances, to see what size knives can be legally carried, to avoid breaking the law or finding yourself in a complicated legal situation.

The Cup or Chalice

The cup, or chalice, is the traditional tool of the Element of Water. Many witches prefer to use a bowl or cauldron of water on the altar for this purpose. Some rituals and spells call for the use of a cup, and often include wine, water, juice, or some other substance that is held in the cup. You may also prepare herbs for your spell and present these in your cup. You can purchase a special cup such as a chalice or wine glass for this purpose, or you can select a cup from a regular housewares store, or you can use a cup you already own, as long as you cleanse and consecrate it before use (which we'll discuss later in the chapter). If you like, you can also make your own cup out of clay in your home or at a ceramic shop or studio. You can also decorate your cup. The Element of Water is associated with emotions, as well as fertility, the Goddess, and the Tarot suit of Cups.

> **Making Magick**
>
> Aurora's first chalice was painted by an artist friend with a Waning and Waxing Moon symbol on it. She glued a moonstone in the middle of it, painted an ankh (the Egyptian symbol of life) on the cup, and glued a jade stone in the ankh.

We know witches who use antique metal wine cups, but if you do this, be careful that you check what kind of metal it is and that it is safe to use. Aurora almost bought a beautiful metal cup in Greece, but when she asked if she would be able to drink out of it, the vendor said, "No. I'd like to sell you this, but I don't want to poison you." The cup was a tourist knickknack, and it had not occurred to the vendor that anyone would want to drink from it.

If you have a cup that you want to use for magick, or if you find one at a garage sale or antique store, you may want to use the following spell to purge it of its previous associations with former owners. Or perhaps it was an ordinary cup in your kitchen. Fill the cup half full with water, the Element it will represent. Tap water is fine. Take it to your altar, light candle(s), and call in the Water Elemental:

> *Powers of Water, come witness this rite, a tool of yours comes into my sight.*

With the cup on your altar, circle around the outside of it (deosil, or clockwise) with your athame (or wand or finger), chanting:

> *Cup of previous associations, be now purged of former thoughts. Former energies all are gone, a magickal chalice stands on my altar.*

Dip your athame (wand, finger) lightly into the water, saying:

> *Blessed be this water and its vessel, that both shall serve purity and goodness.*

Now take a sip of the water, bestowing your bodily blessing on the cup. Your cup is now ready for cleansing and consecration (discussed later in this chapter).

The Wand

Like the athame, the wand is used to direct magickal energy. The wand is associated with the Element of Fire (a wand is a fairly obvious phallic symbol) and with the suit of Wands in the Tarot deck. It is fine to use a wand any time, and it's especially nice to use when you don't want to pull out your athame. Some spirits are not comfortable with metal (some would say this is true of fairies), so it might be best to use a wand when dealing with them. Rituals to do with Fire or summer and relationships are excellent times to use the wand. Wands also come in a variety of materials but are usually made of wood. You can make your own wand by finding a stick of a desirable length (different traditions say that your wand must be a particular length, often the length from the tip of your finger to your elbow, but we think that the most important thing is that the wand works for you) and preparing it for magick by cleansing and consecrating it. You should consider the kind of wood your wand is made of beforehand—learn about the associations of the kinds of wood you can find where you live.

If you make your own wand, try to do so from a stick or branch you find on the ground. If you plan to remove one from a tree, be careful how you go about this—you don't want to be careless or harmful of nature in the name of magick. If you are going to remove a branch from a tree, you will need to develop a relationship with the tree first. Spend time with it over many seasons: Water it, mulch it, communicate with it, and most important, ask its permission. If you are unsure of your ability to receive the answer from the tree, use a divination technique that you like; perhaps a pendulum or Tarot cards. If you remove a branch from a tree, do so in pruning season and definitely leave an offering of thanks, such as tobacco, food or wine, your own hair, or chocolate at the base of the tree.

If you wish to make a wand out of a piece of wood, try this spell to find the right piece. Aurora worked this spell on Summer Solstice, the first day of summer, which is the season associated with the Element Fire. Sensing that it was time to acquire the tool of Fire, Aurora set up sacred space in a wooded area and called the four directions. Then she raised energy, dancing and singing this chant:

> *Wand of Fire, wood of desire, find me now in this sacred hour.*

After the energy was raised, it was sent off into the universe to work Aurora's magick. Aurora took down her circle and began to walk along the trail. After a short time, she saw the perfect stick lying right in front of her. It was the length of her arm from elbow to fingertip, and thick enough to hold the two crystals that were to be embedded in its ends. These were later attached to the wand with a bit of glue and sheathed in strips of red leather. If you try this spell, don't be discouraged if it doesn't work in one day. Just keep your eyes open, and keep taking walks—you might find your wand a week later!

Some witches have multiple wands of different kinds of wood, and some decorate their wands by putting crystals, gems, or other ornaments on them. A wand channels energy from one end to the other, so it is thought to need an energy-channeling device at each end (think of them as the positive and negative poles of a battery). There are those who feel these must be amber at one end and jet at the other. Aurora uses a clear quartz crystal at one end and obsidian at the other. These are simply options, of course.

The staff is a larger version of the wand and, like the sword, is more dramatic and easier to see. If drama and visibility appeal to you, by all means, try a staff. Or perhaps the staff simply is convenient for you because you also use it for walking or carrying things. A staff can be a beautiful hand-carved item that incorporates leather, fur, and crystals—whatever you like to work with.

The Pentacle

The pentacle is a 5-pointed star (a pentagram) inside a circle. It represents the Element of Earth and is associated with the body, prosperity, nature, and the Tarot suit of Pentacles. It is used to bless other things with the energy of the earth, such as the bowl of water that you place on the pentacle while you ritually bless it. You have likely seen this symbol before and will perhaps want one on your altar. While this tool is traditionally a flat metal plate that sits on your altar, you can find pentacles in all sizes and made of any number of materials. The pentacle is often used for protection and healing rituals. It is probably the one least used by most spellworkers, as so many less-abstract things can be used to symbolize Earth (such as a plant, a pot of dirt, or salt). Throughout this book, when we ask you to bless something with your Earth Element representation, you can use a pentacle, but you are also welcome to use whatever you like to represent Earth on your altar: a plant, a stone, or something else. Aurora uses a flat stone that her toddler gave her at the beach, on which she has painted a pentagram. Your altar pentacle could also be made out of ceramic or wax, and it could quite literally be a plate that you also use for serving bread or cakes.

The pentacle is also the main symbol of the craft, and people use it as a sign of their religious affinity. Witches often find and recognize each other by means of pentacles worn as jewelry or as stickers on cars.

You can find everything from stationery to jewelry embellished with pentacles, and you may feel this symbol to be an attractive way of displaying your spiritual involvement with spellwork. Be aware that even if you don't consider yourself Wiccan, if you wear a pentacle, other people will assume you are.

If you wish to make yourself a pentacle for your altar out of clay or wax, you can imbue it with magickal Earth energy by using this spell as you work. First invoke the Element of Earth to bless your work:

> *Earth, Mother, mountain, clay,*
>
> *Come and bless this work today.*

Then, as you form your piece, chant:

> *Earth energy will channel through*
>
> *This gateway that I make anew.*

Any tool that you make with your own hands has such strong alignment with you and your energy that it is bound to work well for you.

Spellcasting _____

You can purchase your magickal tools from a metaphysical store or local craft fair, particularly a craft fair geared toward historical reenactments, such as medieval or Renaissance fairs. The advantage of craft fairs is that you often get to meet and talk to the craftspeople who made the items. Their energy might be the deciding factor for you on whether or not you have found the perfect tool. And who knows—you might strike up a lasting friendship! For specific, difficult-to-find tools, there are many mail-order and Internet stores out there (we've included a few in Appendix B). Or check out *The Complete Idiot's Guide to Wicca Craft* by Miria Liguana and Nina Metzner.

Brooms, Cauldrons, Amulets, and Other Accessories

In addition to these tools, you might see the following discussed in spellcasting or find them in occult stores: brooms, bolines, cauldrons, bowls, ritual clothing or robes, amulets, cords, candles, incense, herbs, oils, jewelry, etc. The broom is used for cleansing a space, marking a meeting space, jumping over at a wedding, leaping for sympathetic crop magic, and of course, sweeping the floor! A handmade broom is also a beautiful, decorative item. The one Aurora's grandmother had hanging in her hallway made a lasting impression on her as a child.

The white-handled knife is a not-very-creative name for a knife that is kept with your magickal supplies but is used for cutting things (candles, cords, cheese) within a magick circle. The name is meant to distinguish it from the athame (which is often black-handled, though of course, that is up to you). Traditionally, a coven would own a white-handled knife; it is not something each witch would have. A Swiss army knife would work fabulously. You could bless it by saying:

When I have need to sever and cut, serve me well O blade of steel.

Another kind of knife that you may see or hear about is a boline. It is a sickle-shaped knife used primarily for harvesting herbs.

Cauldrons are used in that "double, double, toil and trouble" way, but you can find them in much more portable sizes than you might envision when you think about witches creating a potion. Like the cup, the cauldron symbolizes the Goddess. It's usually made of cast iron and is used for everything from creating potions to burning incense. Small bowls will come in handy for working magick, and you will likely need at least two, one for holding water and one for salt (which you use to make holy water for the cleansing of your tools).

If you want to bless your cauldron or bowl with some lines adapted from the bard, try:

> *Double, double, toil and trouble,*
>
> *Fire burn and cauldron bubble,*
>
> *What e'er I shall in you bake,*
>
> *A blessed stew your pow'r shall make.*
>
> *Show the Goddess as you should,*
>
> *Then the charm is firm and good.*

Within some covens, specific clothing and jewelry is used to designate your position within the coven; the particulars on this vary, however. Robes are often used for rituals, or whenever you want to help get yourself into a magickal frame of mind. You can make these yourself. Aurora's first coven told the neophytes to sew robes for their first coven meeting, so she and a friend went to the local fabric store and bought the pattern for the Jesus and Holy Family costumes used for Nativity plays: A robe is a robe is a robe. (You'll find great robe and tunic patterns that are easy to make in *The Complete Idiot's Guide to Wicca Craft* by Miria Liguana and Nina Metzner.)

Some (particularly Gardnerians) prefer to practice magick *skyclad*—this is said to open up the flow of energy. It also equalizes everyone and brings us back to ourselves and away from our mundane trappings. You may want to have special clothes that you use only for magick and rituals, but these don't have to be elaborate—and naked is a simple solution! And, believe us, there is something very magickal (and bracing!) about standing outside on a hill at night buck naked! Menstruating women in the group would be free to choose a garment such as underwear, a swimsuit, or a skirt if they wished. During menstruation is a very powerful time to work magick, as it makes you more open to channeling the Goddess's energy. Some people think it is so powerful that you need to beware! But this is an individual choice; if you feel like working magick, then do so! If you feel like staying home and curling up with a good book, go for it!

Amulets are magick spells made tangible. They are a way of putting a spell into a small, portable form that you can give, wear, or hang in your home or car. You can sew one out of cloth

> **Words of Power**
>
> **Skyclad** means naked. Many witches (especially Gardnerians) prefer to practice magick this way.

> **Words of Power**
>
> An **amulet** is a small, tangible spell, an object invested with magickal power. A rabbit's foot and a four-leaf clover are folk amulets.

and fill it with herbs, crystals, or whatever is appropriate. An amulet could also be a piece of jewelry, a stone that you find, or just about anything that comes to you invested—or that you invest—with magickal power. It gets charged for protection, good luck, weight loss, job opportunities, or whatever you are working toward.

You may find a purpose for items such as cords, candles, incense, herbs, and oils as you create specific spells (we'll discuss these items in Part 3, where we consider magickal correspondences). You may need to visit an occult store, herb shop, fabric shop, or health-food store for these. You certainly don't need to have a cache of these items when beginning to work magick. As we noted in Chapter 3, in kitchen magick, you can use household herbs, spices, and foods to work magick.

Some people really like to accessorize. If you decide to get into practicing magick, you will find a whole subculture of products out there, everything from jewelry to calendars to sleepwear. And let's not forget the books! (The best investment, in our opinion!) You can spend a fortune on all of the accessories available to you as a worker of magick, but again we emphasize that you don't *have* to buy any of them (no matter how cute those PJs would look on you), or you can buy what you like. If you find a piece of jewelry with an amulet that you love, by all means add it to your collection, but don't try to make your magick work better with a fancy athame or expensive robes. Know that the tools and accessories are not what make your magick successful. Your power and how you use it are the keys to successful spellcasting.

Cleansing and Consecrating Your Magickal Tools

Before you use them in magick, you will want to cleanse and consecrate your tools, to make them sacred for the work they will do. To cleanse your tools is to purify them, ridding them of any negative or unwanted energy; to consecrate your tools is to bless or dedicate them to their magickal purpose. Both cleansing and consecrating are performed by ritual. These acts will also serve to focus your mind on the magickal work ahead.

You will cleanse and consecrate your tools when you first acquire them (or intend to begin using them magickally), and then periodically as it seems necessary (it's not necessary to do so before each use), and there are a number of rituals for this. We're including a simple one here for the athame that you can adapt to the tools you have.

CAUTION

For Protection

Don't use your tools for the first time before you have followed a ritual to cleanse and consecrate them—it's important that they be free of any negative energy and marked with your own energy before you begin to work magick with them.

If your tools are handled by someone without your permission (or even with it), and especially if they are mishandled, you will want to cleanse and consecrate them to re-establish their positive energy and purity of purpose, and make them effective for working magick. A change in energy in your tools doesn't have to be the result of purposeful mishandling; even a curious friend can alter the energy of your tools. This, of course, is another good reason to keep all of your magickal tools in a very safe place.

Ritual for Cleansing and Consecrating

Before you can cleanse and consecrate your tools, you will need to cleanse and conse-crate your altar and create your sacred space. (We discuss this in detail in Chapter 2.) You will use the four Elements in this ritual: Air, Fire, Water, and Earth.

Start by cleansing the space (smudge, sweep, sprinkle saltwater, whatever you feel is appropriate). Have a bowl of water and a bowl of salt, a candle, and burning incense either ready or already lit. Cast your circle and call the four Elements: East (Air), South (Fire), West (Water), and North (Earth), or whatever geographical correspon-dences make sense in your area. Call on the Lord and Lady if you wish, or whichever spirits or deities you feel are appropriate—perhaps Vesta, Goddess of hearth and home, if you are dedicating a home altar. Say, *"By the powers of Air,"* circling the in-cense around the altar; *"By the powers of Fire,"* indicating the altar space with the candle; *"By the powers of Water,"* sprinkling a few drops of water with your fingers; and *"By the powers of Earth,"* pouring the salt into the water and stirring. Next, begin sprinkling the saltwater, singing or chanting: *"By Earth, by Air, by Water, by Fire, I charge and consecrate this space."*

Now the space is ready. When you are ready to cleanse and dedicate your athame (or other tool), first smudge it (if you don't like using smudge, which are herbs burnt for the purifying and cleansing aspects of the smoke, use incense instead), then place it on the altar. If you are continuing from the altar-dedicating ritual, you are ready to begin; if you are doing this ritual on its own, you need to cast the circle and call the quarters. When you call the quarters to do a dedication ritual for an athame, you might want to make special mention to the Air Elementals, as you call them, that you call them to witness and bless a consecration of their tool. Then introduce the tool to each direction, first holding it to the East, then South, West, and North. You might say the following: *"Element of Air, behold your tool, the ritual athame. Bless it for its work, that it always cut true."* Then, *"Element of Fire, behold this tool, the ritual athame. Bless it for its work, that its energy be directed truly."* To the West, *"Element of Water, behold this tool, the ritual athame. Bless it for its work, that it always be wielded in love and truth."* And to the North, *"Element of Earth, behold this tool, the ritual athame. Bless it for its work, that its purpose always come from a sound foundation."*

Charging Your Tools

A final step in preparing your tools for use in magick is to *charge* them, or awaken the positive energies in them. A very simple way of accomplishing this is to lay them out under the light of a Full Moon so that they receive the energy of the Goddess. You can repeat this process in full midday sun to also give your tools the energy of the God. You can sit with your tools as they absorb the energy, meditating and visualizing your tools receiving the energy of the God and Goddess (visualize this energy entering yourself, as well). You could bury a tool (or some part of it) in the earth, to charge it with the local Earth energy and the magick of the local spirits of place. For example, you could drive the blade of your athame into the ground during the course of a meditation. During the meditation, visualize the earth's energy flowing up into the tool. You might want to try the following chant (or make up your own!):

> *Goddess and God, draw down your light,*
>
> *Bring your power and might to me,*
>
> *Power of Earth, awaken the life,*
>
> *Fill these tools with your energy.*

Care of Your Tools

The tools you decide to use for your magick are sacred to your work and should be cared for as sacred, spiritual objects. If you own an athame, you are not only responsible for keeping it from harming another person, you must also take care of it, keeping it clean and protected from negative energy. You should purchase or make a sheath for your athame, so that its blade is protected and others are protected from its blade.

You will want to be sure your tools do not become broken or rusted from lack of care or misuse, and you should store them carefully. If you can, keep all of your magickal supplies in one place—perhaps a locked cabinet—you will find this most convenient. You'll also want to keep your tools *organized* (here we go again!). Don't just toss everything together into a box or drawer, so that you have to rummage around the next time you need a candle or some incense. This isn't a respectful way to care for your tools and can cause them to be damaged.

Spellcasting

Most coven work or group rituals use an altar (or at least a candle) at each of the four directions. You don't need to create four altars in your home, but if you're going to do a major ritual or work with a group of people, you might want to consider it. Often for group rituals people are told to bring items to place on the altars. Participants bring items they want blessed or empowered that they associate with Air for the East altar, Fire for the South altar, and so on. It is traditional to light the candle on each altar when that Element is called in (that is, invoke Water, then light the candle on the West altar, and so on).

Your Sacred Altar

Your altar is where you will practice rituals and magick; when working spells, you will lay out the ingredients of your spell on your altar. Altars are most often made from natural materials, such as wood. You can make an altar; it doesn't have to look any specific way, and you can also purchase some very fancy ones. Your altar is a reflection of you and the magick you will work, therefore you should feel comfortable with it. You can build an altar from wood, or arrange stones to represent your altar, or you can use a shelf, a coffee table, or the top of a dresser, any of which you set up as a sacred space. There aren't really any hard and fast rules here, and again, it's what feels best for you, in the space where you're comfortable working magick.

When you're working magick, the idea is that the altar is your anchor, linking you with the mundane world while you are engaging the magickal world. There is much debate about where the altar must be placed (it is often placed to the East); if you're working in a magick circle, the altar should be within the circle, but in exactly what position? Place it where it feels best for you in working your magick.

You can set your altar up each time you prepare to work magick, or leave it set up, keeping candles and other tools there all the time if your living space permits this and you're comfortable with it. If you're going to set your altar up each time, keep your tools together and someplace safe, where you can find them but where they won't be found or used by others. What goes on your altar is also a personal issue.

As we said, you will place the tools for the magick you plan to work on your altar, and when you're working magick, you should avoid clutter and keep the altar about the magick at hand. There may be other objects that are meaningful to you that you want to place on your altar and you can do this if your altar is set up permanently, or you could set up a separate altar for this purpose, perhaps a wall altar—an altar on a shelf or in a niche in the wall, or on your fireplace mantle.

If you have a permanent altar set up, avoid the temptation to use it as a temporary parking place for something you just don't know where to set down. Think of it as sacred space, not another surface on which to spread the clutter of life. When your life is feeling hectic, you might find that going to your altar, rearranging it, refreshing the water and flowers, and replacing the cloth with one appropriate for the coming season will feel like a calming, centering meditation. You may find that the calm and beauty of your altar is inspiring and spreads to the rest of your house! If you only have a few moments to clean, start with your altar. It has a magickal way of distributing loving energy. As you work on your altar, try chanting:

> *Loving energy spread from here,*
>
> *Focus my life both far and near.*

You may want to cover your altar with a decorative cloth, though you should keep in mind that the cloth may get candle wax or incense ash spilled on it when you are working magick, so don't choose something irreplaceable, or use a second cloth on top of the decorative cloth when working magick on your altar. You might also have a representation of the God or Goddess or important gems or amulets on your altar. When working magick, you may want to place a pentacle on your altar (in the center, or above where you will be working magick), and you will need space for whatever else you need for working magick: herbs, candles, your cup, or oils.

The Best Place(s) for Your Sacred Space

We talked about creating a *sacred space* in Chapter 2 and will remind you now that it's important that you choose this space carefully. It can be inside or outside, at your home or in some other location. You have to consider issues of privacy, noise, and access, and if you share your home with other people and plan to create a sacred space there, you will need to discuss it with them so that everyone is comfortable with the idea. The last thing you need is your roommate or spouse accidentally (because you didn't discuss it with them) or purposefully (because they resent your use of the space) interrupting your magick or handling your magickal tools without your consent. If necessary, create a temporary sacred space and a portable altar (one you can pack up and out of the way). You want this space to be one of harmony and power for you. If you have a spare room, you may want to use it for magick—this way you can store your magickal tools in the room and have access to everything you need, as well as the ability to close out the rest of the

Words of Power

A **sacred space** is a place where you feel powerful and confident, and that you have cleansed and consecrated for working magick.

household, if necessary. You could redecorate the room to better express its purpose, but of course, this isn't necessary.

If you choose an out-of-doors sacred space, keep in mind issues of privacy and weather. Unless you live in a very open-minded neighborhood, you probably don't want your ritual to be on public display for the neighbors. And think about whether or not you would really go outside and do your spellwork if the time you choose turned out to be during a downpour. (Of course this may be a message that you should postpone your working.) Ultimately, it is ideal to have both indoor and out-door options for your magick. You can use any public garden or park as a temporary sacred space, and creating a permanent one could be labor-intensive, though ultimately enriching.

Your sacred space should not only be the place where you set up your altar and work magick, it should be a place where you feel confident and powerful, safe and relaxed. You should feel good in this space whether you are working magick there or not, and once you decide to make the space sacred, you will cleanse and consecrate it to your magickal purpose.

Though there are many tools for working magick (and plenty of cool accessories, too), you don't have to spend a lot of money to work magick. Remember that the most important tool you have when casting spells is yourself.

The Least You Need to Know

- There are many tools and accessories available for working magick—you should decide what you need as you go along; don't feel pressured to make a lot of unnecessary purchases to work magick.

- Always cleanse and consecrate your magickal tools before using them for the first time, and do so again periodically as they seem to need it.

- Take care with your magickal tools, and store them locked away and out of the reach of others who might change their energy (or who might harm themselves with your tools).

- You can erect your altar on any number of household surfaces, but be sure to set your altar up in a sacred space.

- You can create a sacred space indoors or out, but remember to choose carefully, working with other household members, if necessary, before cleansing and consecrating the space.

- The most important tool you have for practicing magick is yourself.

The Dedication Ceremony

In This Chapter

- ◆ Dedicating yourself to magick and spellwork
- ◆ What's involved in a dedication ceremony
- ◆ Your magickal name: finding it and using it
- ◆ Dedication doesn't have to be eternal

Dedication ceremonies are done in covens as well as by solitary witches. If you decide to dedicate yourself to spellcraft, you may also want to take a new, magickal name (though you don't have to).

A dedication ceremony is a very personal choice. If you feel drawn to this idea, then go forward with it. If not, skip it for now. The main reason for a dedication ceremony is to give you a feeling of purpose on your path and plug you into a deeper current of connection with the deities and energies of the universe. You can always plan one at a later date, when you're ready.

Dedicating Yourself to the Magickal Path

To dedicate yourself to spellwork is a very serious matter and an important rite of passage in your magickal life. It's much like a church confirmation. When you dedicate yourself, you are saying that you have done some work and considered the work ahead, and decided that the magickal path is right for you: You are making an informed and conscious decision to study and learn about the path. You promise to follow the Wiccan Rede: "*An it harm none, do what ye will*"; and you welcome the Lord and Lady into your life. Within a coven, a dedication ceremony will be performed by a Priest or Priestess and will likely have set requirements of and guidelines for the dedicant. If you are working alone, you can perform your own ceremony, and you can choose to do this privately or to have others present.

Do not plan to dedicate yourself to magick if your only experience of magick is what you've done with this book; have enough time and experience under your belt that you are past the initial flush of excitement and are sure that this is the correct step for you to take. A year and a day of practice is the traditional length of time before dedication, to let things settle and make sure you feel committed to following your spirit down the magickal path. If you are unsure, you might try some divinations on whether or not it is time for your dedication ceremony. You don't have to have a dedication ceremony before working magick, and you'll want to explore magick before you decide to dedicate yourself.

If you are feeling drawn to the idea of a dedication ceremony but not sure whether this is the right time for you to go forward, you might want to try this divination. Go to a place where you feel connected to nature and the universal flow of energy; a sacred outside place would be best. Cast a circle and call the Elements of the four directions. Call personal deities or helper spirits who you feel direct you on your path. You might say:

> *Lord and Lady, you who guide my life and my magickal footsteps, help me to see the correct course of action. Is this the time for me to dedicate myself to this work?*

Pull out a divination method that you prefer, be it Tarot cards, runes, or the I Ching. The first item you pull out should give you a clear image of whether the time is right for your dedication. If you are using the Tarot, for example, a card indicating a person of magickal work and learning would tell you to go ahead with the dedication. A card showing downfall and confusion may indicate caution and a time of waiting. Your first message will probably be right on. And remember, if the indication isn't for going ahead, it is not telling you that you are on the *wrong* path, but rather that the time is not quite right. You can repeat this divination as often as you like, and when the indication is favorable, begin planning your dedication ceremony. After your divination, thank and dismiss the deities and Elements, and lower the circle.

What Happens During the Dedication Ceremony

If you have decided to dedicate yourself to spellcraft, you should plan a dedication ceremony. You can plan and write this yourself, or use the one we include here. You will want to plan your dedication ceremony carefully, selecting a fortuitous time, day, and place for your ceremony, and deciding on the elements and what you will wear (or if you will be skyclad). You may also choose your magickal name before your ceremony (more on this later in this chapter). Work out all of the details ahead of time, as you would for any ritual or magick you might work.

> ### Spellcasting
>
> The New Moon might be a good time to dedicate yourself to magick, if you feel that this is a new endeavor for you. Try the Full Moon if you want it to be especially magickal and powerful, and see your dedication as a culmination of your time of preparation for dedication to the craft. Any time between the New and Full Moon are good times for dedication, too; the important thing is to choose the time that resonates to your intent of practice.

You will begin by setting up your altar for the dedication ceremony. Include on your altar all of the working tools that you use in your spellwork (athame, wand, cup, and pentacle, or some representative of each Element)—whatever you usually use as mainstays of your spellwork. If you don't usually use a wand, don't procure one for this ritual, use the tool that you normally use to represent Fire. You will also want candles for each direction and some incense that indicates rebirth for you (sage and lavender, perhaps, for new endeavors). You may want a rattle, drum, or flute, or another music-making device that helps to put you into a magickal frame of mind. Also include some drink to put in your cup and some kind of food that you can share with the Lord and Lady and other energies that you will be calling. If you are working indoors (and cannot simply pour your libation on the ground), you will want a cup and plate for the offerings to the spirit, as well.

Many dedicants decide to perform their dedication ceremony skyclad, because the ceremony represents a rebirth into the magickal life. If you find yourself concerned that you may be menstruating at the time of the ritual, don't worry. Skyclad can easily be modified to make you comfortable. Choose any garment that will work for you: underwear, a swimsuit, or perhaps a skirt—whatever you feel is right for the situation. If you are menstruating at the time of your dedication ceremony, this would be a very powerful omen. For the Goddess to have given you the gift of extra energy flow at this time shows a special connection with the magickal path. Take it as a good sign!

Next, you should prepare a *ritual bath* for yourself, laying out the robe or clothing you will wear afterward. A ritual bath is an important step before working any kind of magick or performing rituals; it cleanses not only the body, but the mind as well. It helps you to be relaxed and get focused, ridding your mind of negative energy. The ritual bath can also serve as a period of meditation prior to your ritual. Chapter 20 covers ritual baths in detail; read that chapter before completing your plan for this part of your dedication. Choose what sounds right for you from Chapter 20, but make sure your bath includes sea salt and some kind of focusing oil (such as lavender). While in your bath, prepare yourself for your dedication with a chant:

> **Words of Power**
>
> A **ritual bath** is meant to cleanse your body and your mind prior to performing a ritual or magick. It will relax and focus you, preparing your mind for the magickal work before you.

> *Lord and Lady, for you I prepare,*
>
> *Myself to devote to the magickal way.*
>
> *Be with me, guide me, show me my power,*
>
> *As I begin to walk on this sacred path.*

If you are doing the ritual alone, you might try something like this: After you are bathed, lay out your sacred space. You will want to have at least a candle at each cardinal direction; your sacred space might even have room for four altars, one for each direction. If so, you can, place your representations of each Element on their respective altar (feathers, athame, and incense at East; wand, phallic stones, red dragons, and candle at South; cauldron or chalice, bowl of water, and shells at West; pentacle, stones, and plants at North). Next, cleanse the space (and yourself) with smudge or incense, ritual sweeping, asperging, or sound (drumming, bell ringing, or chanting could be used to clear a space of unwanted energy). Here's a chant you might use:

> *Cleanse this space and make it free*
>
> *And clear of negativity.*

Or try this:

> *As I sweep and cleanse this place,*
>
> *By Lord and Lady it is a sacred space.*

Ground yourself with a meditation, tree visualization, or chakra alignment. Begin by standing in yoga's mountain pose with your hands centered before your heart. Breathe deeply and fully as you connect yourself to the energy of the earth. If you'd like, move into yoga's tree pose and evoke the chakra energy of the tree of life to symbolize your growing knowledge of and dedication to your chosen path. Say the following words of sacred grounding, or choose your own resonating words of grounding power:

Center my heart at the start

Of my given path.

May my feet stand firm

And ready as my arms reach

To gather knowledge and wisdom

From the blossoming tree of life

I feel the energy rise

From Earth to sky

In praise of this work.

Mountain pose (left) and tree pose (right).

Cast the circle with your athame (or wand or finger or feather—whatever you like to use). Starting in the East, and moving deosil (clockwise) around the circle, call:

> *Circle of Power, contain this energy,*
>
> *Allow only love to enter, only love to leave.*

Now call the directions, starting with the East, and lighting each candle in turn as the Element is welcomed into your circle. Call the Elements to witness your dedication to working magick. You might say something like:

> *Elementals of the East, bring your gift of knowledge to this new endeavor.*
>
> *Elementals of the South, bring your connection and fierce passion to this dedication.*
>
> *Elementals of the West, bring your gift of intuition to this magickal working.*
>
> *Elementals of the North, bring your gifts of groundedness and stability to this rite.*

Next, call your personal deities with whom you will be working. If you, like us, prefer to work with many deities, you can just call on Goddess and God, or Lady and Lord. Some people like to dedicate themselves to a specific deity (Isis or Hecate, for example); this is a choice you will have to make for yourself. Aurora generally says that she is dedicated to the Goddess's work, whatever she may ask. So the Goddess will manifest in Aurora's life in many different guises, and Aurora will call her by different names. If you are a man, perhaps you will feel more ease in relating to a male deity or deities, though not necessarily. Do what feels right to you. Ask the deity or deities you have decided on to come and bear witness to your dedicating yourself to their work.

An example might be:

> *Great Goddess Athena, you who bring wisdom and strength. Come to this rite and witness my dedication to your work. Welcome Athena.*

Use this method to invoke any other entity you feel needs to be present for your ceremony: ancestors, spirits of place, faerie spirits, tree spirits—whoever is important in your working. For example:

> *Ancestors, you who have gone before, my foremothers and forefathers all the way back to the beginning of time, come! Ancestors of blood and bone and ancestors of spirit, all you helping spirits who wish me well on my path, come and guide my hand, I call you here to witness the dedication I perform today.*

Spellcasting

If your dedication ritual is performed in a coven, another witch will introduce you to the Lady and Lord and each Element as a dedicant. They will introduce you to each working tool, saying a few words about its proper use. Perhaps a specific field of study or goal will be identified for you (such as devoting yourself to the study of Tarot, runes, herbs, or accomplishing certain tasks) before the next step—which might be your initiation.

Now state your intention to all assembled (you are introducing yourself to them, and if you are taking on a magickal name, this is the time to use it):

> *I, Aurora, your priestess and dedicant, am hereby offering to dedicate myself to your work, the magick and spellwork needed by my community, and ask your blessings. May your wisdom and love ever guide me in following the Wiccan path.*

You can mention specific goals, such as finding a coven or group to work with, your future initiation, or learning to be a healer or herbalist or diviner—whatever specific path you hope to follow. If you don't have a specific path or goal, you can ask for guidance at this time, either from the deities, or by using a form of divination at this point in the ritual, using Tarot cards, runes, or another form of divination. Addressing the deities and spirits you called, ask for help:

> *Ancestors, Goddess, God, I ask for your guidance! Guide my hand to help me know my true calling. Which path am I to follow?*

Then pull out a rune (or card or whatever). If you are not yet familiar with the runes or don't immediately see the intention of the card you have pulled, you will have plenty of time later to study and meditate on it.

Now face the East and tell the Air Elementals that you intend to dedicate yourself to magick and spellwork. Once again, you are introducing yourself, so use your magickal name if you are taking one on. If you were working with a coven, this is the point in the ritual when you would be introduced to the working tool of Air, so you might want to pick up your athame, if you have one (or a feather or incense) and state to the Air Elementals that you are familiar with their tools and you hope to always use them with wisdom and respect. Now face the South, West, and North, respectively, and do the same with the tools for these Elements. As you do so, you might say:

> *Element of Air, behold Aurora, dedicant to the magickal path, I dedicate myself today to walking the path of connection, I ask your blessing on my journey.*

(Repeat for each Element.)

This would also be a good time to give a small offering to each Element as you ask its blessing: Offer smoke from incense to the Air Elementals, light an extra candle for Fire, pour some water for the Water Elementals, and place a stone or bit of food on the Earth altar.

When you have completed your round, you can close your dedication ritual with a song or some words to the Lord and Lady and assembled spirits to the following effect:

> *I have dedicated myself to your service,*
>
> *May this be for the greatest good of All,*
>
> *May my ear be ever open to your call.*

Now it's time to share some food and drink with all assembled, putting their portion on a plate and in a cup that you will later place outside in a secure and sacred spot, leaving it there overnight. If you perform this ritual outside, you can simply pour the drink onto the ground and place the bread or cookies or whatever food you have chosen onto a rock, if you prefer.

As you place your offerings, you might want to chant:

> *I offer this food to ancestors, spirits, Goddess, God, all my relations.*

Once you have grounded yourself with the nourishment, you are ready to take down the circle, as the new you, the new dedicant, perhaps with a new name. Dismiss the spirits and deities you have called, thanking them for witnessing this important event. Dismiss the Elements, thanking them for their great contributions to your magickal work. Finally, open the circle by tracing it widdershins (counterclockwise) starting in the East and chanting as you walk:

> *The magick is done, the rite is won.*
>
> *The circle is open, but unbroken.*

After the Ceremony

You've done it—you're a dedicant! You have chosen the magickal path and declared your commitment to the Lord and Lady. You should record your ceremony and your feelings about it in your Book of Shadows. If you drew a Tarot card or rune, now is the time to write down what you selected and perhaps meditate on this. Pay special attention to your dreams this night, and record them, as well.

You might want to celebrate your dedication by doing something special for yourself and for the God and Goddess. Take a day to yourself and go out and enjoy nature; take a hike, spend time reading in a park, or do some gardening. Maybe you'll want to celebrate with some friends—have a celebratory feast, or plan a special visit with a close friend to share your joy.

What's in a Name?

Well, a lot, actually, as I'm sure you know from your own name or nickname. You can cull information on a person from a name: their gender and sometimes their nationality or religion. When you dedicate yourself to magick, you choose your magickal name. This is the name by which other witches, as well as the Goddess and God, will know you. This name might speak of your special affinities (such as with a certain tree or herb or with a particular planet) or perhaps it will relate to a path begun in a past lifetime.

Spellcasting

Is a magickal name just not coming to you? Try looking through books of mythology or astrology, books of plant and tree names, foreign-language dictionaries, and books of baby names for inspiration. But most important, don't worry! When the time is right, the name will arrive.

The Magickal Name: Where Does It Come From?

If you have kids, you know how difficult it can be choosing and agreeing upon a name (at least when finding your magickal name, you're the only one who has to like it!). It's an awesome responsibility. The same is true of your magickal name. You want this name to speak to you, and you want to be aware of what it says about you. It should be a name that you feel strongly connected to, and one that inspires you. Have you heard of Wiccan writers Starhawk or Silver Ravenwolf? Those are magickal names, as is the name Aurora has chosen to use for this book: Aurora Greenbough. You can always use your personal name, if you choose, but most people use renaming as an opportunity to begin establishing their new magickal identity.

Before her initiation, Aurora's High Priest performed a dedication ceremony where he introduced her as Aurora to the four directions and to the Lady and Lord as a dedicant. Then, at her initiation, she was introduced to the rest of the coven as Aurora, the initiate.

Finding your magickal name is very much like rediscovering a truth about yourself that has always been there. It may be a name that your spirit has had for many lifetimes, or perhaps it is time for a new quest, a new direction. You might think of it not as choosing a new name, but as finding a name that you already have—one you just didn't know about.

Making Magick

Your magickal name will often find you in unexpected ways, so keep your eyes and ears open. Perhaps the name will recur in dreams, movies, books, and conversation—it could come to you from anywhere. Pay attention to these little signals. Aurora's name came to her repeatedly over a period of a few years in diverse ways: the Aurora Borealis might be mentioned; it was the name of a crystal she was looking at; it is the name of Sleeping Beauty in the ballet of that name. The name just kept popping up until Aurora could tell it was trying to get her attention.

You should spend some time researching names—don't just choose the first one that comes to mind. If you've ever been dissatisfied with your name or found it limiting, consider this your chance to expand, to reach out and find a new expression of who you are and who you hope to be. How will others see you, and what will they expect from someone named Moondove, as opposed to Prairie or Ares? You can choose more than one name, and use them together as one name or two (like Moondove or Moon Dove). The name you choose will be distinct, and because you use it only in the pagan community, it will also afford you privacy and a new sense of identity within that community.

You don't have to choose a name like Moondove, of course, though names taken from nature are popular choices. Many witches have perfectly normal witch names (like Anna or Henry) that they feel drawn to, perhaps because it was their name in a past life or the name of an ancestor they admire. Perhaps there's a name you're drawn to, or a god or goddess you feel a strong connection with. Be careful of using a deity name of a powerful head of pantheon (how would you feel about someone who asked you to call him Lord Zeus?) or one who might be invoked often in the pagan community (how will you feel about having a couple hundred people chanting your name while drumming and raising energy?).

If you find yourself torn between two or more names, or without a clue as to which name might be right for you, meditate on it. Ask yourself how you feel about being seen as strong, gentle, energetic, or powerful. Think about the gods and goddesses and which ones appeal to you. Also do some research into nature: find out about plants and trees, make lists of your favorite things (including flowers, trees, places, books, cars—anything can lead you to the name you're looking for!). You can even take the names you come up with and rework the letters into new names. We're sure that, as you meditate and work on the problem, you will come across the right name (or it will come to you). Naming is something done for most people at birth in our culture, and you should see this renaming as a kind of rebirth: the birth of your magickal self. Feel free to express who you hope to be and explore another side of yourself—the magickal side.

CAUTION

For Protection _____

Don't choose your magickal name on a whim! You may quickly be sorry you chose to be called Witchipoo or Gandalf. Be sure to research the name you choose before you decide— _donders_ sounds good, but it means _damn_ in Dutch!

Using Your Magickal Name

When you dedicate yourself to spellcraft, you may want to take a magickal name; sometimes, within a coven, you will take a name as a dedicant, and then, one year and one day later, you will take a new, permanent magickal name. It is possible to rededicate yourself and take a new name when you feel you've outgrown the one you have, but keep in mind that this can be confusing to others.

You'll use your magickal name whenever you work magick, and will also use it with others in your circle of pagan friends and acquaintances. If you put your name on your tools, your magickal name is the one you will use. This is the name the God and Goddess will know you by, and it represents your magickal self. It will be inscribed in the front of your Book of Shadows.

Spellcasting _____

Once you've found your magickal name, or perhaps to help you find one, try looking up the name and its meaning in runes or some other magickal alphabet, or do a numerology exercise on it.

The Numerology of Your Magickal Name

In numerology, the letters of the alphabet are assigned a numerological equivalent. You can find out many numerical truths from the name you were born with. You can figure your Destiny Number, the total of the letters in your birth name; your Soul Number, the total of the vowels of your birth name; and your Personality Number, the total of the consonants in your birth name. Here though, we are interested in finding out the numerological meaning of the all-important magickal name you gift to yourself.

Most numerologists will say that if you are choosing a name for a new baby, or if you are changing your own name, you should choose the name _intuitively_, and only figure the numerology of the name *after* it has been decided. The energy of a name should not be forced and there are no "wrong" numbers. So if you've already chosen your magickal name, let's see what numerology has to say about it. If you are still deciding on a magickal name, you may want to try this exercise, but be sure to guide your ultimate choice solely by your inner light.

Letters and Numbers								
1	2	3	4	5	6	7	8	9
A	B	C	D	E	F	G	H	I
J	K	L	M	N	O	P	Q	R
S	T	U	V	W	X	Y	Z	

The letters of your magickal name, like the letters of the first name in your birth name, add up to what some numerologists call the Key Number. The Key Number reveals how you will view your life experiences and gives insights about your future growth on your path. To find the resonance between your first name at birth and your magickal name, you'll want to figure the Key Number for both. If the total you calculate for your Key Number has more than one digit—for example, if it adds up to 13—you'll want to add those numbers together so that your result is reduced to a single digit: 1 + 3 = 4.

Write your first name at birth and its corresponding numbers in the spaces below, calculate the total, and reduce the final result to a single digit:

First name at birth: ___ ___ ___ ___ ___ ___ ___ ___ ___ ___ ___

Numbers: ___ ___ ___ ___ ___ ___ ___ ___ ___ ___ ___

Total = _____ Key Number

Now, write your magickal name and its corresponding numbers and calculate the total, remembering to reduce the final result to a single digit:

Magickal Name: ___ ___ ___ ___ ___ ___ ___ ___ ___ ___ ___

Numbers: ___ ___ ___ ___ ___ ___ ___ ___ ___ ___ ___

Total = _____ Key Number

What do your Key Numbers reveal about your magickal name?

- ◆ **1**   You are a leader, but also a strong individual. In group practice, you could aspire to become a High Priestess or Priest. Or you may find yourself solidly setting off on your own determined path as a solitaire. Whichever path you take, your example will be one of inspiring leadership.

◆ **2** You're a terrific partner and you'll be looking to make harmonious magick for the benefit of yourself and those with whom you share your practice of spell-craft. You possess the warm and receiving energy of the Goddess.

◆ **3** You'll bring joy and enthusiasm to your practice and everyone around you will be inspired by the creative and imaginative expression of your spellcraft.

◆ **4** You are organized, reliable, and a terrific planner. You may be drawn to the more formal aspects of performing ritual. You'll have a terrific Book of Shadows and grimoire of spells for any and all magickal occasions.

◆ **5** You love to try new things and will be curious about the many Wiccan traditions and spellcasting methods. You may find you move from one group practice to another, only to land on the eclectic path. But no matter where (or how) you practice, your dynamic energy ignites the group and inspires action.

◆ **6** You understand the nurturing power of magickal energy and you'll feel a great duty and responsibility to your fellow practitioners, as well as to your family and community. You care deeply and your loving nature infuses your spellwork with warmth.

◆ **7** You are intuitively connected to the flow of magickal energy and perhaps you've always been drawn to the metaphysical and the esoteric arts. You may find most enlightenment through a solitary practice, though what you learn and know about magick will inspire others.

◆ **8** You are an action-oriented achiever and your voracity for learning and leading will probably send you to many teachers on your path until you become the teacher yourself.

◆ **9** You encompass the energy of all the numbers on your path, bringing all together with compassion. You desire a complete and deeply spiritual practice.

For more about numerology, you'll want to read *The Complete Idiot's Guide to Numerology, Second Edition* by Kay Lagerquist and Lisa Lenard (Alpha Books, 2004).

The Chosen Path

Choosing the magickal path and committing to the study of spellcasting and magick is a serious matter, but it isn't a choice you will be bound by for life. You are dedicating yourself to the study of the craft for now, and if, after study and work, you decide the magickal path is not for you, you can ritually tell the spirit world that your studies in that realm are through. This will be your decision to make, and you are responsible for creating your own life. Always be sure that you are making informed, thoughtful choices for yourself.

The Least You Need to Know

- ◆ When and if you decide you are ready to dedicate yourself to a magickal path, you may want to perform a dedication ceremony.

- ◆ Part of your dedication ceremony may include renaming yourself with your magickal name.

- ◆ The ritual bath is performed prior to the dedication ritual to cleanse your body and mind, focusing you for the ritual and magick ahead.

- ◆ You always have the free will to choose another path, if the magickal one turns out to be the wrong one for you.

Chapter 7

Elemental Magick

In This Chapter

- The four Elements: Air, Fire, Water, and Earth
- Studying the Elements
- A look at the fifth Element: spirit or Akasha
- Elements and their correspondences
- Elementals: spirits associated with the Elements
- Elements in daily life

You're already familiar with the four magickal Elements: Air, Fire, Water, and Earth. You may not know about the fifth Element, often referred to as spirit or Akasha, and you may not be aware of the role the Elements play in magick. Working with the Elements is a good place to start your magickal training and spellcrafting practice.

Let's begin by reviewing the Elements and some of their many associations. A detailed study of each Element is a great way to further your magickal studies, and you may want to take some time to do this, but this can also be a lifelong endeavor. And of course, you can work spells with one central Element or with all of them.

Meet the Elements

The magickal *Elements* are the building blocks of all magick. The Elements provide a view of the world that allows us to understand the universe—and life—by looking at its constituent parts and working to find balance through them. We meet the Elements each day in the natural world, and you'll use them in working magick, as well. All spells include at least one of the Elements, drawing on the power of that Element, and asking for its blessing and resources. Many spells seek to balance all of the Elements. This is also true of the magick circle—you'll have representatives of the Elements in your magick circle; you might have your athame, a candle, saltwater, and a pentacle on your altar. The tools you use are also representative of the Elements: The athame is usually linked to Air, the wand to Fire, the cup to Water, and the pentacle to Earth.

> **Words of Power**
>
> The four traditional **Elements** of Western magick are Air, Fire, Water, and Earth.

Let's take a closer look at how you can experience each of these Elements.

Air

Introduce yourself to the Element of Air by going out into nature and spending time enjoying the air and the clouds. If there's an appropriate place nearby, you could go to a high altitude and look out at the world from above—feel the clouds around you and experience what the world is like from the air and sky. Pay special attention to which birds you see and what they are doing. Try facing East, the direction associated with this Element.

> **Spellcasting**
>
> *The Spirit of Place: A Workbook for Sacred Alignment* by Loren Cruden (see Appendix B) is a wonderful book for getting deeply in touch with the four Elements. Cruden guides the reader through intense work on Air from Spring Equinox until Summer Solstice. Then she works on Fire until Fall Equinox, then committing to Water until Winter Solstice. Through the winter the focus is on Earth.

You could bring a tool linked to this Element—perhaps your athame, a flute (such as a pennywhistle or recorder), or some incense—or you could bring or collect objects that you feel link you to the Air, such as a feather. Intellectual knowledge, such as that contained in books, is usually attributed to the Element of Air, so you could bring your journal and a pen as part of your Air package. Put yourself in a place where you can feel the air around you and meditate on this Element and its place in the world. Feel the Air on your skin: Is it warm, cool, cold?

Is there a breeze? Can you see the clouds move across the sky, or a bird flying? Try flying a kite, to feel the power of the wind. Focus on experiencing the Element of Air and introducing yourself to it. If you can, face East at sunrise, chanting:

Winged ones, airy friends,

Bring your knowledge, hear my song,

Winged one, circling round,

Help me see both far and long.

Record this experience and your feelings in your Book of Shadows.

Fire

Introduce yourself to the Element of Fire with fire, if possible. You could set up a campfire or a bonfire (in a safe and appropriate setting—never leave a fire or lit candles unattended), or simply bring some candles to a place of meditation and light them, meditating on the flame. You might have your wand with you, as well, or perhaps some rattles or a drum. Feel free to include other items that speak to you for each Element—perhaps you have a red cloth that you feel links you to the Element of Fire. Bring that with you as you introduce yourself to the Element and face South during your meditation, as this is the direction corresponding to Fire.

Fire is the Element of relationships. Think about all the connections you have with others in your life: your family, friends, lovers, and co-workers. Do any of these relationships need work? Watch the fire consume the fuel (be it wood or wax). Fire connects the material that is burning with the air as it becomes smoke. Fire is a *process*, not a *thing:* a process of transformation that changes one thing into another. Is there anything in your life you want to transform? These are all good things to think about as you meditate on Fire.

If you have a campfire, bring offerings to the Fire Element: herbs, incense, or food. Toss them into the flames while explaining to Fire why you are offering these items. Chant and dance (if you have space):

Fire, flame, warmth,

Warm me, heat me, teach me.

After your introduction, spend some time alone with your thoughts and record the experience in your Book of Shadows.

Water

Introduce yourself to the Element of Water with some water. If you're near a body of water—a lake, a river, or the ocean—that's great. Find a quiet place near the water for your meditation. Bring along your cup and perhaps collect some of the water in it, or bring something to drink that is sacred to you (perhaps water from your own home well or spring, or a special juice or wine—all liquid is symbolic of Water). Water also represents blood, your life force. Take special notice of it as you do this meditation.

If you aren't near a body of water, you could bring a blue bowl of water or saltwater and place it on a cloth for the meditation, or bring some water to drink and feel. Again, focus on the water; touch the water. If possible, take a swim, dangle your feet in the water, put your hand in it, sprinkle yourself with it, drink the beverage that you brought, so that you can experience the sensations of the water: its smell, its feel, how it sounds as the waves lap, or the water splashes or sprinkles. Face West for your meditation if practical, as this is the direction corresponding to this Element. Splash water on your face, chanting:

Water, ocean, sea,

Mother, come to me.

Water, ocean, sea,

Mother, set me free.

Water is also the Element of intuition and divination, so you might want to do a Tarot reading while sitting near your water. See how it feels to exercise your intuition while working on this Element and then record the experience in your Book of Shadows.

Earth

Introduce yourself to the Element of Earth in nature: You might have your pentacle with you, and you could choose to sit in a forest or on a boulder and meditate. Try facing North, which is the direction corresponding to this Element. You could also go into a cave and be inside the Earth, sit with your back to a tree or face a tree, or have someone help you and bury you to your neck so you are truly within the Earth. (This is easy to do at the beach, far away from the tide! Or bury yourself under a pile of natural woolen fiber blankets. However, *never* place yourself or someone else in a position of possible danger where you or someone else cannot move and stand freely.)

You could also bury an object in the Earth, and feel the Earth in your hands as you do so. However you choose to explore this Element, try to experience it firsthand, and meditate on the sensations you have from the Earth: How does the forest sound? How does the boulder feel? What is the tree saying? What do you hear in the cave? How does the Earth smell?

You could bring a cloth with you to sit on, and put something sacred for the Element of Earth on the cloth with you as you meditate. This could be your pentacle, some salt, or perhaps a special stone to represent the Element of Earth. These can be objects or tools that help you feel closer to the Earth, and that also give you a focus for your meditation, which can be done with your eyes open or closed. If you close your eyes, concentrate on your other senses—how the Earth sounds, feels, and smells. If your eyes are open, take in everything around you, and focus on the meaning of Earth in the world.

The Element of Earth also feeds us, so bring some food on your exploration, something basic—perhaps bread. If you baked it yourself, you can focus on putting Earth energy into it; perhaps add some rosemary! As you sit in this Earth-sacred place, weave a spell of connection by chanting or singing:

> *Earth Mother, hold me,*
>
> *Cradle me and rock me,*
>
> *Feed me, nurture me,*
>
> *Until I am whole.*

After you have worked on your attunement with the Earth Element for a while, record your impressions and any communications from the Earth in your Book of Shadows.

Making Magick

Earth has a lot to teach us about community and how to nurture one another. One of Aurora's pre-initiation tasks was to meditate in the West Kennet Long Barrow, a Neolithic passage grave in Great Britain. Nervous when she arrived, Aurora thought this would be a dark and frightening experience, but she found a group of young people camping at the entrance with lit candles everywhere. They willingly stepped outside as she did her magickal work, and found that what the Earth had to say was not dark and lonely, but beautiful and community-centered.

Dedicate Yourself to Study of the Elements

It's a good idea to spend some time exploring each Element, introducing yourself to the Element, and learning all you can about it—its associations, energies, and magickal correspondences. For detailed study, a practical way to do this is seasonally: Welcome each Element by season, and spend time during those months becoming acquainted with the Element and its energy. We suggest performing a dedication ritual first, to ask for the blessing of each Element. You should set up a shrine to each Element within your magick circle, and include articles related to that Element on the shrine. You can do this ritual for each Element as the season—and your study—begins, or, if you're more ambitious (and have the space), you can set up all four shrines and do the ritual for them all at one time.

Dedication Ritual

Here's how to go about it: Set up the shrine (or shrines) within a magick circle (your shrine can be on your altar, and inside your house, if you like). If you set up all four shrines at once, place them in the quarter for the direction with which they're associated. Your shrine might include some of the following:

- For Air, you might include incense, feathers, smudge sticks, your Book of Shadows, quills for writing, and other things that link you to the Air.

- For Fire, include candles, incense, red stones or other objects, your wand if you have one, and anything that connects you with the Element of Fire.

- For Water, you might choose a chalice, shells or stones, and some water. Make sure you can experience this Element by getting wet: Sprinkle yourself with water, or place your hands or feet in a bowl or basin of water and sand.

- On your Earth altar, you might have stones, cedar boughs, your pentacle, some living plants, and any other articles you feel strongly connect you with the Earth.

As you visit each shrine, ask for the blessing of that Element. We've included a chant for each Element, but you can say whatever comes to mind or seems appropriate to you:

> *Element of Air, I ask your blessings on my work.*
>
> *Bring your knowledge, your discernment,*
>
> *The far-sight of the winged ones.*
>
> *Help me to see the fresh new beginning I undertake,*

The sunrise of my path.

Element of Fire, I ask your blessings on my work.

Bring your passion, warmth, connection,

The transformation of the flames.

Help me to dance, love, grow.

Help me to feel my heat.

Element of Water, I ask your blessings on my work.

Bring your emotion, intuition, flow,

The knowing of the finned ones.

You who are the blood of my body,

Help me to swim with the changes.

Element of Earth, I ask your blessings on my work.

Bring me your wisdom, your deep ancestral knowing,

the wisdom of the winter crone.

Help me to know nurturance, sustenance, abundance.

Help me to go within.

If working with a group, you may want to divide up into astrological correspondences (see Chapter 13), so that all those who are of an astrological Air birth sign (Gemini, Libra, Aquarius) will welcome and bless the rest of the group to Air, smudging them, brushing them with feathers, or whatever comes to mind. Then everyone of an astrological Fire sign (Aries, Leo, Sagittarius) welcomes everyone to the Fire altar, brushing them with the Fire stones, blessing them with a candle, showing them the representations on the Fire altar. Water people (Cancer, Scorpio, Pisces) can offer everyone water to drink, dip into, bathe in, and reflect on. The Earth group (Taurus, Virgo, Capricorn) can bless people with boughs of plants, flowers, offerings of food, dirt to sink their fingers into, and most important, hugs! (This is a ritual that originates from Aurora's work with her Dagara shamanic teachers—thanks to them both.)

Spellcasting

Each Element is associated with particular kinds of magick: Air is the Element for study of magickal languages, Fire is the Element for candle magick, Water is the Element for divination, and Earth is the Element for prosperity/fertility magick.

Deepening Your Connection

You should study the Elements in a way that is personally meaningful to you. If you enjoyed spending time outside, introducing yourself to each Element, you might want to do more of this as you study each Element. Think about the Elements and their place in your life, physically and otherwise: Air rules the intellect and communication, Fire rules passion and transformation, Water rules emotion and the subconscious, and Earth rules the home and stability (think Earth Mother). Plan exploratory exercises for each Element.

For example, you might try this spell when you want to feel more connected to Fire: Take a piece of red fabric and sew it into a small pouch, adorning it with fiery-looking beads. Then place stones, herbs—anything related to your work on Fire—in the pouch, which will become an amulet. On Fall Equinox, as the season of studying Fire comes to a close, cast a magick circle around a fire pit and have a bonfire. Call in the Element of Fire and offer it incense and herbs. Tell the Element that you intend to continue your study and work with Fire and ask for blessings on your amulet.

This could be done with each Element. When you feel the need for more Fire in your life, wear that particular amulet. While outside, you can collect objects and decide which Element they feel linked to. Continue collecting objects for each Element and create a medicine pouch for each Element. These will come in handy for working magick when you need objects representative of each Element. You'll have an assortment to choose from for each Element and can do your work with the one that feels right for a particular spell or ritual.

CAUTION

For Protection

If you think you might go into some of these Elemental meditations to the level of trance, it would be best to have someone with you, especially if you choose to work near a body of water or with a live flame.

You could also make a collage for each Element as an exercise, cutting out pictures that remind you of that Element's attributes. As you paste them all onto poster board, see what other realizations about that Element come to mind.

Also try meditating with your Tarot deck, using the suit for the Element you are working on. For example, as you work with Water, meditate on the Queen or King of Cups, or perhaps look at all the Cups cards.

The Fifth Element: Spirit or Akasha

The fifth Element is the Element of *spirit*, also called *Akasha*. Spirit certainly influences you every day and will be a powerful factor in working magick. Spirit is the source of all energy, and it exists in everything around us, as well as within us. Many witches call in the direction of "center" after they have called the East, South, West and North, and you can think of center as where spirit, or Akasha, resides.

Witches also use the pentacle to symbolize spirit being above the four earthly Elements. This is why, in some traditions, witches who are still in training wear the pentagram or pentacle upside down to represent that they have not yet mastered the four earthly Elements. They then right it (turn it around) after their second degree initiation to show that their spirit has mastered the other four Elements (Air, Fire, Water, Earth). This tradition is not used so much in the United States because Hollywood and the media latched onto the upside-down pentagram/pentacle as a satanic symbol, so you may want to be careful about using the pentagram/pentacle in this way. But the idea of the fifth Element, spirit, being the pinnacle of the pentagram/pentacle remains valid and appropriate.

> **Words of Power**
>
> The Element of energy that exists in everything is called **spirit** or **Akasha**. Spirit is represented by the top point in the upright pentagram/pentacle.

Elemental Correspondences

The following table lists the four Elements and some of their correspondences. As we discover more about magickal correspondences in Part 3, we'll go in-depth with each of these areas.

Elemental Correspondences

	Air	**Fire**	**Water**	**Earth**
Direction	East	South	West	North
Tools	Athame, incense	Wand, candles	Cup, cauldron	Pentacle, salt
Season	Spring	Summer	Fall	Winter
Astro signs	Gemini, Libra, Aquarius	Aries, Leo, Sagittarius	Cancer, Scorpio, Pisces	Taurus, Virgo, Capricorn
Colors	Yellow, blue	Red, orange	Blue, green	Green, brown
Lessons	Intellect	Relationship	Intuition	Material needs
Magick	Languages	Candles	Divination	Prosperity/ fertility
Elemental	Sylphs	Salamanders	Undines	Gnomes

In addition, each of the five points of the pentagram corresponds to one of the Elements:

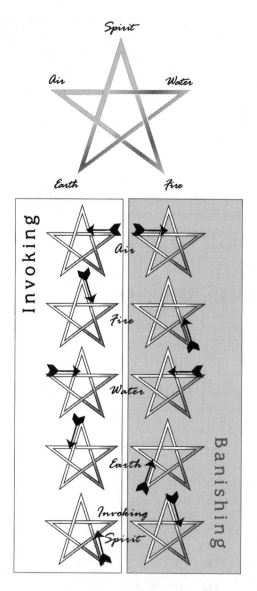

In Wiccan ritual, a person doing an invocation will often end it by "drawing" a pentacle in the air with their athame (or whatever they are using). There are different starting points and directions for drawing the pentacle, depending on which Element you are invoking. This movement can also be used to seal the sacred circle, once you are done casting it, and is often accompanied by the phrase *"So mote it be."* It might be thought of as a closing kiss to a spell. If this interests you, you can study the different invoking and devoking pentacles and learn each one.

It's Elemental

The spirits associated with each of the Elements are called *Elementals*. These spirits may be summoned for working magick. The Elementals should be visualized as the pure energy of that Element, and they have much to teach from their realm. Some traditions use sylphs to represent the Elementals associated with Air, salamanders with Fire, undines with Water, and gnomes with Earth. This symbolism also appears in many Tarot decks.

You can work on any given Element by making offerings to the Elemental spirits, visualizing them, and asking for the lessons of their Elements. Make sure you treat them with polite respect, thanking and dismissing them when you are done! Work with Elementals should be done in a magick circle.

> **Spellcasting**
>
> Elementals are often addressed as "Lords and Ladies of the East" (or South, West, or North). You are speaking to these spirits when you call the directions. You might visualize these energies as royalty of their particular realm, invoking them with something like: *"Lords and Ladies of the East, I call on you to witness my rite. Bring your knowledge, your youthful energy, and guard the Eastern portal."*

The Lord and Lady and the Elements

The Lord and Lady, or Goddess and God, are the All: They encompass all five Elements. They can certainly be called on for their blessings in your work with the Elements; this is simply a matter of personal preference. If you want to do a formal magick circle, declaring your dedication to this study, you might invoke the Goddess and God to witness and bless your dedication. Specific gods and goddesses are associated with each Element, and it would be appropriate to call on them for Elemental work. Yemaya, Caribbean Goddess of the sea, for example, could be called upon for work with the Element of Water, especially if you are at the seashore. Pele, the Hawaiian Goddess of fire and volcanoes, might be called upon for work with Fire.

The Elements in Your Daily Life

When you think about it, the Elements are essential to daily life; we just don't often think about them. Wherever you walk, the Earth is beneath you, and your body is mostly Water. You need Air to breathe, and Fire is the source of our planet's warmth and light. In combination, the Elements provide us with food, clothing, and shelter, not to mention our spiritual energy.

Consider this the next time you walk anywhere, the next time you have a drink or take a bath, the next time you cook and eat a meal, the next time you take a breath. Thanking each of the Elements for their contribution to our lives is a good way to start and end each day and pay respect to the sacred sustaining energy each provides to mind, body, and spirit. When you think of the areas associated with each Element, you can see how the Elements work on a deeper, more profound level in your life as well.

Try this spellcrafting exercise to help remind you of the Elements in your daily life: At least once a day, perhaps when you're on your lunch break or when you can take five minutes to relax, sit in quiet meditation. Focus on your senses and try to discern the five Elements in your surroundings. How does the air feel? Can you hear water? What do you smell? What do you feel? Explore these sensations and find the Elements around you, whether you're in a park or in your office. This spell uses no words, only emotions, sensations, and feelings to work its magick and connect you to the divinity of the Elements and the All.

The Least You Need to Know

♦ The four Elements are Air, Fire, Water, and Earth. Spirit, or Akasha, is often referred to as the fifth Element.

♦ You can introduce yourself to the Elements and begin to study them; familiarity with the Elements will be crucial in working magick.

♦ The spirits associated with the Elements are called Elementals.

♦ You can easily become aware of the Elemental influences in your daily life.

Chapter 8

Esbats and Full Moon Magick: Drawing Down the Moon

In This Chapter

- ◆ Esbats and the power of the Moon
- ◆ Working Full Moon magick
- ◆ Can you work magick on a Blue Moon?
- ◆ Charge of the Goddess: Drawing down the Moon
- ◆ Rituals and spells for the phases of the Moon

The Moon is very important in witchcraft, magick, and spellworking. Most witches perform rituals based on lunar cycles, and spellwork is best when timed with the appropriate phase of the Moon.

Covens often have monthly gatherings for ritual and social purposes that are called Esbats which occur on the Full Moon. Esbats are celebrations of the power of the Goddess that are based on the phases of the Moon. The celebrations may involve magick and ritual, and can be performed alone or with a group.

Esbats

Most covens celebrate an *Esbat* at least once a month and usually on a Full Moon. You can choose to work with Moon energy more often, if you like, perhaps celebrating the Goddess on the Full Moon and the New Moon. The energy of the Moon is Goddess energy, and the power of the Goddess is felt differently during the various phases of the Moon. Many witches celebrate Esbats during the Full Moon because it's then that the Goddess is at her height. If you have magick that needs working, a Full or New Moon ritual is the perfect time, and Esbats are considered prime working time by many witches.

> **Words of Power**
>
> An **Esbat** is a Moon ritual of celebration for the Goddess, usually held on the Full Moon.

Moon Phases

We discussed Moon phases in Chapter 3, when we talked about timing your magick. Here's a quick reminder:

- The New Moon is when the Moon is not visible. It's a great time to start new projects.

- The Waxing Moon is when the Moon is growing from New toward Full, and is a time for working magick for fulfilling goals or for prosperity.

> **For Protection**
>
> Don't work magick on the Full Moon just because it's the most powerful time in the lunar cycle. Be sure you're ready to work magick and that the time feels right to you, and be clear on your intent before proceeding. You may find that a different time in the lunar cycle is best for the spell you need to work.

- During the Full Moon, the Goddess is at the height of her powers. Powerful magick can be worked during a Full Moon, particularly for divination, love, and psychic energy.

- The Waning Moon is when the Moon is going from full back to new. This is a good time to work banishing magick.

Some witches like to celebrate an Esbat for Diana's bow, which is the period about three days after the New Moon, when a small crescent of the Waxing

Moon becomes visible. This is thought to be a good time for working magick related to new projects, and to ask for blessings such as on a new home. You might call on the Goddess Diana, for example:

> *Goddess Diana of the silver bow, huntress of the hounds, come to me this night as I celebrate your Moon. Lady of the hunt, I ask your blessings this night on my hunt for a new home. Help this come to pass, I pray.*

One aspect of the Goddess is reflected in each Moon phase: The New Moon is the Enchantress, the Waxing Moon the Maiden, the Full Moon the Mother, and the Waning Moon the Crone. From these names, you can clearly see how the Moon is associated with women, from youth to old age. The Moon is responsible for the ocean tides on the earth and is linked to the menstrual cycles of women as well. The reflective light of the Moon has also been linked to the hidden arts because they were more safely practiced away from direct light (hidden), and also because the shadow side of reality, such as that explored in magick, is better seen in indirect light; mundane life appears better in the direct light of the Sun.

You will feel this powerful connection with the Moon if you go outside on any night that you can see her. Look up, dance if you can, and sing:

> *Luna, Luna in all your glory: Enchantress, Maiden, Mother, Crone!*
>
> *Honor me with all your beauty, I honor you in all your forms!*

Celebrating Esbats

If you're part of a coven, there will be a set schedule for celebrating Esbats, but you can work Moon magick on your own at other times. An Esbat is a great time for taking care of the individual magickal needs you have and harnessing the energy of the coven or the group you work with, if you have one. You can take care of blessing a new amulet, or consecrating a tool, or working spells for which you'd like to use others' energy.

Drawing Down the Moon

Drawing down the Moon is the traditional ritual within a coven of invoking and drawing the Goddess into the High Priestess. The Goddess will enter the High Priestess, who becomes the Goddess incarnate. The High Priest (if there is one) usually draws the Goddess into the High Priestess, who then channels the Goddess for everyone's benefit. She may recite the "Charge" (discussed later in this chapter), telling the coven to meet every Full Moon to honor her and giving advice on working magick. The coven then works its magick and afterward thanks the Goddess, who leaves the High Priestess. The High Priestess may or may not share the power of the Goddess with the other members of the coven when the Goddess is within her; the power to draw down the Moon is often reserved for the High Priestess of a coven.

Making Magick

At a recent Full Moon ritual Aurora attended, the group decided to draw the Moon into everyone present, taking turns in the center of the circle. Someone was drumming and everyone else was dancing and singing. One by one they came to the center (which in the yurt had the light of the Moon shining through the clear dome above) and everyone present helped draw the energy of the Moon into the person in the center. They then used this experience as inspiration and made magickal masks.

Drawing down the Moon may seem more complicated than it really is—you can draw down the Moon whether you work within a coven, in a more informal group, or solitary. As a solitaire, you have the advantage of connecting to the Goddess directly by drawing down the Moon. Many witches do this. On any Full Moon, stand firmly with your arms outstretched toward the Moon, asking for the Goddess energy to enter you. Visualize the white light of the Moon flowing into you. In this way, you draw her power within you. You could use music, drumming, or dancing during your ritual, and you could also take advantage of the Full Moon to charge tools or amulets, as we described in Chapter 5. You can use your wand or athame, pointing it at the Moon as you draw the Goddess energy, but this isn't necessary. Here's a chant you can use, though you should feel free to compose your own, and say what feels right to you:

> *Power of the Goddess enter me,*
>
> *Filled with your energy let me be.*

Aurora has also used the refrain from a song by Kenny Klein for this purpose, for which we gratefully acknowledge permission (for more information on Kenny Klein, see Appendix B):

> *Full Moon shining bright, midnight on the water;*
>
> *Hail Aradia, Diana's silver daughter.*

Drawing down the Moon can be a very intense experience, but it may also take some practice. It's different for everyone and can be quite emotional. You may find it affects you differently each time you do it. When you draw down the Moon on your own, rather than within a coven, the intent of the ritual is different from that of the coven. In a coven setting, the High Priestess (or High Priest) asks the Goddess to temporarily speak through her for the benefit of the coven. When you do this yourself, you might ask the Goddess to temporarily speak through you for divination or some other purpose, in which case you should devoke (or return to yourself) when you are done. But you will more likely ask the Goddess (the Moon) to infuse you with her energy for a life-force boost.

> **For Protection**
>
> Make sure that if you draw the Goddess down into yourself you are clear about your intentions: Are you looking for a divine boost of life force and connection, or are you planning to channel her words for the benefit of your community? If it is the second, make sure you devoke (or dismiss) her with your thanks at the end of your ritual.

You can draw down the Moon wherever you are, but you will likely find the experience more powerful if you are outside, under the Full Moon, rather than visualizing yourself there. Even if the Moon is hidden behind clouds, the energy is still there to be worked with.

To ask for life-force boost from the Goddess, you might try:

> *Goddess, Moon, Luna, you who have ruled over women's lives since the beginning of time, come to me! I seek to infuse my life with your power, be with me always!*

When working Moon magick, music and dancing are more powerful than words, so try bringing a percussion instrument or pennywhistle—anything you can dance with and play at the same time. Dancing under the light of the Moon with your intent stated is an empowering experience. You might find yourself wanting to do it every month!

You don't *have* to draw down the Moon every month, but it can be wonderfully re-energizing and can empower you for doing magick as well. You don't have to do magick after drawing down the Moon, though. You can just bask in the glow of the energy you have received and spend some time meditating in the light of the Full Moon.

Once in a Blue Moon

There is a Full Moon every 27½ days, so there are 12 or 13 Full Moons each year—giving you that many opportunities to draw down the Moon. In the following table we've listed the monthly Full Moons and some of the traditional names they have been given. Note that when a year has thirteen Moons, the thirteenth will be called a Blue Moon. This doesn't happen every year (as in, "that happens once in a Blue Moon"!). The explanation for Blue Moons is a little complicated, and we won't try to describe it fully here, but essentially, when a season has four Moons rather than the traditional three (one per month), the third Moon is called the Blue Moon (this leaves the other Moons with their traditional names falling at the right time of the year). We told you it was complicated!

Generally, if a month includes more than one Moon, which sometimes happens because of the number of months we have that extend to 30 or 31 days (remember, the lunar cycle is 27½ days), the second Moon is called a Blue Moon. The Blue Moon is also sometimes called a Goal Moon, and it is considered a good time to work on long-term goals and planning, and to work magick around these issues. To find out when the next Full Moon is and what it's called (as well as the other phases of the Moon), check a lunar almanac. We've included a Blue Moon spell you can use or adapt, as you wish. Let it inspire you to write your own spells for any of the specific named Moons of the year.

If you have the opportunity to work a spell under a Full, Blue Moon, why not take it? Use this time to think about where your life is and where it is going. If you have some long-range plans that have felt a bit too far-fetched, perhaps this is the time to dust them off and take a good look at them. Maybe you can further your education after all? Or seek that more-enticing career you've dreamed about? Or maybe it is time to see the intense beauty in the life you have? Either way, a Blue Moon spell is a wonderful way to empower these thoughts. Be playful, and think of everything blue: Bring blue food, a blue candle (in a votive cup so it won't blow out), a blue stone, maybe a blue cloth, and anything else that occurs to you. Lay your items out in a spot where you can see the Moon (or the cloudy sky if it is overcast) and chant:

> *Moon that comes but ne'er so often,*
>
> *Take my wild dreams, make them soften;*
>
> *Blue as you I cannot be,*
>
> *But take my thoughts and set them free!*

Then state clearly what your spell is for, such as, *"Blue Moon, help me get the job I seek! So mote it be!"*

Make sure to leave offerings of the food and drink you have brought and any other offerings you feel like leaving in the spot where you performed this spell. Stones and herbs are always fine for offerings, but please don't leave anything in nature that is not biodegradable!

Month	Names for Full Moon
January	Winter, wolf, rowan
February	Trapper's, snow, chaste, ash
March	Fisherman's, worm, seed, alder
April	Planter's, pink, hare, willow
May	Spring, flower, dyad, hawthorn
June	Midyear, strawberry, mead, oak
July	Summer, buck, wort, holly
August	Dog days, sturgeon, barley, hazel
September	Fall, harvest, wine, vine
October	Harvest, hunter's, blood, ivy
November	Hunter's, beaver, snow, reed
December	Christ's, cold, oak, elder, birch

The Charge of the Goddess

The *Charge of the Goddess* is usually spoken by the High Priestess after drawing down the Moon. The Goddess is drawn into the High Priestess and then she speaks the words of the Goddess, called the Charge. The Charge is the promise of the Goddess to all witches that she will teach and guide them. There are many versions of the Charge; the one we've included here was first published in 1897 in *Aradia: The Gospel of the Witches*, by Charles Leland. You can use this one or create your own.

> **Words of Power**
>
> The **Charge of the Goddess** is a speech often used in Wiccan rituals. It is the words of the Goddess, who entreats her followers to be joyous and free.

> *When I shall have departed from this world,*
> *Whenever ye have need of anything,*
> *Once in the month, and when the moon is full,*
> *Ye shall assemble in some desert place,*
> *Or in a forest all together join*
> *To adore the potent spirit of your queen,*

My mother, great Diana. She who fain
Would learn all sorcery yet has not won
Its deepest secrets, them my mother will
Teach her, in truth all things as yet unknown.
And ye shall all be freed from slavery,
And so ye shall be free in everything;
And as the sign that ye are truly free,
Ye shall be naked in your rites, both men
And women also: this shall last until
The last of your oppressors shall be dead;
And ye shall make the game of Benevento,
Extinguishing the lights, and after that
Shall hold your supper thus.

The many different Wiccan traditions tend to have their own versions of the Charge. Gerald Gardner's High Priestess, Doreen Valiente, created a very popular version of the Charge, and there's also one adapted by Starhawk that is particular to the Reclaiming tradition, for example. If you are invoking a particular deity with your Charge, she may have a particular message for you. For example, if you invoke the Goddess Aphrodite, expect to hear something about love! If it is Athena you have called upon, perhaps the focus will be on wisdom. We've included a general Charge of the Goddess that Aurora has used, but remember: The infinite Goddess will speak to you, too! Whatever she says is the Charge. Once you have drawn her into you, try letting go of any inner judgment, and what comes out of your mouth is the Charge of the Goddess!

Hear now the words of the Great Goddess, who has been known by infinite names. Whenever ye have need of anything, come to me, for I will comfort and nurture you. Whenever you need me, come together in the magick circle and call my name. I shall come, and teach you all my secrets. Know that all acts of love and joy are my rituals.

Keep your heart always pure, let no one turn it aside for ill.

My gifts are the wisdom of the Cauldron of Cerridwen, the Holy Grail of Immortality. Drink in my gifts, and you shall experience the joy of the earth, for I am the loving Mother of all living things, and I am the soul of nature.

Seek wisdom and understanding in me, yet know that your seeking will avail you not if you find me not within you. For I have been with you from the start, and this is the greatest mystery.

Rituals for the Phases of the Moon

Each Moon phase lends itself to particular types of magick, and you can use this aspect of timing to make your spellwork more powerful and successful. Let's try some spells you might work for each Moon phase.

New Moon ●

As we have mentioned, the New Moon is a good time to do spellwork on starting something new. Let's say you are going to begin a new project—writing a book, perhaps—and you want to give it a magickal boost and blessing. At the New Moon, bring something that represents your project to your sacred space, perhaps a notebook or folder with notes for the book, or a notebook in which you have written the title of the book you are writing and some hopes for how it will turn out. Cast a circle and call the quarters, then call an appropriate deity for the project; you might call Athena, Goddess of Wisdom, for help putting down your words with wisdom. Place the representation you are blessing in the center of the circle and chant:

> *Goddess, spirits, Elements four,*
>
> *Bless this project on the floor.*
>
> *Make it blossom, make it sing,*
>
> *Guide my hand in everything.*

After raising some energy with this chant, pick up the object and take it to your altar, blessing it with each element by holding it over the incense, candle flame, water, and pentacle or plant and saying in turn:

> *By Air, by Fire, by Water, by Earth,*
>
> *This spell is sealed, I give it birth!*

Spellcasting

Get a lunar phase calendar, like that by Snake and Snake Productions (www.snakeandsnake.com), to keep you in touch with the Moon. If you are a mensing woman, keep track of your menstrual cycle, or Moontimes, on the calendar and see how you feel about working different kinds of spells during your Moontime as well as the various phases of the Moon.

Waxing Moon ☽

Spells for starting something new could also be done during the Waxing Moon. This is the time when projects you've initiated grow and evolve. Your spell can be one that tracks the progress and positive energy of your project. This is also a good time for working spells related to prosperity. Let's say you've recently planted a garden, and you want to use the growing energy of the Waxing Moon to boost your garden's growth.

To help your garden grow in health and fullness, try this spell: Go to the center of the garden in the evening of a Waxing Moon. Bring with you something that your garden would recognize as food, such as water, compost, grain, or organic fertilizer. If you choose water, it would be great to use collected rainwater, but tap water will also do (just don't use saltwater). Take off your shoes so that your bare feet are touching the ground. Hold your offering (water or food) up to the Moon, channeling Earth energy up through your feet and Moon energy down from the sky into the offering that you are holding up. Once the offering is charged, become a human sprinkler of blessing, throwing the charged offering around you while chanting:

> *Garden, garden, you will grow*
>
> *Grow strong, grow full, together we grow.*

When you are done, you will have a very happy and well-loved garden. It should feed you well.

Full Moon ○

The Full Moon is a very powerful time, making it a good time for working all types of magick, especially magick to bring a project to fruition. Divination and magick related to love are also well worked during a Full Moon.

If you have a project that you are ready to bring to fruition, try this spell. Place a representation of the project in the center of the floor. Cast a circle and call the quarters, then call an appropriate deity (perhaps Aphrodite if you are seeking a loving relationship, or Hestia if you are seeking a home). Now raise energy for your project by dancing around it singing:

> *Full Moon energy charge this spell,*
>
> *As I call, you shall work well.*
>
> *Goddess, God, Elements four,*
>
> *Complete this* [the representation of the project] *upon the floor.*

When the chanting has done its job, pick up the object and take it to your altar, blessing it with each Element by holding it over the incense, candle flame, water, and pentacle or plant and saying in turn:

> *By Air, by Fire, by Water, by Earth,*
>
> *This spell is sealed, it shall go forth!*

Waning Moon ◑

During the Waning Moon, you could work spells for dispelling negative energy, getting rid of unwanted habits, and so forth. We'll cover such spells in greater detail in Chapter 18. Let's say you wish to curb your addiction to coffee. You could place some coffee (beans or grounds, not brewed) in a cup in the center of your circle and chant:

> *I am through with your control,*
>
> *Over me your power won't hold.*

The Least You Need to Know

- Esbats are celebrations of the power of the Goddess.
- You can draw down the Moon alone or within a group, on any Full Moon.
- The Full Moon is a powerful time for working magick. Each calendar year has 12 or 13 Full Moons.
- The Charge of the Goddess is traditionally spoken after drawing down the Moon in Wiccan rituals.
- There are rituals you can work during the different phases of the Moon.

Chapter 9

Sabbats: Circling the Wheel of the Year

In This Chapter

◆ Celebrating Sabbats

◆ The Wheel of the Year

◆ Sabbat spells and rituals

◆ Your link to nature

The major Wiccan holidays are called *Sabbats*. In the last chapter, we discussed Esbats, which are celebrations based on the phases of the Moon. Sabbats are based on the annual cycle of the Sun and celebrate the turning of the Wheel of the Year.

If you like holiday festivities, you might look at the Sabbats as an opportunity to plan a party. Because the Wiccan holidays are based in nature, you won't need to make fancy arrangements to celebrate the Sabbats—look no further than your own backyard for all the inspiration you'll need. Many Wiccan communities have large celebrations on the Sabbats. For example, some communities host May Day celebrations with flowers and a maypole, or have fall harvest celebrations or fairs. We'll look at the traditions of each of the eight Sabbats in this chapter.

Sabbats

You'll notice that the Sabbat dates are near those of major holidays, and some of the ritual elements of the two holidays are the same—these have been carried over from the pagan holidays into more mainstream or otherwise religious holiday celebrations (such as Halloween, Easter, and Christmas). If you are doing a ritual with a large group, focus on the celebratory aspect, or general (as opposed to personal), magick. These times of group celebration are not best for working personal magick—not everyone will be focused on consecrating your amulet; save that for an Esbat—but dancing the maypole is weaving a community spell.

Words of Power

The Wiccan holidays are called **Sabbats.** The **Wheel of the Year** depicts the natural cycle of life and death through all eight of the Sabbats.

The seasons of the year are marked through the Sabbats, which follow the cycle of the *Wheel of the Year* and the life cycle of the Goddess and God. The names we've used for the Sabbats are fairly common, but each Sabbat is known by a number of names, from many different languages. If you belong to a coven, you may learn the Sabbats by different names.

Wicca's Sabbats: The Wheel of the Year.

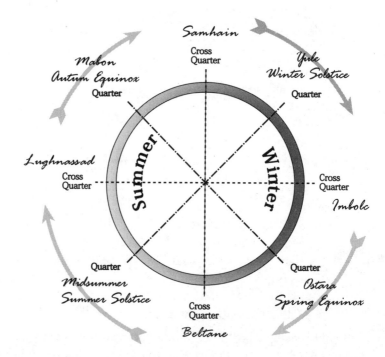

Samhain (Halloween): October 31

You likely know October 31 as Halloween; this is a direct descendant of the pagan Sabbat and includes some of the same ritual elements (such as witches!). For Wiccans, Samhain is a hallowed day, a day to honor the dead. The Catholic Church calls Samhain the Eve of All Saints, and November 1 is All Saints Day (November 2 is All Souls Day and is celebrated as Day of the Dead—Dia de Los Muertos—in many Latin American Catholic countries).

Samhain (pronounced *Sow*-wen or sah-*veen*) means "November." It is one of the major Sabbats—those that fall on the midpoints between the Solstice and the Equinox, called the cross quarters. These four Sabbats mark the change of seasons through the year and follow the same date year after year.

Samhain is the ancient Celtic New Year's Eve. This is where the pagan year begins. Because this is the start of the new year, the night of Samhain is not of this year or of last year. It is the night when the veil is thinnest between the seen and the unseen worlds, or between the living and the dead, and so is a perfect time for divination and to pay homage to the honored dead, ancestors, and anyone on the other side.

This was a time of insecurity for some of our ancestors, who likely worried about the future: Winter is coming—is enough grain stored? Are enough of the livestock left to breed next spring? Has enough been culled that we can feed the rest? These important decisions and preparations must already be made by Samhain, which became a time to hope for blessings through the winter.

Making Magick

One of Aurora's initiators used to say, "The Sabbats are for everyone." By this he meant that the Sabbats should be times for an entire community to come together and celebrate (the harvest, the start of planting, dancing the maypole, etc.). Don't plan anything too complicated for your Sabbat celebrations; rather, if you celebrate with others, try to get everyone involved and working together to make the celebration a community event.

Celebrating Samhain

Samhain is a great time for divination, for putting out a meal for the spirits, or for holding a *dumb supper*. Other ways to celebrate Samhain might include carving a jack-o-lantern and placing a candle inside, planning a dinner and preparing the food, creating masks, making a broom (the witch's broom is called a *besom*), or creating an altar in honor of deceased loved ones. You might also perform your own Day of the Dead ritual: visiting loved ones at a cemetery, taking time to clean up the gravesite, leaving offerings of food or flowers, and having a picnic among the dead.

Samhain Rituals and Spells

This is the perfect day to do some scrying or divination of any kind. (Scrying is a term meaning divination by permitting your eyes to see shapes or forms in a hazy object, and it allows for communication with the other side.) The Goddess is now the Crone, and you might ask her to share her wisdom. If you wish to try scrying, you can use a mirror draped with a black veil or a crystal ball. You can also drip candle wax into a cup or bowl of cold water and look at the shapes it hardens into—try to interpret the shapes.

As you prepare to scry, raise energy while chanting:

> *Ancestors, honored dead, let me know,*
>
> *Help me to see what you will show.*

Remember, scrying is not about foretelling the future; it is simply communication with other realms. Maybe your ancestors or other helper spirits have been trying to tell you something about your path that would help you along—here's their chance!

The minor Sabbats may change date by a few days each year; our calendar—the Gregorian calendar—is standardized, and doesn't account for the actual astrological occurrence of these events. Consult an almanac for the exact dates of the minor Sabbats.

Yule (Winter Solstice): December 21

Solstices and Equinoxes are the minor Sabbats. Dates of the Solstices and Equinoxes vary slightly year to year, but are often celebrated on the twenty-first; they may fall from the twentieth to the twenty-third of the month (check an almanac to find out the exact date for these each year).

Yule is Old Norse for "wheel"; this Sabbat is all about the turning of the Wheel of the Year. Yule marks the shortest day (and longest night) of the year, but it is also the turning point: After this day the days begin to grow longer. The Sun is reborn—and the God is reborn from the Goddess. Some witches keep vigil through the night to make sure the Sun will return.

Yule is the end of the waning year, ruled over by the Holly King (this is where those images of Santa Claus come from: an old man with holly in his beard). He is defeated on this day by his brother the Oak King, who then rules over the waxing year until he, in turn, is defeated at the Summer Solstice by the Holly King. Many covens like to reenact the kings' fight, with the Holly King staging a theatrical death after a valiant swordfight.

You may be used to decorating a tree in your home at this time of year; this is a very old pagan tradition. Druids decorated the Yule tree with what they wanted the year to bring. Evergreen wreaths, holly, and mistletoe are also common Yule decorations. Most witches decorate a Yule tree to honor the tree that is filled with life at this time of year. Many Wiccans also exchange gifts at Yule.

Making Magick

The Holly King and the Oak King are two sides to the Celtic God of fertility Cernunnos, the Horned God. In Celtic lore, the Holly King (representing the waning year) and the Oak King (representing the waxing year) duel each Yule. The Holly King wins this battle, and he is defeated at their second annual battle, at Summer Solstice. The Holly King's rule is a time to be introspective and reflective. The Oak King's rule is a time for action, beginning new projects, and working on self-improvement and growth.

Celebrating Yule

To celebrate Yule, you might want to get up to witness the sunrise and see the Wheel turn, honoring the newborn God and the mother Goddess. You might also plan decorations for your home from traditional materials: make a wreath to represent the Wheel of the Year; take a walk in the woods and harvest some holly or mistletoe to place in your home; cut down a tree and decorate it in your home or decorate a tree in your yard, rather than cutting one down. Remind yourself of the cycle of nature, and be thankful for the plants and animals that remain through the winter.

Yule Rituals and Spells

A commonly used spell during Yule is the burning of the Yule log. If you don't have a log that sits securely, cut a log in half so that it sits comfortably on its flat surface. You can decorate it with holly, ivy, red candles, or anything that feels right to you and is nontoxic to burn. While you make it, concentrate on what you wish to bring to your family, community, or town on this day of celebration. While concentrating, chant:

> *As you burn, this spell's set free;*
>
> *As I will so mote it be.*

When you place the Yule log in the fire, all your good magick will go to work as you enjoy the feast day with family or friends.

As a group spell for Yule, have everyone bring an ornament that represents something they'd like to bring into their lives in the coming year. Place all the ornaments on the tree and join hands around it. Circle around the tree, charging your ornaments and singing this chant written by Aurora's good friend Liguana (check out Liguana's *The Complete Idiot's Guide to Wicca Craft*; see Appendix B):

> *The seasons change and then,*
>
> *We turn the wheel again.*

(Repeat.)

> *And we grow, and we grow, and we gro-o-o-o-ow.*

(Repeat.)

At the end of the merriment, everyone can take their ornaments home with them for their own altars or trees.

CAUTION

For Protection

Don't burn a Yule log in an unsafe environment (stick to the fireplace), and always be sure that the decorations on your Yule log are nontoxic and safe to burn.

Imbolc (Candlemas): February 2

This major Sabbat is associated with the Goddess Brigid (later re-iterated as Saint Brigid). Imbolc means "in the belly"—as in the year is now quickening in the Goddess's belly. She's pregnant with the new year, buds are beginning to come up, and there are signs of oncoming spring. The days are growing longer as the young God grows stronger, and there is hope for spring.

Imbolc is also called Candlemas, and it is a festival of light. Candles feature strongly in the celebrations of this Sabbat, sometimes even being set into a crown worn on the head. Groundhog Day is also related to Imbolc (in other countries it is sometimes a different animal), which is about being patient for spring to come. It's unlucky to be impatient, which is why winter will last longer if it is sunny and the animal sees its shadow. Valentine's Day is related as well; love and romance feature prominently in our anticipation for spring!

Celebrating Imbolc

To celebrate Candlemas, you might want to try your hand at making candles (it's surprisingly easy, and all the necessary supplies can be found at your local crafts store). If you're not that craftsy, you could simply meditate to the light of a candle or take a relaxing bath by candlelight.

You might also celebrate the coming spring by starting some seeds inside to prepare for spring planting. If you aren't planning a garden, you might try forcing a few bulbs inside—paperwhites or hyacinths, perhaps.

Imbolc Rituals and Spells

This is a good time for spring cleaning, so why not do some internal spring cleaning? This is a spell that you might consider spring cleaning for your soul. Think of those negative messages you send to yourself (I'm not good enough or smart enough; I don't practice my spellcasting enough) and resolve to clean this negative thought out of your psyche. You will focus on self-love, and as this is also a time for love (Valentine's Day grew out of the Roman holidays for this month after all), this spell will help love flow into your life in a variety of ways.

Get a red candle and bless it for self-love and the removal of unwanted negative feelings you have about yourself. Rose quartz is a good stone for self-love, so if you have one, place it in front of the candle. You may want to carve a rune (perhaps Ansuz; see Chapter 14 for more on runes and magickal alphabets) for love or a heart into the candle. Now bless the candle with each Element, asking for that Element's help in cleaning out the negative and leaving only love. Light the candle and build energy as you chant:

> *As you burn, only love shall be*
>
> *Left in my heart and soul for me.*

Watch the candle burn for a while focusing your intent on this internal spring cleaning. Then you can let the candle burn while you go about other business, making sure you don't leave it unattended. If you need to, you can finish burning it another time.

For a group spell at this Sabbat, you can take the spring cleaning idea a bit further. Have one person hold the coven broom (if you have one), another saltwater, one with incense or smudge, etc. Others can do the "psychic sweeping," pretending to hold a broom while energetically sweeping the area. Throw into the middle of the room your words for what you are cleaning out of your life (such as "I'm not good enough"). When everyone has done this, start circling while sweeping, smudging, asperging, and so on. Everyone can sing:

> *Sweeping out the negative,*
>
> *Setting myself free.*
>
> *As we clean we leave only*
>
> *Love for you and me.*

You'll get your temple cleaned while working a nice springtime spell!

Eostara (Spring Equinox): March 21

At Eostara (Oh-*star*-ah) the God is becoming stronger; day and night are of equal length. The name of this Sabbat sounds like Easter, doesn't it? They both come from the German Goddess Eostar. The non-Christian aspects of Easter are remnants of the pagan Eostara—Easter eggs, for example. The egg symbolizes the fertility of the Goddess and the new life coming with the spring. As the days grow longer, the God is now a young man.

Spellcasting

Look ahead to Chapter 10 for some information on the symbolism of color before you dye your Eostara eggs, and choose colors that are meaningful for you or represent your hopes for the coming spring.

Celebrating Eostara

To celebrate Eostara, you might dye some Eostara eggs to celebrate the new life coming with spring. You can also get yourself in tune with spring by going outside and really seeing the changes taking place in nature. Are there flowers blooming now? Which ones? Daffodils? Tulips? What do they look like? What do they smell and feel like? What else do you notice? Is grass coming up? Do the trees have buds? Leaves? What does it feel like outside? Can you smell the earth?

Eostara Rituals and Spells

Spring is a time of year associated with new life, and eggs are a prime symbol of new life. For this ritual, blow an egg by pricking a small hole in each end of a raw egg and then blowing into one hole to remove the insides. You can scramble the egg innards that come out, or use them as an offering to the Earth by burying them in your yard! Once the eggshell is hollow, you can dye it a bright, life-giving color with regular food dye and decorate it with egg paints. It's a bit tricky to get the hollow egg down into the bowl of dye because it now floats, but you can gently push it under and roll it around so it gets covered.

Think of a new project you wish to start this spring, and paint symbols on the egg that represent that project. This egg will now be a magickal talisman for your new endeavor. Bless the egg at your altar, asking each Element for its blessings on your project. Hold the egg and chant:

> *New life, new starts, new eggs in spring,*
>
> *Bless this endeavor in everything.*

With a long needle, you can thread a string through the eggshell and hang it over your altar, until you feel the magick has worked and the project is well underway. Then ritually thank the talisman, crush it, and bury it in your yard.

For a group spell, it's fun to do an egg hunt at this time of the year. The one described here is part spell, part divination. (One year at Eostara there was snow on the ground where Aurora lives, and the group had a great time nestling the colorful eggs into the snow. Someone brought strawberries, too, and affixed these to the ends of the tall, dead grasses. It looked very festive.)

Have everyone in the group arrive with an egg that has been dyed and blessed (and perhaps marked with a rune or other symbol) for some specific purpose. Perhaps one person feels drawn to making an egg for peace, or prosperity, or love. No one knows for whom they are making their egg; make yours for whatever you feel drawn to do. It is best if these are hard-boiled eggs, as blown ones are quite fragile. Assign one or two people to be the "rabbits"; they will assemble everyone's eggs in a basket and then go outside (or into another room) and hide them. When the hunt begins, each person is allowed only one egg. The one they find represents what they need most at that moment. After the hunt, everyone can relax and share the stories of who got whose egg and what it was charged for. You may discover that what you really need is peace of mind when you thought you needed a new job!

Beltane (May Day): April 30

Beltane is a major Sabbat; the name simply means "May," and the holiday begins at sundown on April 30. This is a joyous and carefree Sabbat, opposite Samhain on the Wheel (after Samhain, it is the second most important Sabbat). As at Samhain, during Beltane the veil between the worlds is thin, making contact between them possible.

Beltain is a festival of fertility, and it used to be a time when trysts in the woods went unnoticed and unheeded, a time when otherwise unbreakable rules could be broken. The sexual union of the Goddess and God happens at Beltane: The God has grown into maturity and as he and the Goddess are united, the Goddess becomes pregnant. The maypole is a symbol of May Day, a phallic symbol honoring the virility of the God.

Celebrating Beltane

Beltane is traditionally celebrated with a maypole dance, a great group spell. Have each person bring a length of ribbon around four yards in length and attach them to the top of the pole (preferably before the pole is erected). The pole can be topped with flowers and any springtime decorations you prefer. Have each person hold the end of a ribbon and step back to the edge of the circle (as far as the ribbon will allow). Now have everyone count off aloud, alternating: "one, two, one, two …" Then everyone who said "one" turns to the right, and everyone who said "two" turns to the left. Start with the ones going over the twos. Next, the twos will go over the ones. This simply alternates: over, under, over, under. If someone can drum or play a pennywhistle, that would be great; otherwise the dancers can sing as they dance. One traditional and ancient song follows:

> *Hal an tow,*
>
> *Jolly rumble-o!*
>
> *We were up,*
>
> *Long before the day-o!*
>
> *To welcome in the summertime,*
>
> *Welcome in the May-o!*
>
> *Summer is a-comin-in,*
>
> *And winter's gone away!*

Other group or solitary Beltane celebrations could include making a wreath or crown out of the flowers that are blooming, or decorating your altar with flowers and fruits to celebrate and honor the Goddess's fertility.

> **Spellcasting**
>
> The Great Rite is the Wiccan ritual honoring the ultimate magick: sex. It is performed between a priestess and a priest who are already married or are partners in life. Often it is done in symbolic form, where the athame represents the male and the chalice represents the female. This is also the way of blessing the wine (or juice) before sharing it around. The Great Rite is often enacted at Beltane, usually in private, if sex is part of the ritual; or with the whole group, if done symbolically.

Beltane Rituals and Spells

The dancing of the maypole is really a community spell, weaving a web of connection and love between the people dancing. If you don't have a group to dance a Maypole with, why not do a cord spell yourself? Get three beautiful ribbons in colors that make you think of spring and love (also see Chapter 10 for color symbolism). Focus on something you want to bring into your life at this time. It could be love (if so, keep it nonspecific; love in general, not a particular person you want to make love you), or it could be a new job, a new place to live, etc. Attach the ends of the ribbons to something stationary (a chair, or your toes!) and braid them. As you braid, focus your energy while you chant:

> *As I braid, I bring in May so dear,*
>
> *Bring me _____ all through the year.*

Insert what you are working on in the blank space (love, peace, prosperity), and wait for your spell to work.

Litha (Summer Solstice): June 21

The Summer Solstice, or midsummer, is the longest day of the year—the God is at his peak, and the Goddess is his bride. After this date on the calendar, the days will begin to shorten, and the power of the God diminishes. This festival honors life, the fertility of the Goddess, and the bounty of crops, animals, and the natural world, as well as the power of the God.

Celebrating Litha

To celebrate Litha, see the sunrise on its strongest day. Then enjoy some time outside, in the light of the God. Perhaps spend some time in your garden, appreciating the bounty of the earth. Pick a bouquet of flowers that you can bring inside as a reminder of the power of the God.

Litha is also a popular time for weddings (ever hear of the June bride?). The Wiccan wedding ceremony is called a handfasting. It refers to the hands of the two people being "fasted" together (as in, "Give me your hand in marriage"). Handfasting is also often used to mean a kind of engagement ceremony performed a year and a day before the legal wedding is planned. If you're planning, participating in, or attending a wedding near this time of year, think about the celebration of bounty and light. You might give a gift embodying this: a living plant or a bundle of candles, for example. See Chapter 15 for more on handfasting.

Litha Rituals and Spells

Midsummer is when the reign of the Oak King comes to an end, as he is defeated by his brother the Holly King, who will reign over the waning year. As at Yule, many covens will reenact this battle—one coven we know did this with water pistols!

This Sabbat is sometimes looked at as the marriage of the Goddess and the God. A wedding at this time of the year would certainly be a powerful spell. Solstices also deal with the turning of the wheel, and often flaming wheels are used to symbolize this. This is a good day to do Fire spells: If you can, light a fire outside. If you don't have a safe place to do that, use a candle instead. If you want to bring more Fire energy into your life (action, transformation, dance, or relationships), make a talisman out of red cloth and consecrate it at the Summer Solstice, again asking the blessings of each Element, but especially speaking to Fire. Then raise energy over the talisman, chanting:

The wheel turns round, summer comes in,

Fire bring the _____ in.

For a group spell at Litha, it's nice to have a bonfire outside, but if you can't, use a cauldron with some votives burning in it. Have everyone write on small pieces of paper something in their lives that they want to be done with. Dance and raise energy around the fire until the time is right. Then everyone should use his or her passion about the thing written on the paper to throw it into the fire, letting the fire consume and remove that thing.

Lughnasadh (Lammas): August 1

Lughnasadh (pronounced *Loo*-nus-ah), a major Sabbat, means "August." Lughnasadh is the first of the three harvest festivals, and usually refers to the grain harvest. The God is beginning to lose his strength at Lughnasadh, and rituals include the use of the first harvested grain in preparing food and making an offering of this grain as thanks for the bounty of the harvest.

Celebrating Lughnasadh

You might celebrate Lughnasadh with one of the traditional grains of this harvest: corn. Plan a feast, featuring corn soup or corn bread. Perhaps there is a local farmer's market where you can purchase fresh corn, after which you can shuck the husks from the corn and see the corn through its stages from plant to meal, appreciating the grain and the God and Goddess for their work in providing you with this harvest.

Lughnasadh Rituals and Spells

For the most appropriate spell at this time, try some kitchen magick and bake a loaf of bread! ("John Barleycorn" is a fabulous song to sing during this Sabbat.) If you're up for something more challenging than a simple loaf, try a braided bread. This Sabbat also deals with sacrifice, so you might want to bake an extra loaf that you give away to someone. As you knead and bake, focus your thankfulness for the harvest and your love that you are willing to sacrifice for others into your work. As you work, you can chant:

I give of myself to this bread,

The goodness of harvest, in this bread.

Here's a hearty recipe you can try:

Oat-Nut Bread

- ½ cup warm water

- 2 tsp. active dry yeast

- 5 cups whole-wheat flour

- 1½ tsp. salt

- ¼ cup honey

- ¼ cup vegetable oil

- 2 cups cooked oatmeal

- ½ to ¾ cup toasted nuts and/or seeds (sunflower or flax seeds and chopped walnuts work well)

In a cup or small bowl, combine the warm water and yeast. Mix until the yeast dissolves completely.

In a large mixing bowl, combine the flour, salt, honey, oil, and cooked oatmeal. Add the yeast mixture. With a large spoon or your hands, mix the ingredients thoroughly. Knead the dough with your hands until it is springy and smooth. Add the nuts or seeds and knead them into the dough. Make a ball of the dough.

Place the dough in a bowl and cover with a damp cloth. Let rise in a warm spot for 1 hour, or until doubled in size. Press the dough down flat and then shape into a ball again. Allow it to rise again, this time for about 30 minutes.

Shape the dough into two loaves and place in greased bread pans (8 × 4 inches). Let the dough rise until it is about 1 inch above the rim of the pan (usually 20–40 minutes).

Bake at 350°F for 35–45 minutes, or until the top is brown. Let cool in pans for 10 minutes, and then place onto a cutting board or wire rack to cool completely.

If you have a group to work with, you could get together and make a scarecrow at Lughnasadh. Place onto this scarecrow everything that you give to your community (your love, your good intentions, your nurturing, or your time). It will then be ritually burned at the Lughnasadh bonfire while the group thinks about the sacrifices needed of everyone to make a community work. This is a spell to prepare for the oncoming winter, banding the group together to help each other get through any difficulties ahead.

While you burn the scarecrow, try chanting:

> *Fall, Fall, the Fall comes in,*
>
> *Let the harvest now begin!*

Mabon (Autumn Equinox): September 21

Mabon (pronounced *May*-bon) is another harvest celebration. Day and night are again equal; it is a time of balance between the light and the dark. However, the dark is gaining, and winter is definitely on the way. Some people think of this holiday as the pagan Thanksgiving, because the American Thanksgiving in November is late for a harvest festival in many regions.

Celebrating Mabon

Enjoy some of the fruits of the fall harvest in your Mabon celebration: Go out and pick apples, pumpkins and gourds, and nuts, and bring them home and make a meal from them. If you live where this is possible, you might also go out and experience the fall leaves as they change color. Perhaps collect some from the ground and decorate your home or altar with them. If you have a garden, your harvest may be finished; spend some time in your garden, perhaps cleaning it out in preparation for the garden you will plant next spring.

Mabon Rituals and Spells

Mabon is often seen as a fruit harvest. Take a fruit that is in season where you live—if you grew it yourself, so much the better; or maybe you can purchase it directly from the person who did (as at a farmer's market). In a magick circle, consecrate the fruit, asking the blessing of each Element on it, to bring the magick of the season and of the harvest into you. Think about all that you are thankful for. Raise energy while chanting:

> *What I reap this I will sow,*
>
> *Day of balance, let it flow.*

Then eat the fruit, savoring the magickal energy in it!

A variant of this spell that could be done with a group would be to have a basket of apples or other in-season fruit in the center of the circle. The group dances around the basket singing the previous chant, focusing the desired energy into the center.

Then everyone sits down and picks one fruit from the basket, eating the magick within the circle.

The Wheel of the Year

Celebrating the Sabbats can be a powerful way of strengthening your ties to nature and to the natural world. Many of us do not spend as much time in nature as we might like, and simple recognition of the cycles of nature can remind you of your link to nature, whether you live in the country, the city, or somewhere in between.

The Least You Need to Know

◆ Sabbats are the eight Wiccan holidays based on the solar calendar and celebrating the natural cycle of life throughout the year.

◆ Many of the Sabbats share symbolism with popular holidays, such as Halloween or Easter, which stems from their shared pagan roots.

◆ The Sabbats can be celebrated alone or with a group.

◆ Celebrating the Sabbats can remind you of the power of nature and your link to the natural cycle of life.

Part 3

Spells Manifesting Magickal Correspondences

Spells can include a wide variety of variables, and the more you learn about the options you have in working magick, the more powerful your magick will be. In this part, we'll give you magickal correspondences for color, herbs and botanicals, oils, incense, stones, and magickal symbols and alphabets. We'll offer some spells that use them, as well. You don't have to memorize these correspondences, because the tables are always available to look things up, but you may find some become second nature to you. Using these correspondences in your magick will empower and enrich your work, as well as deepen your understanding of the connections in the universe.

Using Colors, Candles, and Incense

In This Chapter

- ◆ Using color in your spellwork
- ◆ Auras: the color of your energy and health
- ◆ Working candle magick
- ◆ Incense and the scents of spellwork

Spells often include the use of color, candle, and incense magick, all of which we'll discuss in this chapter. While it's not necessary to consider color when planning your spell, it can be useful—just like timing—in making your spell as powerful as possible. And color can be used in many different types of magick, from poppets and cords to candles and ritual baths.

Candle magick is very simple and easy to work, and incense is great for purifying a space and moving your mind into a more magickal place. You can use these separately or in combination with other ingredients when working spells.

Color Correspondences

Color is created by light: Light waves bounce off of objects to our eyes. When this happens, we see colors. Colors really do have vibrational energy, and it is this energy that we try to use when we select a particular color for working magick.

The contents or ingredients of any spell are there to focus your mind. They might also serve the purpose of emphasizing your spell's focus to any spirits that you may be calling. Anything you can use to remind, focus, emphasize, or highlight your intent will help you in your spellwork. Especially if you are a visual person, color is a central element of preparing yourself to work magick. Following is a table of colors and their magickal correspondences. Before you look at it, take a few moments to think about color and answer the following questions:

What is your favorite color? _____

What color do you least like? _____

What color would you not be caught dead wearing? _____

What color is your car? Your house? Your bedroom?

_____

Is there a color you feel drawn to, one that makes you feel calm or energized?

_____

Now take a look at the table and think about why you might be drawn to some colors and not others, and how colors make you feel. If green is your favorite color (as it is Cathy's), what might this say about you?

The Magickal Correspondences of Color

Color	Correspondences
White	Peace, truth, healing, the ultimate, Monday
Black	Banishing, protection, fertile soil, unseen forces, Saturday
Green	Prosperity, abundance, health, fertility, Earth, growing things, material wealth, Thursday
Blue	Hope, tranquility, spirituality, protection, Water, healing, emotion, Friday
Red	Strength, energy, will, passion, Fire, Tuesday
Orange	Success, strength, Fire
Yellow	Creativity, intelligence, Air, Sunday

Color	Correspondences
Purple	Spirituality, healing, psychic power, Wednesday
Lavender	Intelligence, peace, spiritual growth
Brown	Stability, home, Earth
Pink	Love, friendship, harmony, nurturing
Gold	Wealth, abundance, Earth, Air, metal tools, connection with the divine, solar influences, the God
Silver	Lunar influences, Water, Air, prosperity, healing, the Goddess

Creating Spells Using Color Correspondences

You can use the table we've provided when planning your spells to help make your magick more successful, or you can use the colors that occur to you intuitively for your purpose. If you want to work a spell to create prosperity, including green (or gold or silver) elements in your spell might make the spell work better than using purple or red, for example. If you were feeling upset or anxious, a spell to calm yourself (or others) could include the color light blue. You might light a light blue candle, visualize the color in your mind's eye, and chant:

Calming blue of purest light,

Align my soul with your pure might.

If you wanted to make this spell material, or solid, to enable you to take it with you (perhaps in your car if you deal with frustrating traffic), you could sew a small blue silk pouch and fill it with herbs, crystals, and other items that work for calming (for more on crystals, see Chapter 11; for more on herbs, see Chapter 12). Then bless and consecrate your amulet in a sacred circle while chanting the previous invocation. You might bless the amulet with all the Elements as we have discussed in previous chapters or just use the Element or Elements that you feel are most appropriate (perhaps Earth and Water in this example).

Now your blue color magick is portable and ready to take with you. You can touch it, smell it, or hold it to your forehead whenever you

Making Magick

Before going into a potentially dangerous situation, Aurora made a black amulet for protection, sewing a small black silk pouch and filling it with herbs, resins, and stones that would help strengthen her psychic defenses. Just feeling it hanging around her neck and knowing it was there made her feel stronger.

feel you need its calming strength. You could also let a child hold it if you felt he or she needs calming—but be sure your pouch contains no small objects a child might choke on, and no herbs that would be harmful if ingested. Children tend to put things in their mouths!

Color Spellwork

While it's wise to consider the use of color when creating your spell, you should also remember it is your own energy that is most important in working magick, and as always, you should follow your instincts. If you feel that the color yellow is the right one for the spell you are working, or you are drawn to a blue cord, don't fret over whether the meaning is exactly right for your spell. You are likely feeling a connection to this color for a reason, and you should go with what works for you. Now for another sample spell!

> **Making Magick**
>
> Have you ever wondered why Yule-time colors seem to favor red and green? Red is the color of the Element Fire, which includes the Sun. It is the Sun's return that we celebrate at Winter Solstice. Green is the color of the evergreen trees that we honor at this time of the year—those that keep their vitality and their beautiful green color throughout the cold, dark winter.

Let's say you are going into a bureaucratic office and you feel that you need to muster all your personal strength to cut through the red tape and not get pushed around. You may want to call on Fire or Earth for help with this. If you decide to do a Fire spell, you might light a red candle, create a red amulet as discussed earlier, and bless the amulet with Fire (over the candle) while chanting:

Fire burning in my soul,

Travel with me, make me bold.

Auras and Magick

Auras are the color of a living thing's energy. An aura is created by the secondary chakras—there are thousands of these energy centers in the body that channel energy into the primary seven chakras. Influenced by emotions, an aura changes color accordingly. Some people can see auras, and with practice, you may be able to do so as well. You can begin by noting what you *feel* a person's aura to be upon seeing them. When you get a first impression of someone, or you have a feeling about him or her, what you are sensing is the person's aura.

The colors that you will see in various people's auras tell you a lot about how they are doing or feeling, but it has more to do with how the color "feels." Does it look or feel like a sickly color? Perhaps the person needs his or her health boosted. Is it a vibrant, glowing color? This person is no doubt feeling strong and well. If you see a mix of colors, but the main color is blue, this person might be very spiritual and emotional; if the main color you see is red, the person might be quite strong-willed and passionate.

You can use auras in spells to boost your own or someone else's well-being by focusing your mind (perhaps with an appropriate color candle) and strongly visualizing the person's aura turning a strong, healthy, vibrant color. For example, say you notice your friend surrounded by a weak, sickly yellow or green aura. With the person's permission, light a candle of a strong, healing color (blue or red if strength is needed) and visualize your friend's aura taking on these glowing, healthy hues. If someone is feeling worn down by money concerns, you could use the same spell technique to visualize your friend surrounded by gold and feeling prosperous.

Candle Magick

We discussed candles briefly in Chapter 3. Candle spells are generally simple and practical spells to create. Candles are easily (and inexpensively) purchased in a variety of colors (you don't need a particular kind of candle to work magick), and the burning candle and your meditation or chant can become the spell—it can't get much simpler than that. Candle spells are good for anything that you want to send "out there": distance healing, peace, or prosperity. If you needed a spell for your own strength, you might create an amulet you could take with you, but to send a spell to another person or another place, a candle spell would be perfect, because the fire of a candle creates energy that goes into the ether to carry the spell.

Preparing to Work Candle Spells

We've been through the basics of candle spells already in Chapter 3, but we'll retrace some of those steps here. First, even for a simple spell, be sure of your intent and consider the timing of the magick. When you are ready, you will select the candle for

the spell you want to work—perhaps a blue one for a calming spell like the one we did earlier in the chapter—and you will then imbue the candle with your intent. You could *dress* the candle by adding essential oils or herbs to the candle (be careful with this, and make sure you watch the burning candle carefully if there are flammable materials nearby). You can also write or carve what you want to achieve

Words of Power

Dressing a candle refers to preparing it for its part in a spell. This may include inscribing it with words, runes, or other symbols, or adding oils or herbs.

with the spell directly into the wax of the candle (perhaps the words calm or health). If you think you will not want to burn the entire candle for this spell (this can take a long time), make a mark on the candle to indicate the point at which the spell will be complete.

You can ask for the blessing of all the Elements, or of the Elements you feel are most important to this work. With the calming spell we mentioned earlier, you might ask for the aid of Water.

You might want to consecrate your candle, introducing it to all four Elements on your altar and as you do so, chanting:

> *By Air, by Fire, by Water, by Earth,*
>
> *Burn and let my will be done.*

You can create another chant to go with your particular spell, and you should repeat the chant with your consecrated candle at hand. Once you feel your energy building and you are ready to release it, you will light the candle, sending your energy into the candle and its flame. Burn the candle to the point you indicated for the completion of the spell, if you are not burning the entire candle. You can focus on the candle as it burns to the point of the spell's completion, meditating on your goal and picking up your chant again, if you like; you could also go about other business while the candle burns. The candle sends out the spell and focus that you put into it—you could be knitting or doing the dishes while your spell is still working away. Once the candle reaches the mark you've made, your spell is complete and you should snuff out the candle with your finger and thumb (blowing out the candle will disperse your magickal energy).

CAUTION

For Protection

When working a candle spell, once you've lit your candle, *don't leave the room for any reason* without first snuffing out the candle. You may go to answer the phone or cook dinner and forget all about the candle. This can be extremely dangerous and is a serious fire hazard. If you must leave the room, snuff out the candle and relight it later to complete your spell.

If you used a large pillar candle, you could use it again for other spells. If you are using a taper, it is probably done with its useful life and you might want to use it as a fire-starter for your fireplace or just burn the rest for light.

You can purchase candles for spellwork anyplace, from the local new age store to the grocery store. While color can be important to the success of your spell, so can the candle itself: Choose one you are drawn to, based on its size, color, and smell. Candles are available in many scents, and you may be meditating to the burning candle, so be sure you buy one (scented or not) that you like the smell of. Don't let the scent of a candle distract you while doing spellwork. You can choose fancy candles or candles in special shapes. If you see a candle shaped like something that seems just perfect for the spell you are about to work, by all means buy it! But if you use candles often in magick, as we do, a good selection of plain tapers in different colors is really your most flexible purchase. Votives can also be used, but remember, a votive must always be contained in a glass or ceramic cup made for the purpose of burning it. And they generally take much longer to burn than tapers.

You can also make your own candles—it's really quite easy to do. When you do this, you can add materials to the wax for working a spell; you can make the candle a specific color or add essential oils or herbs relevant to your spell to the molten wax. See Appendix B for some resources on candle making.

CAUTION

For Protection

Many scented candles are scented using artificial perfume oils. These will probably not be helpful in your spell and may give you a headache! If a candle is made with pure essential oils the scent is a natural product, coming from a plant. It may be strong, so be sure it is correct for the purpose of your spell. (Don't use a strong eucalyptus candle for calming or psychic work, for example, because it will probably make you feel energized.)

Candle Spells

Now let's try a few spells using candles. First, a community blessing spell. Many of us live in communities that are fractured or disjointed—just a group of people who don't really have that much to do with each other. To bring your community together so that all can function to be supportive of each other, try the following candle spell. Use a large pillar candle to represent the group, and several small tapers to represent either separate groups, families, or individuals. Bless the pillar with the four Elements before you begin, asking for unity in your community. Inscribe a symbol on the candle that represents unity to you. Then take the tapers that you will be using and bless them with each Element, asking that Element to help them all come together. Green or brown candles would be appropriate for this spell, because Earth is the Element traditionally associated with holding community together. Each night for seven nights perform this ritual: Light the pillar, then light the tapers from the pillar, chanting:

From one light we fan the flames,

On one earth we all draw nourishment.

> *From one sky we all draw breath,*
>
> *From one sea we're all washed clean.*

Focus on your wishes for your community—choose some concrete goals: perhaps a group barbecue, block party, community garden, or cookie party during the holidays. These are all good ways of bringing people together. Snuff the candles with finger and thumb after they have burned a little bit each night until the week is up, at which time bury any remaining candles in the ground outside.

To bring in prosperity, you can use a large pillar candle and four coins. Traditionally, these would be silver coins, so you might want to use dimes, but pennies would do also. Bless one coin for each Element, showing it to the Element and asking its blessing for the prosperity that you need. Then light the pillar until the wax at the top of it is soft enough that you can push the coins into the top of it. Burn the candle each night for seven nights, pushing the coins down a bit each time the wax is soft enough.

Place the candle (with the coins) in a place that you walk by every day; perhaps by your front door or some other place in your house. When your windfall comes, bless the candle with all four Elements to be a candle of gratitude, and burn it, giving thanks to the Elements and deities for helping you with your need.

You can use the next spell if you are looking for a new house or a new place to live. You will need one green taper and one brown taper. The green one is for your resources and the brown for stability, or home. Tie the candles together with twine, string, yarn, or embroidery floss in a color that seems appropriate to you (maybe gold, silver, green, brown, or black). The idea is to melt the candles together so that your resources and your new home become forever intertwined. While tying them together, focus your will on these things coming together, chanting:

> *New shelter, new home, new place to rest,*
>
> *Make yourself clear to me, and be it for the best.*

Light the two candles and watch them until the wax from the two begins to melt together. In this spell it's not desirable to burn the candles all the way down, just to the point where their energies intermingle; your resources and your new home are now intertwined. Then snuff out both candles with finger and thumb, and when they have cooled, bury them in the ground on the property of your current residence. This brings the energy of the Earth and your current home into play, combining with the spell for your new home.

> **CAUTION**
>
> **For Protection** _____
>
>   For working candle magick, select a candle holder made of a nonflammable, nontoxic material such as ceramic or glass (not paper or wood), and never work candle magick on the bare ground outside, unless you're using a fire pit or other space designed to hold fire (a cauldron, pot, or bowl filled with sand or soil works well also). If working candle magick outside, be sure your flame is completely extinguished when you are done.

Incense and Magick

Smell is also an immensely important sense. Using incense and essential oils does an amazing job of focusing the mind on the spell at hand and helping it along energetically. Just as meditating on the flame of a candle can be a wonderful focus, so can the smell of incense—the change of scent can distract your conscious mind, and over time, as you use incense in working magick, it can act as a trigger, telling your subconscious mind that it's magick time!

Incense works particularly well for divination or trance work; anything that involves placing your mind in an alternative state would be a good time to use incense. Incense is associated with the Element of Air; when incense is burning, it also becomes linked with Fire. You may want to use incense on your altar and in rituals to symbolize these Elements.

Some pagans believe that smoke carries our thoughts to the gods; incense can serve this purpose. Pleasant odors are thought to attract the gods; unpleasant ones are repellants and can be used in banishing spells (spells used to remove unwanted energies, habits, etc.).

> **CAUTION**
>
> **For Protection** _____
>
>   Allow yourself to get used to working with incense gradually. If you aren't used to it, you may feel dizzy or sick at first. If you or someone you live with or work magick with suffers from a respiratory ailment (such as asthma), do not work with incense without a doctor's approval.

Creating Spells Using Incense

Practically speaking, aside from the many scents you have to choose from when it comes to incense, there are a number of forms of incense such as joss sticks, cones,

Words of Power _____

A **censer** is a receptacle used for burning incense; often, censers are swung on chains.

and powder. You'll need an incense holder—you may want to use a *censer*. Use something appropriate—and thereby safe. You can always just use joss sticks, for which many simple holders are available. These are simple to deal with and readily available; their only drawback is that they don't last as long as cones, so for longer rituals you might want to get cones, resin, or powder. You can choose the form of incense based on what you like or what's practical for you. Joss sticks are easy to take with you anywhere and sink easily into the earth (always use them in a safe place). Cones, resins, and powders have to be burned on charcoal, which is usually sold in small rolls wherever incense is sold. The best way to light the charcoal is to hold it with some small tongs, which are good things to have in your ritual gear. The charcoal will need to be placed on a surface that can withstand very high temperatures, such as ceramic, or in a cast iron cauldron.

There are hundreds of incense scents to choose from, and you can select one that appeals to you (the charts of magickal correspondences of herbs and oils in Chapter 12 might also be helpful). Don't get too caught up in choosing the right scent—there likely is no one "right" choice.

Incense Spellwork

For the following space-cleansing spell, myrrh is traditionally used. It is a great incense for cleansing and purifying your ritual area. Use a small censer or appropriate holder with a piece of charcoal. First, light the charcoal, holding it with tongs, and wait until it sparks so you are sure it's going. Then place it in the holder and sprinkle the myrrh on top of the charcoal. You can purchase myrrh as little resinous chunks, which is nice because it's closest to myrrh's natural form. Move around the space in a clockwise direction, carrying the incense and directing it into all the nooks and crannies. Walk around the space three times, singing or chanting:

> *Power of myrrh, cleanse this space:*
>
> *It is a purified ritual place.*

The use of incense is natural for any divination ritual because it serves both to put your mind into the ritual, receptive frame it needs to be in, and adds a bit of smoke to the room, which serves to help you "dim" your eyes (and logical, linear mind) so that you can "see" in a divinatory way.

With no light but candles in the room, have a bowl with a good divination incense (such as patchouli, sandalwood, or copal) ready next to your favorite divination tools. You could use a scrying ball, runes, Tarot cards, or a pendulum—whatever you prefer. After you have created sacred space, light the incense, chanting:

> *Bring to me the second sight,*
>
> *Power of* _____ ["copal", or whatever you're using] *with all your might.*

Once the incense is going well, watch the smoke curling up through the air. Breathe it in at the proper distance (so that you smell the incense, but it doesn't overwhelm you, and you can still breathe freely). Once you feel you have the frame of mind you need, pick up your cards, runes, or whatever divination method you are using. You are now ready to clearly state out loud your question. Do so, and then gaze or draw out cards or runes until you feel you have an answer. You might need to stop in the middle of your reading to purposefully breathe some more incense to help your mind clear of preconceptions and help you to interpret what you are getting from your tool.

After a successful reading or scrying, you might want to make some notes to yourself on what you have received. Then thank the spirits present and take down your sacred space.

Colors, candles, and incense may be parts of any spell you will do, so it is good to familiarize yourself with their correspondences. If you know which color of candles you want, which symbols to inscribe on them, and which incense will be appropriate for a given spell, you are already well on your way to successful spellcrafting. As you become more familiar with magick, all of these choices will become second nature to you. For now, craft simple spells or use the ones here to get yourself used to how these elements work for you. Notice how looking at a certain color of candle makes you feel. Notice how the scents of different incense make you feel. Then begin to use the colors, scents, and correspondences that make the most intuitive sense to you. Now you're making your own magick!

The Least You Need to Know

- ◆ Color associations can help you to work successful spells.

- ◆ Auras are the color of a person's energy.

- ◆ Candle magick is very simple and easy to work.

◆ Incense is a good way to put your mind into a ritual state.

◆ Be sure of your intentions and consider the elements of timing even when working a simple candle spell.

11

Using Gems, Stones, and Crystals

In This Chapter

♦ Spellwork with the power of stones

♦ Working with the energies of stones you find in nature

♦ Stone correspondences and energies

♦ Divining and empowering with gems and crystals

♦ Make the stone's energy your own

Gems and crystals are stones, and come from the earth. (Crystals are a particular kind of stone, distinguished by their structure; for our purposes, however, a stone is a stone is a stone.) As such, they have Earth energy, and you can work with this energy to strengthen your magick.

Stones can be used for divination, to create amulets, and much more. Familiarity with the magickal correspondences of stones will help you work them into your spells in ways that empower your magick. Whether you choose to work a spell with diamonds or tourmaline or a stone you collect on a hike, you can use the power of stone magick. The mineral kingdom has much to offer.

Stone Magick

Stone spirits are powerful beings and should always be treated with respect. Before picking up any stone, ask if it wants to come with you or work with you. Once you fine-tune your sensitivity, you will hear the answer. If a stone *does* want to work with you, it will tell you what it is to be used for. You may not have known that you needed to work a certain spell, but if a stone tells you that its purpose is healing or reconciliation or something else, then that is what you need to be working on. Stones that you need in this way will usually find you, whether at the beach or in a New Age store.

Spellcasting

Stones and crystals are magickally associated with gnomes, because they are Earth creatures. Many Tarot decks show these associations.

Also remember that stone, as well as bone and antler, were the first hard materials that humans had for making tools. Often connecting with our magick involves connecting with our ancient origins. Some stones (such as obsidian) carry that wisdom, and if this interests you, study it further.

You can choose to work magick with many kinds of stones, which come in any number of colors, shapes, and sizes. Stones may also be called gemstones or crystals; for practical purposes, we'll call everything stones. You can select your stone based on its magickal correspondences (we've included a table for some of these, later in the chapter), including its color, though you may decide to work magick with a stone that is meaningful or feels powerful to you. As always, do what feels right to you. Don't work a spell using quartz because a chart says that it has the best meaning for your spell if you don't feel the energy of the stone is right for your purpose.

Stone Energy

The energy of a stone can be either aggressive or receptive, direct or indirect. These are the basic energies of everything, the traditional feminine/masculine *Yin/Yang* energies of the universe. It may be useful to you in harnessing and directing the energy of stones to know what energy your chosen stone has. We've included the energy of the stones in the table later in this chapter.

Stones with yang energies—active, external—work best with magick related to the conscious mind, killing disease and giving one strength, and are associated with the Elements of Fire and Air. Stones with Yin energy—receptive, internal—are well used for magick related to the unconscious mind, spirituality, and wisdom, and are associated with the Elements of Earth and Water. You may not know the energy of a stone you collect from nature (and some stones have some of both kinds of energy), though

you may have a sense of the energy of a
stone. Meditate holding the stone for a while
and see what comes to you. If it matters, the
stone will let you know. If you don't know the
stone's Yin/Yang correspondence, this is fine. As
with most things, this information may be helpful to you, but is not meant to be the deciding
factor in creating your spell.

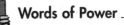

Words of Power

Yin and Yang are
names for the receptive and
active (feminine/masculine,
inward/outward, subconscious/
conscious) energies in the Universe.

Charging Your Stones

If you are planning an important spell, you may want to cleanse and charge the stone
you are going to use first. You can cleanse it with smudge or incense. Charging could
be done at your altar, by blessing the stone with each Element as described when
blessing talismans, or you can do this under the light of the Full Moon. You might
also bury the stone in the earth, while meditating, to allow the stone to absorb the
Earth energy (we described charging your tools in Chapter 5). Try chanting while
you meditate:

> *Bless this stone, my mother Earth,*
>
> *Empower it to work my will.*

Finding and Collecting Stones

You can find stones of all kinds in nature, but if you decide to concentrate on working
stone magick, you may find you need to purchase some particular stones. You can
purchase stones at occult and New Age shops, and also at many craft shops and at
rock and gem shows and fairs. You may actually find inexpensive stones at the latter
venues, though they might be more out of the way for you. Some museums sell
stones, and there may also be a shop for rock and mineral collectors in your town.
Check out all the options before investing a lot of money in stones for magick. And,
of course, be on the lookout for stones in surprising shapes and colors the next time
you're in the park or at the beach taking a walk. You can work powerful spells with
stones you find in nature, perhaps even in your own backyard. Here is a divination
spell using a stone you have collected in nature—a stone you feel connected to in
some way.

Aurora learned the following divination spell while studying at the Foundation for
Shamanic Studies and adapted it for you here. Find a rock about the size of a large
grapefruit. Make sure you ask it if it wants to come with you to answer a question in a
divination spell.

It's nice if you can do this spell with a partner, taking turns so that one person can record while the other person looks at the rock. If you are doing the spell by yourself, just be careful to put the rock down each time while you are taking notes in such a way that you remember which side you were just looking at.

Sit in a comfortable place. Hold the rock up to your forehead and ask it aloud the question you would like an answer to. Now put the rock down on the ground in front of you. Look at the side that is facing up as you naturally put it down. Pick it up so that you can look more closely at that side. See what the shapes, lines, and variations in color on that side of the rock seem to be forming. What pictures come to you? You can try both focusing and blurring your eyes and see what works best. Record the images that come to you.

Turn the rock over and do the same thing with the opposite side, recording these images. Now look at one of the "ends" of the rock, considering that you have just been looking at the "sides." Record these images. Then look at the opposite "end" and record those images. When you are finished, put the rock down and look at your notes.

Usually some kind of pattern emerges from all the images that were observed in the order they were observed. If you are doing this exercise with a partner, he or she might notice connections you don't notice yourself. A string of responses, if not answers, to your question should emerge.

Thank the rock formally, in whatever way feels right to you. You can offer it food or tobacco (tobacco is the traditional offering for this continent) overnight, then place it back where you found it (or as close as possible).

> **CAUTION**
>
> ### For Protection
>
> Always try to give to Earth whenever you take something from Earth. If you find stones you want to pick up, put down an offering of yourself. If you don't have anything with you (tobacco, chocolate, other stones), you can always use one of your own hairs. This way the Earth spirits won't feel that you only take and never give.

> ### Spellcasting
>
> A stone spell is a wonderful way of helping someone else, because it is an easy and small item to give someone. If someone you know asks you for a spell for a safe voyage, for example, he or she might enjoy carrying a small, charged stone along.

Gems and Crystals

When you think of gems, what first comes to mind may be diamonds, rubies, emeralds, and sapphires. While you can use these to work magick, a lot of other gems will work as well. Like any other stone, gems come from Earth and carry Earth energy. Some gems are more rare than others (which makes them more expensive); this doesn't make them better or more powerful for working magick. You may also want to take into consideration where the gems come from. Many expensive gems are mined under none-too-pleasant conditions. Do some research if you plan to do magick with them!

Crystals may suggest more magickal meanings—you may associate crystals with New Age beliefs. Crystals have actually been revered by people since the dawn of time. In a way, they are the earthly manifestation of universal energy. That is why crystals, with their amazing, repeating structure, are often used by witches, shamans, and magicians.

Making Magick with Gems and Crystals

There are far too many named stones for us to list them all here. The following table lists some common stones and their magickal correspondences. While this informa-tion can be helpful, especially when you are planning a spell, don't feel bound by these correspondences. Always trust your own instincts and don't work magick perfunctorily, based on a recipe only—your energy is what makes magick work, and if you are not connecting with the energy of your chosen gem, select another!

Making Magick

A great, in-depth book for reference and further reading on stones is *Love Is in the Earth: A Kaleidoscope of Crystals Update* by Melody (Earth-Love, 1995).

The Magickal Correspondences of Stones

Stone	Energy	Correspondences
Agate	Yin/Yang*	Strength, courage, love
Alexandrite	Yin	Luck, love
Amazonite	Yin	Luck, success
Amber	Yang	Protection, love, beauty
Amethyst	Yin	Healing, peace, intuitive power
Apache tear	Yang	Luck, protection
Aquamarine	Yin	Peace, courage, intuitive power
Aragonite	Yin	Grounding, healing
Aventurine	Yang	Mental acuity, prosperity, luck
Azurite	Yang	Healing, intuitive power, dreams
Beryl	Yin	Intuitive power
Bloodstone	Yang	Healing, strength, courage

continues

The Magickal Correspondences of Stones (continued)

Stone	Energy	Correspondences
Calcite	Yin/Yang	Peace, prosperity, joy
Carnelian	Yang	Courage, sexual energy
Cat's eye	Yang	Beauty, wealth, luck
Celestite	Yang	Healing
Chalcedony	Yin	Health, protection
Citrine	Yang	Intuitive power, protection
Coral	Yin	Protection, health (especially children's)
Diamond	Yang	Strength, healing, courage
Dolomite	Yang	Peace, relief from sorrow, stamina
Emerald	Yin	Love, prosperity, intuitive power
Flint	Yang	Protection, healing
Fluorite	Yin	Mental acuity, stability, health
Fossils	Yin	Protection, past lives
Garnet	Yang	Protection, energy, strength
Geodes	Yin	Fertility, childbirth, dreams
Granite	Yang	Balance, clarity, protection
Hematite	Yang	Healing, grounding, intuitive power
Heterosite	Yin	Purity, self-expression, healing
Iolite	Yin	Intuitive power, healing
Jade	Yin	Love, prosperity, healing, gardening
Jasper	Yin/Yang	Healing, protection, beauty
Jet	Yin	Protection, intuitive power, healing
Kunzite	Yin	Love, grounding, peace
Lapis lazuli	Yin	Healing, love, courage
Lava	Yang	Protection
Lepidolite	Yin	Peace, protection, spirituality
Malachite	Yin	Protection, power, energy
Marble	Yin	Protection, meditation, success
Meteorite	Yin	Spirituality, strength
Mica	Yang	Protection, intuitive power
Moonstone	Yin	Love, protection, sleep, gardening

Stone	Energy	Correspondences
Obsidian	Yang	Grounding, protection, absorbs negative energy
Onyx	Yang	Protection, self-control, strength
Opal	Yin/Yang	Intuitive power, beauty, power
Pearl	Yin	Love, faith, peace, prosperity
Peridot	Yin	Health, prosperity, sleep
Pumice	Yang	Banishing, protection, insight
Quartz	Yin/Yang	Intuitive power, protection crystals
Rhodocrosite	Yang	Energy, peace, love
Rose quartz	Yin	Love, joy, peace, emotional healing
Ruby	Yang	Prosperity, protection, power
Sapphire	Yin	Intuitive power, love, inspiration
Serpentine	Yang	Grounding, healing
Smokey quartz	Yin	Healing, absorbs negative energy, balance
Sodalite	Yin	Healing, peace, wisdom
Staurolite	Yin	Luck, prosperity, healing
Steatite	Yang	Energy, healing, peace (soapstone)
Sugilite	Yin	Healing, intuitive power
Sunstone	Yang	Protection, sexuality, health
Tiger's eye	Yang	Prosperity, protection, luck
Topaz	Yang	Protection, healing, prosperity
Tourmaline	Yin/Yang	Love, protection, friendship
Turquoise	Yin	Protection, prosperity, courage
Zebra stone	Yang	Energy, healing
Zircon	Yang	Protection, beauty, healing

When both energies are indicated, the energy of the stone varies according to its color and other attributes. Try asking the stone if you need to know.

Gem and Crystal Spells

As you can see from the table, most stones have numerous meanings, and many stones share the same meaning. If you consider the color of the stone (see the table in

Chapter 10), you'll come up with even more possibilities for stones to use in your spells. Let's look at some examples of spells using stones.

When a friend is pregnant and ready to find out something about the child she carries, Aurora has performed the child spirit ritual. (Thanks to Sobonfu Somé for the inspiration here!) The mother lies down comfortably and is placed into a trancelike state with drumming and incense. She channels the spirit of the child to tell us what the child's spirit is coming here to do, and what it might need to help it remember that path after birth on the earth plane. Aurora always has a pouch of various stones with her, and she asks the mother to put her hand in the pouch, then allow the child's spirit to guide her hand to the stone most needed by the child. She makes a note of which stone the mother pulls out. This stone or a stone of this type can then be made into a rattle or other gift for the child, so that he or she will have that stone's energy close by.

As in the previous spell, in the divination energy spell you use a pouch of various stones to divine the specific nature of the energy you need to answer a question. Place a selection of stones with the specific energies you are curious about in a pouch. Place the pouch on your altar or prepare another sacred space of quiet and reverence in which you can ground and center yourself to receive magickal energy. Place your hands over the pouch of stones and chant:

> *Sacred stones lend your wisdom*
>
> *to this seeker of open mind and heart.*
>
> *May your ancient energy guide,*
>
> *and my needed truth impart.*

As you reach into the pouch to draw out a stone, ask the specific question you'd like the stone's energy to help you answer. Some general examples might be, "What kind of energy do I need right now?" or "What energy will help resolve the circumstances surrounding a current situation or relationship?" Once you've chosen a stone, cleanse and charge it using the method given earlier in this chapter. You can carry the stone with you, put it on your altar, make a wand using the stone, use the stone's message for self-care (if you've drawn rose quartz for self-love you might buy yourself some roses or prepare a ritual bath with rose petals), or use the stone to do more spells to work with that stone's particular energy.

Let's say that you've performed the divination spell and drawn citrine, used commonly to help break addictions. Or you've chosen to work with this stone because there is a particular addiction you'd like to overcome. Aurora admits to an addiction to caffeine, and she has also used citrine to work with a friend who wanted help to stop smoking cigarettes. Cleanse the citrine and charge the stone with the elements to give added power. Then ask for blessing and strength:

> *Lord and Lady,*
>
> *Bless and strengthen this citrine.*
>
> *Increase its intuitive power*
>
> *to break the chains of addiction.*
>
> *Mind, body, and spirit again*
>
> *free to honor self and thee.*

Ask the person to carry the citrine with him or her, put the stone by the bedside, or place the stone on your altar and ask that its energy travel with the person who needs its energy. If this spell is done for another person's benefit, you still want the person's permission; most people are willing to let you give them a stone to carry. Some more adventurous people may let you put the stones on their body and bless them. For example, during meditation to break a smoking addiction, the citrine could be placed on a ribbon and worn around the throat chakra or over the lungs.

> **Spellcasting**
>
> You can use gems in jewelry for working magick, with jewelry you already own or jewelry you buy for a specific purpose. This doesn't have to be jewelry you buy at an occult or New Age store—the stone is what matters. So if you want to carry a stone for protection and you have a turquoise ring, cleanse and charge it and wear it for protection!

Magickal Stones

You can work magick with any of the gems or crystals we've listed in this chapter, or you might choose to use a stone you find at the beach (a rounded stone that soothes you) or in the mountains (a sharp-edged stone that gives you energy). When choosing the stones to work magick with, remember that it's not the meanings associated with the color and type of stone, but rather how the stones make you feel, and what you intuit the energy of the stone to be. Use your own energy and the energy within the stones you choose to work powerful spells.

The Least You Need to Know

◆ Stones are living entities and you must ask their permission before using them.

◆ Stones generally carry the energy of the Earth, but can carry many other energies as well.

◆ Valuable gemstones and rocks you find in your local park can be equally powerful to you in spellcasting.

◆ Multiple stones have similar magickal correspondences, giving you a wide range of choices for spells utilizing stones.

◆ When looking for the right stone for your spell, trust your instincts, and the right stone will find you.

Chapter 12

Using Herbs, Oils, and Power Animals

In This Chapter

- Growing, harvesting, and making magick with herbs
- Magick with oils: dressing *and* aromatherapy
- Cooking up some kitchen magick
- Finding your familiar
- Calling on the spirit of your power animal

Witches have long been herbalists, and have worked magick using plants and oils in healing spells and potions. Plants and oils can be used to dress candles, make incense, and work kitchen magick, to name just a few of their magickal uses. Use the magickal correspondences of plants and oils to help you plan your spellwork.

In this chapter, we'll look at the basics of using plants and herbs in spellwork, and we'll also consider the importance of animal spirits in working magick. Power animals and familiars can work with you and the energies in nature to boost the potency of your magickal work.

Herbs

Herbs and other plants have been grown, harvested, and used for their healing powers for centuries, and modern medicine still relies on plants for their medicinal powers. Herbal magick is really an art and a science, and we could write a whole book on it (many people have—see the resources listed in Appendix B). Here we'll talk about the basics of herbal magick, to familiarize you with it. If you find yourself drawn to this kind of magick, you can do further work on it, perhaps becoming a full-fledged herbalist!

Making Magick with Herbs

What makes an herb magickal? Herbs—all plants, for that matter—are living beings and have living energy. As you would anything in nature, ask the plant its permission before taking it. If you sit in quiet meditation for a while in front of a plant, you can expand your awareness to include the spirit of the plant and communicate with it. Ask it what its uses are and whether it wants to work with you.

The boline, a curved knife, is the traditional Wiccan tool for harvesting herbs, but a straight blade or a pair of garden shears will work just as well. Make sure you leave an offering when you harvest a plant; your offering can be tobacco or anything you value, or if you have nothing else, one of your own hairs.

You might use plants to create an amulet, make incense, or whip up a cup of magickal herbal tea—all of these can be used in spellwork. There are three methods of extraction in preparing herbs for use in magick:

♦ Decoction uses boiling water

♦ Infusion also uses water (not boiling), for steeping

♦ Tincturing uses alcohol to create a tincture or infusion

Most of the plants you'll use in working magick are quite common, and you may already grow a number of them in your yard: Do you grow roses or have columbine or daisies in your flower garden? Perhaps violets are a favorite, or you have a pot of basil in your kitchen. All of these may be used in spellwork.

Most of the plants you'll want to use—and herbs especially—are quite easy to grow, though you can also purchase many of them in a health-food or metaphysical store, and, depending on the weather and your location, you can collect some of them on strolls through your neighborhood or local park. It takes fairly specialized knowledge of plants to harvest herbs from nature. To avoid mishaps, only harvest those you're sure of, like common flowers and herbs. If you aren't sure the plant you brought home is hyssop, don't use it in your spell.

Spellcasting

Wash your fresh herbs in water and blot them dry. Then hang them upside down in a cool, dark place for two or three weeks to dry out. Store dried herbs in a cool, dark location, out of direct light, to make them last longer. Be sure your herbs are labeled and that any toxic herbs are clearly marked as such and kept out of reach of others. Use airtight containers for storage—glass works best to preserve your herbs.

Some plants can cause allergic reactions, and the oils of many plants are absorbed into the skin, so be careful handling your herbs. If you are aware that you have an allergic reaction to mint, don't use it in your spellwork, not even in a spell to heal your allergies! Also, prolonged exposure to herbs and their dust can bring on allergic reactions that may not have been apparent before. Be careful of dusty, dry herbs—it may be wise to wear a dust mask if you are working with them a lot.

If you decide to do more herb harvesting on your own, there are many good books (both Wiccan and general botanical books) on plants and specifically herbs. You might enjoy gardening and find growing plants for working magick a relaxing and peaceful way of integrating magick into your everyday life. It is also an important way of getting in touch with the earth and the plant spirits around you. But if you can't do it all right away, don't worry—it's fine to buy the herbs you need for your magick, either fresh or dried.

As do colors and stones, herbs have traditional associations and energies, and you can use these to help you select appropriate herbs for your spellwork. In the following table we've listed plants you might use for magick followed by their energy and some of their magickal correspondences. Use this table as a guideline; the charted energy of the plant might be useful, but if you have a strong *feeling* that chamomile is what you should use in your spell, and the associations don't seem to fit, trust your instincts and use the herb you're drawn to.

Making Magick

Gardening can be a spell in itself. Like Cathy, you may find digging in the earth to be magickal and meditative. If you're growing plants for use in magick, you'll feel this connection even more—and you'll have a ready source of herbs and flowers for use in spellwork, to cook with, and to brighten your home.

The Magickal Correspondences of Herbs

Plant	Energy	Correspondence(s)
Almond	Yang	Love, luck, money, prosperity, sex
Aloe vera	Yin	Luck, protection
Amaranth	Yin	Healing, protection
Anemone	Yang	Healing, protection
Angelica	Yang	Healing, protection
Anise	Yang	Luck, protection, purification
Apple	Yin	Healing, love
Ash	Yang	Healing, protection, prosperity
Aster	Yin	Love
Balm of Gilead	Yin	Love, healing, protection
Barley	Yin	Healing, protection
Basil	Yang	Success, harmony, love, prosperity, protection, purification
Bay leaf	Yang	Healing, mental acuity, prosperity, protection, strength
Bergamot	Yang	Balance, prosperity, protection
Bittersweet	Yang	Healing, protection
Black cohosh	Yang	Courage, love, protection
Bleeding heart	Yin	Love
Bluebell	Yang	Luck, funerals, grieving
Borage	Yang	Courage, intuitive powers, strength
Buckwheat	Yin	Prosperity, protection
Burdock	Yin	Healing, protection, purification
Calendula	Yang	Love, prosperity, consecration, vision
Camellia	Yin	Prosperity
Camphor	Yin	Divination, healing
Caraway	Yang	Mental acuity, protection
Cardamom	Yin	Love
Carnation	Yang	Protection, strength, vitality
Catnip	Yin	Beauty, love, happiness
Cedar	Yang	Healing, money, protection, purification, success

Plant	Energy	Correspondence(s)
Celandine	Yang	Happiness, protection
Celery seed	Yang	Lust, intuitive power
Chamomile	Yang	Harmony, love, prosperity, purification
Chicory	Yang	Frugality, obtaining favors
Chrysanthemum	Yang	Protection
Cinnamon	Yang	Healing, love, prosperity, protection, intuitive power, success
Cinquefoil	Yang	Health, love, luck, prosperity
Clove	Yang	Love, protection, purification, strength
Clover	Yang	Fidelity, prosperity, protection, success
Columbine	Yin	Courage, love
Comfrey	Yin	Healing, protection (travel)
Coriander	Yang	Healing, love
Cotton	Yin	Healing, luck, protection
Cowslip	Yin	Healing
Cumin	Yang	Fidelity, protection
Cyclamen	Yin	Fertility, protection
Daffodil	Yin	Fertility, love, luck
Daisy	Yin	Love
Dandelion	Yang	Divination
Dill	Yang	Love, prosperity, protection
Dogwood	Yin	Protection, Moon, harvest
Dragon's blood	Yang	Love, protection, purification, strength, stress relief
Echinacea	Yang	Used to strengthen spells
Elderberry	Yin	Healing, love, prosperity, protection, purification
Eucalyptus	Yin	Healing, protection, invigorating
Euphorbia	Yin	Protection, purification
Fennel	Yang	Healing, protection, purification
Fern	Yang	Luck, protection
Fig	Yang	Divination, fertility, love
Flax	Yang	Beauty, healing, protection, intuitive power

continues

The Magickal Correspondences of Herbs (continued)

Plant	Energy	Correspondence(s)
Fleabane	Yin	Protection
Foxglove	Yin	Protection
Frankincense	Yang	Dispels negative energy, protection, spirituality, stress relief
Gardenia	Yin	Healing, love, passion, peace
Garlic	Yang	Healing, love, protection
Gentian	Yang	Love, power
Geranium	Yin	Fertility, healing, love, protection
Ginger	Yang	Love, power, success
Ginseng	Yang	Beauty, healing, love, lust, protection
Goldenrod	Yin	Divination
Goldenseal	Yang	Healing, prosperity
Hawthorn	Yang	Fertility, protection
Heather	Yin	Fertility, luck, protection
Heliotrope	Yang	Healing, prosperity, purification
Hemp	Yin	Healing, love
Hibiscus	Yin	Divination, love
Holly	Yang	Luck, protection
Honeysuckle	Yang	Protection, intuitive power
Horehound	Yang	Healing, dispels negative energy, mental acuity, protection
Horse chestnut	Yang	Healing, prosperity
Hyacinth	Yin	Love, protection
Hyssop	Yang	Protection, purification
Ivy	Yin	Healing, protection
Jasmine	Yin	Dreams, love, prosperity
Juniper	Yang	Love, protection
Larkspur	Yin	Healing, protection
Lavender	Yang	Harmony, love, prosperity, protection, stability
Leek	Yang	Love, protection
Lemon balm	Yin	Healing, love, success
Lemongrass	Yang	Intuitive power, lust

Plant	Energy	Correspondence(s)
Lilac	Yin	Protection
Lily	Yin	Protection
Lily of the valley	Yang	Happiness, mental acuity
Linden	Yang	Love, luck, protection
Loosestrife	Yin	Peace, protection
Magnolia	Yin	Fidelity
Maidenhair fern	Yin	Beauty, love
Mallow	Yin	Love, protection
Mandrake	Yang	Fertility, love, prosperity, protection
Marigold	Yang	Love, protection, intuitive power
Marjoram	Yang	Love, prosperity, protection
Masterwort	Yang	Courage, protection
Mint	Yang	Healing, protection
Mistletoe	Yang	Fertility, love, protection
Morning glory	Yang	Happiness, peace
Mugwort	Yin	Divination, healing, protection, intuitive power, strength
Mulberry	Yang	Protection, strength
Mullein	Yin	Courage, protection
Mustard	Yang	Fertility, protection
Myrhh	Yin	Healing, protection, purification
Nettle	Yang	Healing, protection
Nutmeg	Yang	Divination, fidelity, healing, love, luck
Oak	Yang	Fertility, healing, luck, prosperity, protection, strength
Oats	Yin	Money, prosperity
Oleander	Yin	Love
Olive	Yang	Fertility, healing, protection
Onion	Yang	Healing, protection
Orchid	Yin	Love
Orris root	Yin	Divination, love, protection
Parsley	Yang	Prosperity, protection, purification
Passionflower	Yin	Balance, calm, friendship, peace

continues

The Magickal Correspondences of Herbs (continued)

Plant	Energy	Correspondence(s)
Patchouli	Yin	Fertility, protection, sensuality
Pea	Yin	Love, money, prosperity
Pennyroyal	Yang	Protection, peace, strength
Peony	Yang	Protection
Periwinkle	Yin	Love, mental acuity, protection
Persimmon	Yin	Healing, luck
Pine	Yang	Fertility, healing, prosperity, protection
Pineapple	Yang	Luck, money, sex
Poke	Yang	Courage
Poppy	Yin	Fertility, love, luck
Primrose	Yin	Love, protection
Purslane	Yin	Love, luck, protection
Quince	Yin	Love, protection
Rhubarb	Yin	Fidelity, protection
Rose	Yin	Beauty, fertility, love, luck, protection, intuitive power
Rosemary	Yang	Beauty, healing, love, protection, purification
Rowan	Yang	Healing, intuitive power, protection
Rye	Yin	Fidelity, love
Saffron	Yang	Happiness, healing, love
Sage	Yang	Prosperity, protection, purification, stress relief, wisdom
Sandalwood	Yin	Healing, mental acuity, protection, purification
Sassafras	Yang	Healing, prosperity
Slippery elm	Yin	Protection (especially from gossip)
Snapdragon	Yang	Prosperity, protection
Sorrel (wood)	Yin	Healing
Spearmint	Yin	Healing, love, mental acuity
St. John's wort	Yang	Healing, protection, strength
Star anise	Yang	Luck, intuitive power
Strawberry	Yin	Love, luck
Sunflower	Yang	Fertility, friendship, prosperity, wisdom

Plant	Energy	Correspondence(s)
Sweetpea	Yin	Courage, friendship, strength
Tansy	Yin	Healing
Thistle	Yang	Healing, protection, strength
Thyme	Yin	Healing, love, intuitive power, peace, strength
Toadflax	Yang	Protection
Tobacco	Yang	Dispel negativity, healing, purification
Tonka	Yin	Friendship, love, prosperity
Tulip	Yin	Love, prosperity, protection
Uva ursa	Yin	Intuitive power
Valerian	Yin	Love, peace, protection, purification
Verbena/vervain	Yin	Healing, love, luck, prosperity, protection, purification
Vetivert	Yin	Love, prosperity, protection
Violet	Yin	Healing, love, luck, protection
Walnut	Yang	Fertility, healing
Wheat	Yin	Fertility, prosperity
Willow	Yin	Divination, healing, love, protection
Witch grass	Yang	Happiness, love
Witch hazel	Yang	Beauty, protection
Wolfbane	Yin	Protection
Wormwood	Yang	Protection, intuitive power, love
Yarrow	Yin	Love, intuitive power, protection
Yerba santa	Yin	Beauty, healing, intuitive power
Ylang-ylang	Yang	Calming, love

A few words of caution: Before ingesting any plant, make sure it is edible and will not cause any adverse reaction, such as inflaming allergies or interacting negatively with any medications (prescription *or* over-the-counter) that you are taking. If you are taking *any* medication, always check with your physician before ingesting any particular herb. Be aware of any medicinal properties of the herbs you use so that you are not surprised by negative side effects, and remember that the oils in the herbs can be absorbed into your skin—you might want to wear gloves when handling the plants you use for working magick.

Herb Spells

Herbs can be useful in many kinds of spells, and one of the simplest kinds of magick to work with herbs is kitchen magick (magick you work with ingredients you find in your kitchen). Herbal teas can be a wonderful tool for raising magickal energy in spellwork. For this spell you will choose the herb for your tea that possesses the appropriate energy for your purpose, and you'll also time your spell to the best season or Moon phase to achieve the desired result. Of course, the herb you choose must be suitable for ingesting as a tea! You can do this spell for your own benefit or you can serve the tea to yourself and a guest, which means the two of you will participate together in the spell. Rose and hibiscus are lovely choices for spring and love. Other magickal purposes might be for cleansing, fertility, or luck for a project, and you'd want to choose an herb for each that corresponds to that particular purpose and/or energy.

To begin, brew your tea. It's fine to use tap water, or whatever water you would ordinarily drink. If you wish to bless the water first, you could hold the tea kettle up, and say, *"I ask the blessings of purity upon this creature of water, by the Lady and Lord."* If you can, use loose herbs for your tea instead of tea bags. Take the loose herbs before you put them in the tea ball or sack and say a brief spell such as:

> *By power of Earth, strengthen these plants,*
>
> *Bless them with* [love, healing, abundance, joy]
>
> *Augment their powers, make their work strong,*
>
> *As I will, so mote it be!*

When the tea is ready, go ahead and drink it. You may want to drink the tea as a simple morning or evening ritual in your favorite chair, or drink it in a sacred outdoor space or before your altar. If you use loose leaf tea, read the leaves that remain at the bottom of the cup once the tea is drunk. Swirl the cup three times, look at the pattern the tea leaves settle into, open your heart, breathe deeply, and intuit what the pattern says to you. Record your impressions in your Book of Shadows.

If the herb you have chosen is safe to drink as a brewed tea every day continuously for a week, repeat your tea spell for seven days. Choose the week (and if you can, the season) for your tea spell that is most appropriate to your magickal purpose. For example, a spell for a new love would be good to do during the week of a New Moon. If after your week has passed, you're not seeing the result you want from your tea spell, then figure out if what you really need is a new direction or magickal purpose. Or take a break and try the tea spell for a week again on the following Moon. Or try a new herb for your tea.

If this spell includes another person (whether or not that person is a practicing Wiccan—or whether *you* are!), invite your partner to participate in the ritual of brewing the tea and allow the herbal tea to infuse its beneficial energy to the good of whatever aspect of the relationship the two of you are working on together. Remember, if you do this spell with someone else, you need to have his or her full consent and participation. You can't just hand a cup of "love tea" to the gorgeous guy or girl in the next cubicle, or a cup of "give me a raise" tea to your boss—believe us, these would backfire!

CAUTION For Protection

If you plan to grow plants for working magick, be careful what you grow and where—especially if you have small children or pets. Some plants, such as the common flower foxglove (from which the potent drug digitalis is made), are poisonous and can be fatal if ingested in large enough quantities. Foxglove can be useful for working magick, and in lore, this plant is the traditional home to faeries.

Oils

Oils found in your kitchen—olive oil, for example—and those essential oils created from plants and used in making some perfumes can all be used to work magick. Those plant oils we cautioned you about earlier can be tools for making magick. Use gloves to keep the oils from your skin, avoiding any adverse reactions. You might want to use a *carrier oil* for your essential oil, to make the oil less toxic and to stretch out your supply of the essential oil as well.

Even more so than with plants, the scent of essential oils can be overpowering. When mixing oils, or when mixing oils with other ingredients (herbs or stones, perhaps), you'll want to pay attention to the scent and how the mixing changes it. Perhaps you love the smell of jasmine, but when it's mixed with your carrier oil and some dill for your love spell, the scent isn't your favorite; notice your response to the oils you use. A spell using essential oils in a bath is aromatherapy magick! If you have a favorite perfume (or perhaps you wear an essential oil), check the table in the next section for its magickal associations.

Words of Power

A **carrier oil** is one used to dilute an essential oil. Good carrier oils include almond, jojoba, and vegetable oil.

Making Magick with Oils

As we mentioned in our discussion of incense in Chapter 10, oils use the powerful sense of smell to help you in your magickal work. The power this sense has on your mind is probably greater than you realize. When doing a spell or some magickal work involving trance, for example, try having a bit of essential lavender oil handy to help ground you and bring you back when the trance work is over. (This might also be useful after doing a guided meditation on a tape.) Tiny containers for essential oils (such as beads with a bit of cotton stuck into them) are available for purchase that you can wear around your neck. These are handy for this kind of purpose.

Some essential oils are quite pricey, and you might want to substitute, based on the meaning of the oil or the scent, rather than invest in a lot of costly oils you won't often use. The following table lists some essential oils and their magickal correspondences. Use this to help you plan spells using essential oils.

> **Spellcasting**
>
> Store your essential oils in glass containers and out of direct light to preserve them longer. Always label your oils and indicate the date you purchased them on the label. Smell your oil before working with it to be sure it hasn't gone rancid while in storage (it's more likely that your carrier oils will go rancid than your essential oils). Rancid oil will not work toward the success of your spell.

The Magickal Correspondences of Oils

Essential Oil	Correspondence(s)
Acacia	Intuitive power, protection
Basil	Harmony, peace, prosperity, purification
Bergamot	Prosperity, protection
Camphor	Healing, purification
Cardamom	Love, vitality
Carnation	Healing, strength
Cedar	Courage, dreams, success
Cinnamon	Prosperity, intuitive power, purification
Clove	Courage, protection
Coriander	Healing, love
Cypress	Healing, protection
Eucalyptus	Healing, invigoration
Gardenia	Healing, peace, love

Essential Oil	Correspondence(s)
Garlic	Love, healing, protection
Geranium	Love, protection
Ginger	Courage, love, prosperity
Honeysuckle	Intuitive power, protection
Hyacinth	Love, protection
Jasmine	Love, peace, intuitive power
Lavender	Healing, love, relaxation
Lemongrass	Intuitive power, purification
Lilac	Protection
Lotus	Healing, luck
Magnolia	Love, intuitive power
Mint	Healing, protection
Myrrh	Healing, meditation, purification
Neroli	Happiness, protection
Olive	Fertility, healing, peace
Orange	Luck, purification
Patchouli	Intuitive power, prosperity, protection
Peppermint	Intuitive power, prosperity, purification
Pine	Healing, prosperity, purification
Rose	Beauty, love, peace
Rosemary	Healing, love
Sandalwood	Healing, intuitive power, spirituality
Tangerine	Power, strength
Tuberose	Calm, intuitive power, peace
Vanilla	Love, intuitive power
Vetiver	Luck, prosperity
Violet	Healing, love, luck
Ylang-ylang	Love, healing, peace

Oil Spells

Now let's try a spell using oils. Again, kitchen magick can use oils, but so can many other kinds of magick. For kitchen magick, how about olive oil infused with crushed fresh garlic cloves? As you crush the garlic cloves and infuse them into the oil, chant a brief love spell, repeating it as a mantra. You may want to call respectfully on Aphrodite or whatever deity of love resonates for you. The words of your spell can be whatever is appropriate to you in the moment, as words given to you by the Lord and Lady. Or you can chant these words:

> *Ancient strength of powerful herb*
>
> *Infuse our meal and our bodies*
>
> *For healthy partnership and loving intent.*

Then serve the garlic oil for dipping bread when eating with your lover. Now, if this is a first date and your partner doesn't know you're a witch, you can do this spell ethically if you let your date know before the meal that you've said a blessing over it for the benefit of your relationship. Remember, though, it is one thing to do a spell for the best and the greatest good for the partnership, and another to do a spell to bewitch your partner into a seduction. The best scenario is one where your partner knows your Wiccan practice and is ready to participate in the love spell with you! (Learn more about love spells in Chapter 15.)

Becoming Familiar with Familiars

Have you read the *Harry Potter* books? If so, you'll be familiar with Harry's familiar, Hedwig. No, she's not a member of his family—she's his *familiar*. The cat you always see accompanying the stereotypical witch is her familiar. This is different from a power animal, which you'll learn about in the next section.

Your familiar, should you be lucky enough to have one, is an animal whose spirit wants to work with you. The animal will be helpful to you in many ways, particularly in working magick. Your familiar is simply an animal that you have a special relationship with. Probably any pet that you are close to (dog, cat, or lizard) has great familiar potential. Are you listening with your spirit to what your pet is trying to tell you? Perhaps the main thing you need to learn is how to slow down and listen. Magick is about tuning in and listening to the whole universe, most of which is not human.

Animals are great teachers. If you don't have an animal that you think you can identify as your familiar, perhaps the birds, chipmunks, squirrels, or other animals living outside your door have things to teach you. If you long for a closer relationship with a specific animal, it's okay to seek one out. We'd like to tell you where to go for your familiar, but alas, no shops (that we're aware of) specialize in familiars. Your familiar really has to find *you*—but you can ask for guidance! The following spell will help you draw a familiar to yourself.

If you know the animal you want to draw to yourself, bring an herb associated with that animal or its powers. For example, if you seek a dog, which is associated with loyalty, unconditional love, and intelligence, you could bring bay leaf, cardamom, and rye. Otherwise bring an herb associated with what you seek: love, otherworldly connection, etc. Also, bring some food as an offering, and any other offering that you feel called to bring. Go to an outdoor ritual space that you feel safe in. Call in all four Elements, asking their blessings on your search for a familiar. Then call in whichever spirits you usually call to: Lord and Lady, ancestors, perhaps a specific spirit or deity associated with an animal (such as Diana for a dog or Bast for a cat). Ask for an appropriate familiar to find you. Present the herbs and offerings, and leave them there.

Look around for the next few days—an abandoned kitty might find its way to your door, or you could go to the local animal shelter and see what animal speaks to you there. Tune in to your psychic abilities to receive your familiar's invitation, and use a pendulum or other divination device if you are unsure. Once you have your familiar, give thanks to the entities you called when you did your finding spell, and be sure to thank your familiar for finding you! Although animals have varying needs and abilities in the human-built world, remember that spiritually your pet is your equal (or superior!), and treat your familiar as such. Humility is one of the great lessons animals have to teach people.

> ### Spellcasting
>
> If you feel drawn to a large tropical bird or iguana or other animal, make sure you read everything you can on it before welcoming it into your home. Visit a museum or zoo and ask all the questions you can of the keepers. Large birds may have special needs and often outlive people—even common house pets such as cats can live 15 or more years. Taking any animal into your life is a huge responsibility: You are promising to care for this animal for the rest of its life, so be prepared to do just that!

Power to the Power Animals

A familiar is a bit different from a power animal; the familiar is a specific animal, like a pet to a practicing witch, and a power animal is a *representative* animal. It is a spirit helper, connected with all the animals of its kind. You might feel a connection with a particular animal—cats, horses, or perhaps you've always been drawn to butterflies— and even feel that this animal in some way represents you. This animal might be your power animal, and you can ask this animal to help you when you're working magick.

When you were born, or perhaps as a small child, an animal spirit volunteered to help you on your life's path. If you don't immediately know what that animal is, you can do a journey (or meditation) such as the following power animal spell to find out and reinvigorate its connection to you. This is another piece of magickal work that is best done in pairs, with partners working for each other, though you can do it on your own, as well.

Create a relaxing, safe, sacred space where you know you won't be disturbed. Call in the quarters, asking for their assistance and protection as you journey to the other-world. You can drum or rattle for each other, or you can use prerecorded shamanic drumming if you feel it will help. It is certainly possible to journey in silence as well. You might want to burn incense or use an essential oil that helps you induce trance (such as sandalwood or patchouli). Lie in a comfortable position and close your eyes. See yourself going into the earth, perhaps through a cave or by climbing down the roots of a sacred tree. Keep your eyes open for the animals you meet. Whenever you meet an animal, or perhaps after you have encountered the same animal a number of times, ask it, "Are you my (or my partner's) power animal?"

If you find an animal that says yes, it is the power animal that you seek. Throw your arms around it and quickly journey back to the upper world through the same path that you came down. You can then "blow" the animal into your partner's or your own chest by cupping your hands around your mouth and blowing. Your trance is done. Thank your power animal for coming back with you and "feed" its power by dancing with it. With prerecorded music, or with a friend playing an instrument, allow the animal's movements to come through your body as you dance. Do this periodically throughout your relationship with any power animal.

Keep in mind that this method does not get you a new power animal—it reacquaints you with one you already have. Obtaining a new power animal involves a lengthy quest and is not within the scope of this book. For more on this technique, see Michael Harner's *The Way of the Shaman* (see Appendix B).

You can certainly call on the qualities of any animal in your magickal work regardless of whether it is your specific power animal or not. For example, if you want to be a strong, protective mother, you can ask a bear spirit to aid you. The following table lists some animals and their characteristics as spirit helpers.

Animal	Characteristics
Badger	Fierce courage, self-sufficiency
Bat	Magick, psychic hearing, spiritual travel
Bear	Strength, mothering, protection

Animal	Characteristics
Beaver	Industriousness, building
Bee	Love, fertility, hard work, cooperation
Bull	Virility, Goddess connection
Butterfly	Transformation, blessings, enlightenment
Cardinal	Beauty, ceremony, awakening
Cat	Independence, magick
Cow	Docility, nurturing
Coyote	Fool, trickster, survival, creativity
Deer	Magick, grace, purity, life force, quickness
Dog	Fidelity, protection
Donkey	Gentleness, stubbornness
Elk	Bravery
Fox	Cunning, community, quickness
Hummingbird	Joy, quickness, confidence
Lion	Courage, confidence, hunting
Lizard	Wisdom, divination
Monkey	Agility, curiosity, playfulness
Otter	Playfulness, confidence, freedom
Pig	Intelligence, warrior
Porcupine	Caution, defensiveness
Rabbit	Quickness, Moon magick, fertility
Skunk	Defensiveness, balance
Spider	Creativity, weaving connections
Squirrel	Resourcefulness, community, sports
Woodpecker	Resourcefulness, removal of obstacles

The Least You Need to Know

- Herbs and oils have been used for healing purposes—and for working magick—for millennia.

- You can choose the plants and oils you use in your spells based on their energy, their magickal correspondences, or what feels (or smells) right to you.

◆ You can use plants and oils together and/or with other ingredients (such as stones and candles) to create your spell.

◆ If you listen to the animals around you, you may find that you already have a familiar.

◆ Power animals can also be called upon to add to the effectiveness of your spell.

13

Using Astrology and the Planetary Hours

In This Chapter

- How the planets can help you with your magick
- Do you know your Sun sign?
- Every hour of the day: planetary hours
- Timing your magick with Moon signs
- Asteroids, meteors, and other heavenly bodies

As with other facets of timing, you can maximize the power of your spell by taking into consideration astrology, including Sun and Moon signs and planetary hours. The planets can affect your magick in many ways, and we'll look at the power of the planets and their correspondences in this chapter.

Astrology can get fairly technical, but if you take the time and energy to familiarize yourself with the fundamentals, your efforts will be worthwhile. Wiccans who harness the heavens in their spells (going beyond the Moon to the planets and asteroids) dramatically increase the effectiveness of their magick by working in tune with the celestial harmonies.

Astrology and Its Magickal Connection

Astrology is the study of the heavens and all of its planets and stars. You might already know a little about astrology—perhaps you check your horoscope in the paper. You are probably aware of your Sun sign; that's the zodiac sign at the time of your birth. You may have even had your *birth chart* done. If so, you know that the planets and their position in the sky can tell you a lot. Their placement in your birth chart can tell you a lot about yourself, and their placement when you work magick can help (or hinder) the successful working of your spell. The following table lists the planets, their symbols, and their correspondences, followed by a table of the Sun signs, their symbols, and the planets and energies associated with them.

Words of Power

A **birth chart** is a chart showing the position of the planets at your exact time and place of birth. Your birth chart has 12 houses, which correspond to 12 areas of your life. Each house is ruled by a planet or planets (depending on the position of the planets when you were born). You can learn a great deal about yourself from the information in your birth chart.

Planetary Associations

Planet	Correspondences
Sun ☉	Self, creativity, will
Moon ☽	Emotions, intuition, unconscious
Mercury ☿	Mental acuity, communication
Venus ♀	Love, beauty, money, harmony
Mars ♂	Physical energy, action, courage, desire
Jupiter ♃	Abundance, wisdom, growth, luck, success
Saturn ♄	Discipline, responsibility, structure
Uranus ♅	Sudden change, intuition, liberation, originality
Neptune ♆	Subconscious, intuition, spirituality, idealism, dreams
Pluto ♇	Power, transformation, destruction, regeneration

Sun Signs

Sign	Dates	Planet(s)	Energy/Element
Aries ♈	March 21–April 20	Mars, Pluto	Yang/Fire
Taurus ♉	April 21–May 21	Venus	Yin/Earth
Gemini ♊	May 22–June 21	Mercury	Yang/Air
Cancer ♋	June 22–July 22	Moon	Yin/Water
Leo ♌	July 23–August 22	Sun	Yang/Fire
Virgo ♍	August 23–September 23	Mercury	Yin/Earth
Libra ♎	September 24–October 23	Venus	Yang/Air
Scorpio ♏	October 24–November 22	Pluto, Mars	Yin/Water
Sagittarius ♐	November 23–December 21	Jupiter	Yang/Fire
Capricorn ♑	December 22–January 20	Saturn	Yin/Earth
Aquarius ♒	January 21–February 19	Uranus, Saturn	Yang/Air
Pisces ♓	February 20–March 20	Neptune, Jupiter	Yin/Water

These are the basics to think about when working with astrology and magick. How do the two relate? Well, looking at the associations of a particular planet, you may decide to call on its energies to help you with magick. Saturn might be helpful if you're trying to become more disciplined about exercising. If you decide to call on Saturn, you might work your spell on a Saturday, and you could work your spell during an hour ruled by Saturn (sunrise, perhaps—see the discussion of planetary

Making Magick

Aurora's Wiccan teaching partner Liguana had some friends who wanted her to perform their handfasting ceremony. They chose a date during Taurus, a sign that corresponds with the planet Venus, associated with love. They also got the stability of the bull totem and Earth energy combined.

hours later in this chapter). Likewise, you might call on Neptune to help with your intuitive powers.

Working with the Planets in Spellcraft

Let's look at a few spells that use astrology and planets. Perhaps you're trying to lose weight. To represent this shrinking of your body, burn a candle over the course of a few days. Do this during a time when the Moon is in Saturn, a planet that corresponds to self-discipline. (The Moon visits each sign for about two and a half days each month—check an astrological almanac to find out when.) At the end of several days (while the Moon is still in Saturn), and at the appropriate day and time (Saturday, during a Saturn hour—see the upcoming section on planetary hours—if possible; if not, choose the most opportune day and time you can), take the candle and wrap it in cloth or paper on which you have written your intent (in this case, to curb your appetite and lose weight), and then bury it in the earth in a place you pass by often. After burying the candle, chant:

> *Mother, take my words to heart,*
>
> *My better fitness now will start.*

Don't make the burial spot obvious—you don't want to mark it so that you are consciously aware of the place when you pass it; but rather, its presence should be a subconscious reminder for you of your goal and your intent.

You can easily adapt this spell for a number of purposes. With a few changes, you can make this into a spell to help you quit smoking, for example: Bury an ashtray upside down with a cigarette under it, focusing on your intention and chanting the chant above as you bury it.

Now let's try a spell that uses the planet known for prosperity, Jupiter. (Jupiter, you may also be interested to know, is the planet of weight *gain*.) The best day for a Jupiter prosperity spell would be a Thursday, though you could also work this magick on a day when the Moon is in Sagittarius, the sign of the archer (check your astrological almanac!), to great effect. If you can plan to work your magick during one of Jupiter's planetary hours, you'll be enhancing your spell even more. And if you can work this spell in waxing moonlight, so much the better.

You'll need a green candle and a green ribbon or cord of some type for this prosperity spell. During each of the three days, light the candle and tie a knot in your ribbon or cord. On the first day, while the candle is burning, tie a knot in your cord and chant:

> *Moon come.*

Burn the candle until the wax on the top of the candle is softened, and then blow out the candle and dip your cord in the softened wax, coating the knot (be careful not to burn yourself!).

On the second day, repeat this process, chanting:

> *I have no wants.*

Again, blow out the candle and coat your second knot in the softened wax.

On the third day, repeat the process a final time, chanting:

> *A prosperous life I have called to me.*

Coat the final knot in the softened wax. Also on the third day, repeat all three chants:

> *Moon come,*
>
> *I have no wants,*
>
> *A prosperous life I have called to me.*

Then end with a fourth chant:

> *Lord and Lady hearken to me,*
>
> *As I have spoken, so mote it be.*

Now take the cord with its waxed knots and burn it; your Jupiter prosperity spell is cast.

Retrograde Planets

Retrograde is an astrological term used to indicate when a planet seems to be moving backward through the heavens when viewed from Earth. This is an illusion caused by our view of the planets from Earth as they orbit the Sun. Ancient astrologers regarded retrograde planets as an ill omen, but these days, we believe retrograde planets represent slowed energy or a decrease in the planet's influence. After a period of time, each planet will cease its retrograde motion and, after stationing for a brief period, resume its forward, or direct, motion.

CAUTION

For Protection

Avoid working magick when Mercury is retrograde! Mercury is the planet of communication, and when it is retrograde, communication is stalled. This is a time when your e-mail might be on the fritz, your cable goes out, or you and your spouse miscommunicate. Your intention might not be carried out correctly, or the magickal energy might backfire during Mercury retrograde.

In doing spellwork, the direct motion of a planet emphasizes action; this is a good time to do spells for accomplishing goals. Spells performed during a particular planet's retrograde might focus on redoing or revisiting something to do with that planet's energy—for example, a prosperity spell done during a Jupiter retrograde would focus on turning inward to understand and reverse the source of financial difficulties. Spells done while a planet is stationed, or seemingly motionless, may not go anywhere! Wait until the planet is moving again, if you can, and plan your spellwork in harmony with its motion, direct or retrograde.

Planetary Hours

In Chapter 3 we discussed timing for spells, including general time of day. In astrology, each hour of the day is also associated with one of the planets, and the planets have particular qualities and energies. This information can help you find the most fortuitous time to work your spell. While there are 24 planetary hours in each day, and 12 are considered daytime and 12 nighttime hours, these hours are based on the position of the planets in the sky, and therefore the length of each planetary hour varies according to the time of year.

The first planetary hour of each day begins at sunrise, and the first planetary hour of each night begins at sunset. We mean precisely at sunrise and sunset, so you'll have to check an almanac. There is a great website for the U.S. Naval Observatory (aa.usno.navy.mil/data/docs/RS_OneDay.html#forma) that lets you plug in a date, city, and state, and then provides you with Sun and Moon data for your location (you can also use the site for locations outside the United States). If you know the exact time of sunrise and sunset, you can estimate the length of the planetary hours for that day by figuring out the number of minutes between sunrise and sunset and dividing by 12 (the number of hours in the day and the night).

Here's an example: Say sunrise today was at 7:23 A.M. and sunset is at 4:48 P.M. The time between sunrise and sunset is 9 hours and 23 minutes, or 565 minutes. This means that the planetary hours between sunrise and sunset on this day will last approximately 47 minutes (565 divided by 12). To figure out the length of each nighttime planetary hour, you can find out when sunrise the next day is and do this process again, or, figuring on a 24-hour day, subtract 565 minutes from 1440 minutes (which is 24 hours). This, 875 minutes, is the minutes in nighttime; divided by 12, it gives you the length of the nighttime planetary hours: approximately 73 minutes.

How do we know which planet to start the day with at sunrise? Well, again in Chapter 3, we mentioned that each day of the week is associated with a planet. That planet is the planet for the first hour of the day. If today is Saturday, following the next table, the first planetary hour of the day is ruled by Saturn.

Day	Planet	Energy	Magick
Sunday	Sun	Yang	Power, health, prosperity
Monday	Moon	Yin	Divination, fertility, dreams
Tuesday	Mars	Yang	Conflict, leadership
Wednesday	Mercury	Yang	Communication, arts, fears
Thursday	Jupiter	Yang	Success, abundance, desires
Friday	Venus	Yin	Romance, loyalty, trust, friendship
Saturday	Saturn	Yin	Divination, illness, binding

Here's the order of the planets, which you'll need to know to figure out what planet rules each of the other hours of any given day: Sun, Venus, Mercury, Moon, Saturn, Jupiter, Mars. But wait—that's only 7 planets, and we need 12 for each planetary hour! After Mars, repeat from the Sun again (do this for the entire 24-hour day). If you're starting with sunrise on Wednesday, your first planetary hour will be ruled by Mercury. To figure out the rest of the planets, continue in the order listed previously:

The second hour will be ruled by the Moon, followed by Saturn, etc. It really isn't that complicated, though there is a lot to keep track of (days, hours, times, planets). With your knowledge of the planetary hours, you can plan your magick down to the hour for its best chance of success! Record data for the planetary hours of important days in your Book of Shadows.

> **Spellcasting**
>
> These two websites can help you determine the planetary hours for any day. The first calculates sunrise and sunset, which you'll need for the second: www.sunrisesunset.com and www.planetaryhours.com.

Moon Signs

Back in Chapter 3 we discussed the phases of the Moon. In addition to the Moon phases, you might look into the Moon sign of a day that you plan to work magick. The Moon generally passes through each zodiac sign each month and will likely be in a different sign every few days. Each astrological sign has different associations, so the Moon in each sign will also have specific associations. We list some of these in the following table. To figure out what sign the Moon is in, you'll need a lunar or astrological almanac.

Moon Signs

Sign	Correspondences
Aries ♈	Energy, leadership, new projects
Taurus ♉	Love, money, prosperity, harmony
Gemini ♊	Communication, travel, new projects
Cancer ♋	Emotions, nurturing, home
Leo ♌	Fertility, courage, power, creativity, legal matters
Virgo ♍	Health, self-improvement, mental acuity
Libra ♎	Emotional balance, karma, spirituality
Scorpio ♏	Transformation, desire, power
Sagittarius ♐	Exploration, legal matters, abundance
Capricorn ♑	Career, recognition, organization, discipline
Aquarius ♒	Creative expression, problem-solving, friendship, growth
Pisces ♓	Healing, dreams, telepathy, spirituality

When the Moon is between signs, having left one and not yet entered another, it is called *void of course*. This is not the best time to start a new project or work magick, as the energy of the Moon is somewhat diluted and unclear at this time. Use the void of course Moon to relax, meditate, and plan future workings.

Use your knowledge of the Moon signs to help you in the timing of magick. Perhaps you plan to create an amulet of protection to carry with you on your travels—you might do this during a day when the Moon is in Gemini. Here's a spell for such a protective amulet.

First, gather the materials you'll use in the amulet. For protection, you might choose some relevant herbs: chrysanthemum, lilac, or peony petals or rosemary or sage; stones: a piece of coral, flint, or turquoise; oils: clove or lilac oil. Select ingredients based on what you have handy or what you have access to, as well as what you feel drawn to use. We will use comfrey and a piece of coral. Ask the blessing of each of the Elements upon your ingredients:

> *Air, bless this protective amulet,*
>
> *For my safety it will beget.*
>
> (Repeat this for each Element.)

Place the materials in a small black pouch to create an amulet, and bless and conse-crate the amulet in a sacred circle. Now you're ready to take the amulet—your protective spell—with you on your trip. You can rework this spell to create an amulet for any number of purposes, based on the magickal correspondences we've discussed in other chapters. You might want an amulet to help you get the courage to ask for that raise (for which you might use a red pouch with an aquamarine or some columbine) or to create harmony in your family life (a brown pouch, some dolomite or kunzite, neroli or basil oil, and chamomile or passionflower).

Here are some examples of the kinds of spellcasting you might try when the Moon is in each sign:

- **Moon in Aries.** Do spellwork involving freedom and adventure-seeking. Call forth the perfect vacation for yourself! This is a time of self-centered energy. You may also feel a bit impulsive. *These are not the best days for spellcasting.*

- **Moon in Taurus.** Work spells calling for stability and patience. This is a fair time for love spells and spells for improving your surroundings or finding a new home.

- **Moon in Gemini.** This is a time for spells involving communication and intellect. Use this time for spells improving business associations and enhancing public speaking.

- **Moon in Cancer.** Work magick about home, friendship, and loyalty. This is a good time for improving any partnership. You may feel a desire to impose your will on others right now. *Don't do it!*

- **Moon in Leo.** Do spellwork for winning in any conflict and for influencing those around you. Again, remember your magickal ethics! This is a good time for letting spell work help you change your outward appearance and the way you come across to others.

- **Moon in Virgo.** Work spells to bring knowledge and understanding. This is another good time to seek business success and a fair time for prosperity spells and for bringing order to chaos.

> **Making Magick**
>
> Liguana once told Aurora about a time when there was discord in Liguana's coven, with much bickering taking place. Everyone decided they needed a community peace-making ritual. The coveners picked a day when everyone could attend, but then noticed that the Moon was in Scorpio that day. A good time for power grabbing, just the problem they were already having! So the meeting was postponed until the Moon was in Sagittarius, and the outcome proved peaceful and harmonious!

◆ **Moon in Libra.** Do spellwork for peace and partnerships. This is a good time for romance spells and spells seeking good things for other people. You put forth a positive flow in these days of balance. Use it well!

◆ **Moon in Scorpio.** Work spells of passion and love. This is also a good time for business success or to win in court. This time gives a lot of force to your spells. Remember, you seldom have to beat someone into the ground to make a point. In magick and life, try to be subtle while the Moon transits this dynamic sign.

◆ **Moon in Sagittarius.** Do spellwork for luck and material gain. This is also a good time for spells to enhance friendship, though not as good for romantic partnerships. Focus on doing good for the world and all of humanity at this time.

◆ **Moon in Capricorn.** Work magick for business success and home security. It is a very good time to overcome obstacles and clear a path for success in any endeavor. Family closeness can be enhanced now.

◆ **Moon in Aquarius.** Work spells for divination and seeing the correct path to take in any situation. This is also a time to work on friendship spells and humanitarian causes.

◆ **Moon in Pisces.** Do spellwork for improving intuition and psychic ability. Creativity and compassion are more easily accessed for your magick at this time. *This is definitely not a good time to do business spells.*

Asteroids and Meteors

In addition to the influence of the planets (and the Sun and Moon, which aren't planets but are treated as such for the purposes of astrology), there are many other heavenly bodies whose energy you might call upon when working spells. Asteroids are known as minor planets, and more than ten thousand of them have been named orbiting on a belt between Mars and Jupiter. The asteroids are material left over from the creation of our solar system, and a number of them are named after Roman goddesses (the asteroids have a very Yin energy). Four well-known asteroids and their symbols and correspondences follow.

Asteroid	Correspondences
Ceres ⚳	Mentoring, parenting, nurturing, natural cycles, fertility, Cancer, Virgo, and Taurus
Juno ⚵	Partnerships, control, Libra, and Scorpio
Pallas Athene ⚴	Intelligence, strength, understanding, competition, Leo, Libra, and Aquarius
Vesta ⚶	Fulfillment, service, power, loyalty, Scorpio, and Virgo

What about the other heavenly bodies? The energies of meteor showers and comets can also be called upon in working magick. Comets are not often visible to the naked eye; we think of them as a bright light in the sky with a tail trailing after it, but these are relatively rare and occur only every decade or so. Halley's comet is a well-known one that is visible on average every 76 years. It will next be visible in 2061. Comets are made of ice and dust. They don't usually come very close to the earth and so appear to move more slowly than meteors.

Meteors are what we describe as a shooting or falling star. They move very fast and look like streaks of light in the sky. We generally see these for just a few seconds before they burn up completely. The parts of a meteor that don't burn up as the meteor enters the earth's atmosphere and land on the earth are called meteorites.

Using the Asteroids and Meteors in Spellwork

When working a spell, you might call upon the energies of one of the goddesses associated with the asteroids, much as you might ask for the assistance of the Goddess or other deities. You might also work with the energies of a known meteor shower to enhance your magick. Pay attention to the news to learn of upcoming astronomical events so that you can plan spells in harmony with their timing and energies.

The Geminid meteor shower travels a regular circuit, just like the planets, and its visibility peaks each year from December 12 through 14. It was first spotted in the 1860s, and the energy of the Geminid shower is that of Gemini, making this a good time for working magick related to communication and new projects. If you can, try going outside to work this spell; up on a hill would be best, away from the lights of any city or town so that the night sky is clearly visible.

The following spell to do during the Geminids is for public speaking. Use this if you have a speech or presentation to make for which you need a little help. Take a ring (a finger ring or a bracelet will work well) and imbue it with your intent, to communicate better or to be a better public speaker. Touch the ring to your lips three times and then hold it up to the sky. Try to see three of the Geminids through the ring as you hold it up. Then touch it back to your lips and chant:

> By this sign I will know,
>
> My public speaking skills will grow.
>
> By this ring I will see,
>
> All my listeners drawn to me.

Now wear the ring or bracelet as an amulet during your presentation and feel the power of the Geminids boosting your confidence and your communication or speaking abilities.

Here's another spell using the meteors; this one calls on the Leonids, which peak from November 12 through 14 and carry the energy of Leo for courage, creativity, and power. This spell will give you courage and help you with your sense of personal power. If you have a cat, take him or her outside with you, or brush or comb him or her beforehand—you'll need some cat hairs for this spell!

Chant the following, while holding the hairs up to the night sky, presenting them to the Leonids:

> By the bravery of the lion,
>
> By the power of the storm,
>
> Fetch to me the lion's spirit,
>
> Inner fire stoked and warm.

Spellcasting

If you'd like to learn more about astrology, see *The Complete Idiot's Guide to Astrology, Third Edition*, by Madeline Gerwick-Brodeur and Lisa Lenard (Alpha Books, 2003).

Then take the cat hairs, which have now been charged, and place them in a medicine bag, a pouch you have made (perhaps out of red or orange cloth), and wear this amulet over your heart—tuck it into your shirt or wear it as a necklace—for courage and personal strength. This amulet would also be a good one for winning a court case, as Leo is relevant for legal matters.

The Heavenly Bodies in Your Spellwork

You can use astrology in other ways in working magick—you might inscribe the symbols for the astrological signs, planets, or asteroids on candles and other tools of magick to call on their energies. (For more on symbols, see Chapter 14.) Astrology is a metaphysical science that you could spend a lifetime studying, and we have only given you an overview of the some of the ways it might be relevant to your spellwork. Use astrology to enhance your spells and give them an extra boost of energy, but remember that your energy and your focused intent are most important to working spells with success.

The Least You Need to Know

- ◆ Sun and Moon signs can be used to help you plan effective spellwork.

- ◆ To figure out the planetary hours for a given day, you'll need to know the time of sunrise and sunset for that day, as well as what day of the week the date falls on.

- ◆ Moon signs can indicate when it's a good time to work magick on specific subjects.

- ◆ You can work with the energy of asteroids and meteor showers to work magick.

Chapter 14

Using Magickal Alphabets and Runes

In This Chapter

◆ It's all Greek to us: magickal alphabets

◆ Writing in Theban script, Pictish swirl, and Phoenician

◆ Runes: the Viking Oracle

◆ Astrological and other magickal symbols

◆ You can create your own magickal language

Spells that use iconic symbols and imagery to work their magick have an added visual element as well as a little extra magickal energy. How do you know what symbols to use and how? That's what this chapter is all about.

There are many choices. Any language can be magickal for you—one you speak fluently (such as Italian) or one that's not spoken (such as Theban script). What's important is that magickal languages and symbols have the ability to remove you from the mundane and carry you into the magickal. They also connect you with the past and possibly with your ancestors.

Magickal Alphabets

There are many alphabets other than one you are likely most familiar with—the Roman alphabet. You don't have to become fluent in any other languages, or familiar with symbols, but you may sometimes want to use something other than your spoken language—for most of us that's English—when working magick. Why? Well, just as you might use meditation or chanting to distract your conscious mind so that you can access your powerful subconscious, the use of letters and symbols that are apart from your everyday communication can serve to distract you or act as a trigger for your conscious mind. After repeated use, your use of Theban, Greek, or some other language can signal to your subconscious mind that it's magick time!

The Witches' Alphabet: Theban Script

Theban script is sometimes called the witches' alphabet and is also known as *Honorian script*. It may be medieval, though some researchers believe it to be much more recent. It has been used for writing secret messages and in magick, but it is not linked to any spoken language. Gardnerian witches (those who follow the teachings of Gerald Gardner; see Chapter 1) often use it in rituals, and many witches use it to inscribe their tools. It's a magickal alphabet and using it can add an extra bit of *oomph* to your spell.

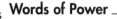

Words of Power

Honorian script is another name for Theban script. In the sixteenth century, Cornelius Agrippa (in his *Three Books of Occult Philosophy*) attributed the Theban alphabet to Honorius.

Once you've become familiar with Theban script, you may want to use it in your spellwork, for inscribing your tools, and perhaps even for writing in your Book of Shadows. Using a magickal alphabet of any kind can help you focus your energy and send it out to work your spell. Following is the alphabet in Theban script. Practice writing your name—or your magickal name—in Theban to get the feel for it. It's a very fluid alphabet.

You can download a Theban script font from a number of websites, which will allow you to write quickly in Theban, should you like. This is especially useful for those who keep their Book of Shadows on their computers.

The following poppet spell utilizes Theban script. You can use a poppet as a symbol for some*one* or some*thing*; if the poppet is meant to be some*one*, be sure you have that person's permission before working magick. The poppet can also be a representative of the God or Goddess, whose powers you call upon to help work your magick.

Theban Script

Theban script.

A ⚹ H ⚹ O ⚹ V ⚹

B ⚹ I ⚹ P ⚹ W ⚹

C ⚹ J ⚹ Q ⚹ X ⚹

D ⚹ K ⚹ R ⚹ Y ⚹

E ⚹ L ⚹ S ⚹ Z ⚹

F ⚹ M ⚹ T ⚹

Mark for end of sentence; period.

G ⚹ N ⚹ U ⚹

This spell is often done in the fall and may be a ritual for Lughnasadh, Mabon, or Samhain, but you can do it at any time of the year. A Waning Moon is best, though, for banishing. You'll need a poppet in the shape of a man, meant to represent the God. Make your poppet, leaving an opening for the objects you want to place inside (see Appendix C for a simple poppet pattern). Directly on the poppet, in Theban script, write the following:

Lord, take these negatives far away and do not bring them back.

Then, on slips of paper, write the things you want to leave behind—jealousy, perhaps, or nail-biting, nervous tension, or fear. If you're up to it, write these in Theban or some other magickal language (this is where that computer font might come in handy!). Roll these papers up and place them inside the poppet, along with corresponding herbs, such as sage for healing. Close your poppet by sewing the open edge.

Now burn the poppet—in a safe place, of course. If you place a bit of activated charcoal inside the poppet (this is the kind used for burning incense), it will help it to burn easily. While it burns, chant:

Lord of cut hay, take this away,

Banish, banish, banish.

Be creative in your use of Theban script, which can be incorporated into just about any kind of spell for myriad magickal purposes.

CAUTION

For Protection

When using fire in a spell, be sure to burn things in a safe place, and when the burning is finished, make certain the fire is fully extinguished.

Words of Power

Pictish swirl is a variation on an old Pictish form of writing based on the Latin alphabet. The Picts lived in northern Scotland as early as the third century.

Other Magickal Alphabets

There are numerous other alphabets you can use to work magick, including Phoenician, Hieroglyphics, and Greek, as well as *Pictish swirl*. A table of some of these follows. More can be found on the Internet, and many websites will allow you to download magickal fonts for free. Type in "magickal alphabets" as your search parameter and enjoy exploring the range of symbols and meanings you can use to enhance your spellwork.

Greek, Hieroglyphic, and Phoenician alphabets.

Runes: Magickal Symbols

Runes are sometimes called the Viking Oracle. They are an ancient tool of divination used by the Vikings, given to them by the Norse God Odin. Like your athame or candles or herbs, runes are tools you can use in working magick. The word *rune* means *mystery* in Old English and Old Norse. There are many variations of runes, though the main ones you'll see are Germanic, Norse, and Anglo-Saxon. There are 25 runes in the Germanic runic alphabet, each associated with a simple meaning.

You can use these individually or in combination to achieve the meaning you intend. The symbols and their meanings are listed in the following table; you can buy a set of rune stones in occult and New Age shops, for use in working magick and divination, or you can write the runes out yourself. If you plan on doing much work with runes, we recommend making or buying a set, because the stones give your work with them a specific tactile experience—they are *stones*, after all, not *papers*. As you can see, runes are created from straight lines, which makes them less difficult to write than some alphabets. Runes comprise a very bold-looking alphabet.

Runes

Rune Symbol	Rune Name	Meanings
	Feoh or Fehu	Good fortune, prosperity, wealth, power, fulfillment
	Uruz or Ur	Strength, healing, stability
	Thorn or Thurisaz	Conflict, change, overcoming obstacles, contemplation
	Ansur or Ansuz	Communication, learning, divine inspiration, transformation, receiving messages
	Rad or Raidho	Travel, change, action, communication
	Ken, Kano, or Kenaz	Creativity, music, opportunity, change

continues

Runes (continued)

Rune Symbol	Rune Name	Meanings
	Geofu or Gebo	Generosity, gifts, love, partnerships
	Wynn or Wunjo	Happiness, joy, love, success, attaining goals
	Hagall or Hagalaz	Change, self-growth, disruption, frustration
	Nied or Naudhiez	Restriction, anxiety, future success, need
	Is or Isa	Wait, stagnation, gestation
	Jara or Jera	Harvest, success, fruition, new beginnings, birth
	Yr or Eihwaz	Protection, endurance, transcendence, inspiration
	Peorth or Perdhro	Financial success, magick, personal power, secrets
	Eolh or Algiz	Protection, luck, success
	Sigel or Sowolu	Faith, success, vitality
	Tir or Tiwaz	Honor, justice, bravery, victory
	Beorc or Berkana	Nurturing, woman, intuition, fertility, new beginnings, rebirth

Rune Symbol	Rune Name	Meanings
	Eoh or Ehwaz	Change, psychic power, action, transition
	Mann or Mannaz	Relationships, communication, cooperation, self
	Lagu or Laguz	Creativity, imagination, intuitive power, sensitivity, rhythm
	Ing or Inguz	Power, success, happiness, fertility, possibility
	Daeg or Dagaz	Balance, security, new beginnings, enlightenment
	Othel or Othila	Stability, family, home, money, tradition, prosperity, separation
	Wyrd	Mystery, fate, death

You might want to inscribe a rune on a candle for candle magick, or carve one on the handle of your athame. If you find that one of the runes or some other symbol—one you've seen or one you created yourself— seems to speak to you, you may wish to use it as a sort of talisman, perhaps crafting a piece of jewelry with the symbol upon it. As with most things magickal, you really must trust your intuition. If you are drawn to a rune or other symbol that does not seem to match your intention, trust your instincts, and use the symbol that *feels* right.

> **Spellcasting**
>
> You can create your own symbols, ascribing to them the meanings of your choosing. Don't allow your imagination to be constrained by what already exists!

Rune Spells

You can use runes in a variety of ways in magick—you might choose to use runes in a spell, carve runes into a candle for abundance, use them in a chant, or try divination with them. Here's a spell we think is pretty nifty. It uses runes to help you locate your magickal name—a form of divination. (Review Chapter 6 for more information on choosing your magickal name.)

Lay out your rune stones, or write the runes on index cards or slips of paper and spread them out before you. Sit in meditation, focusing on your magickal name and what you need to know right now. When you feel focused, and without looking at the runes, reach out and select two. You can use these two runes as your magickal name or part of it or as a stepping stone to your magickal name—if you select Kano and Is, for example, you might use both of these as your magickal name, or combine them into one part of your magickal name, or use one and take the other as a starting point for finding your second name. (The rune Is might lead you to step back and wait for the rest of your name to present itself!)

You aren't bound by these choices, of course, and if they just don't feel right to you, put your runes away and try again another time. If you do decide to use one or more runes in your magickal name, you can put these symbols on your Book of Shadows and inscribe them on your tools, as well.

You can also use runes as talismans. Perhaps you are planning a trip to Las Vegas for a bit of gambling; pull the rune Sigel and write it on your arm (your dice-throwing arm!). Or make a necklace for yourself or a loved one with a ring on which you have wood-burned the rune Wynn. If you're traveling a long distance, you might choose to wear runes on your feet (again, on ankle bracelets, sewn into your socks, or written on your feet) representing your foundation (perhaps the rune Othel). You can choose to use other symbols in this way as well.

Here's another rune spell; this one is a very simple house blessing. Write the rune Wynn on index cards and place the cards on the doorframe of each door that is an entrance to your home. When placing the cards, chant:

> *Lord and Lady by this sign,*
>
> *Safeguard well this home of mine.*
>
> *Goddess, by this sign of Wynn,*
>
> *Draw success and joy within.*

You might choose another rune—perhaps Eolh—for this spell, or another symbol altogether.

Perhaps you want to inscribe one of your magickal tools with one or more symbolic runes—you might have taken these as your *sigil*. We'll use the staff as our example, though you might also inscribe your wand or the handle of your athame. The staff represents your magickal path and your walk of life. You should choose runes that represent what you hope for in your life's path or the progress you hope to achieve on your magickal path. You may find what you need in the runes, but you might also choose various symbols of the Goddess and/or God, astrological or planetary signs, or other symbols important to you.

Words of Power

A **sigil** is a magickal symbol, a stamp or seal that you use as your magickal signature. You don't have to have a sigil, but in time, and after much spellwork, you may feel drawn to one.

The process for inscribing or carving the symbols into your tool will take some care. You should cast a formal magick circle when working with your magickal tools. Before cutting into the tool, spend some time within your circle focusing your positive energy and intent on the tool. Think of this as a positive endeavor and not a violent one (you are cutting, after all). You can do the cutting with your white-handled knife, but if a knife is not the appropriate tool for the material you are cutting into, use whatever tool is appropriate for the material. Anoint your tools by placing some oil on your hands and rubbing the oil into the tool by moving your hand in one direction only—the direction in which energy will flow through the tool. Moving your hand back and forth on the tool can cause the tool to deliver unfocused energy. In general, direct the flow deosil to approximate a clockwise motion, used for positive energy.

Now, with care, carve the runes or other chosen symbols into the tool. While carving, chant:

> *Lord and Lady in this hour,*
>
> *See these runes and give them power.*

After you are finished, seal the carving by dripping melted wax into the symbol (perhaps from a blue or purple candle) or by rubbing the symbol with oils for blessing (heliotrope, myrrh, or sandalwood). Now you can reopen your circle.

This next rune spell is a little different. It's one you might do for your children on their first day of school. You can work magick for your own children without their knowledge and consent because you're their guardian, but you might want to discuss it with them beforehand, without telling them exactly what you'll be doing (which will throw the spell off).

This spell requires some dirt outside your home that your child will walk on. Outside the door to your home, on the path your child will be walking on, write the runes for success and happiness—Feoh and Wynn, perhaps—or other positive runes into the dirt. Write them small: You don't want your child to notice them and linger over them, which will press the blessings down into the earth. After your child has passed over the runes, scoop up a bit of the dirt in your hand and toss it behind your child, sending the protective spell into the air. Chant:

With Earth and Air my blessings throw,

Now with my children bid you go.

You can strengthen this spell a bit by filling in the runes with iron filings, which will make the blessings symbolically stick to your child.

This spell can be adapted for many occasions, using different runes (and chants) to represent communication or health on days when a family member has an important presentation or doctor's visit. Remember, though, if you do the spell for a family member who is not your child or for a friend, obtain that person's permission to do this blessing without telling them exactly what you will be doing. This way they won't be distracted by the runes on their path, stopping there and leaving the blessing behind.

Other Magickal Symbols

There are a lot of other symbols out there that you may find appropriate for magick, including astrological symbols, which we discussed in Chapter 13. You may use symbols as a kind of shorthand, inscribing them on your tools and writing with them in your Book of Shadows—choose or create a symbol for each of the four Elements, and use them when writing spells; inscribe a symbol for the Goddess on a tool; or inscribe a symbol for prosperity on a green candle for a prosperity spell (like the one we worked in Chapter 13). These symbols can work to help you focus your energy and enhance your magick; they can add an empowering (and interesting) visual element to your spell.

This spell is to bless a new home. It can be done with a group of people and it makes a wonderful housewarming gift! Start with a white candle and anoint it with some myrrh or sandalwood oil (or other appropriate oil) for purification and cleansing.

Next, starting at the top of the candle and using a needle (which, because of the eye, represents the Goddess—a pin would represent the God), carve a symbol of your choice into the candle. If a group of people is doing this, take turns carving various symbols into the candle, imbuing it with positive energy for the household and its inhabitants. This is a really great activity for a housewarming party—you can set out the candle and some needles, as well as sheets of symbols (with or without their meanings), and set the party guests to work. Have them write the symbol they choose and the meaning of that symbol to them as a kind of key to the candle. If there is leftover space, create a spiral down the candle. Leave the candle for the new homeowners/dwellers, along with the cards of symbols and meanings. Thereafter, at every Full Moon, the recipient should burn the candle, focusing on the blessings that will come into their home. You might suggest they burn the candle at mealtimes during the Full Moon, extinguishing the candle afterward. The candle can serve to nourish their spirits as the food they consume nourishes their bodies.

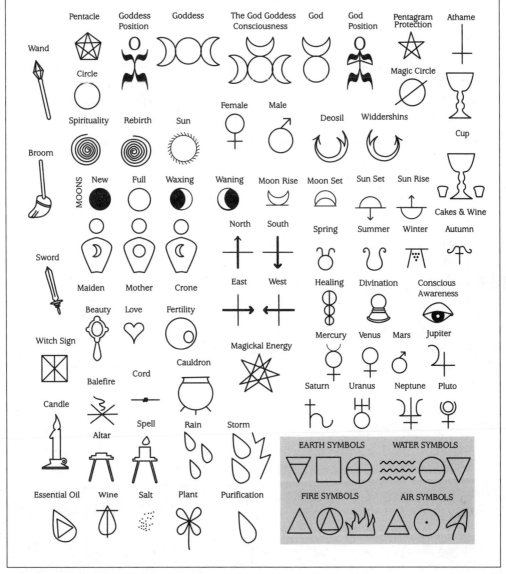

Have fun working spells that use magickal symbols to enhance their power.

Making Magick

Finger painting can be a great way of freeing up the creative mind. Try it yourself: Set up some paper and paints, and either dip your hands into the paint or place some blobs of color onto your paper. Then start painting—swirl your fingers around, close your eyes, and feel the paint on your hands. Try this outside, where you can feel the spirit of nature. You might wait for inspiration or ask for assistance. (Help me create a sign I can use for _____.) When you're done, see what your painting looks like. You may find that you've created a new symbol or symbols you can use in working powerful magick.

Here's a spell you can do to change the weather. Children can work this magick as well. If it's a rainy day and you long for some sun, simply draw a symbol of the Sun onto a piece of paper or an index card and put the paper with the symbol facing outside in an Eastern or Southern window (a Northern exposure works best if you're asking for snow). Put the symbol up in the morning, if possible, and chant when you do so:

> *Be there no harm, let it be warm.*

or

> *Let it harm none, let there be Sun.*

For Protection

When working a spell to influence the weather, be aware of how many people the weather affects and don't cast such spells lightly. Also remember that when we work magick, we are working *with* the energies of nature—don't work *against* them by asking for snow in July, unless that's common for your climate.

You can make up a different chant if rain or snow is what you're wishing for. Each morning for three days, go to the window where you've placed your symbol and repeat your chant. If there's no change in the weather after three days, recognize that it may not be the best time for the weather you desire.

You can adjust this spell to ask for certain weather on a specific date—perhaps the day of an important outdoor event. Write the day and date on a card, using the alphabet of your choice, along with a symbol of the weather you would like. Write this symbol on this date on your calendar, as well.

Take the card to the place of the event, if possible, and hold it up to the sky while visualizing the weather you hope for, chanting:

> *An it harm none,*
>
> *On June fifteenth bring forth the Sun.*

or

> *On the seventeenth of May,*
>
> *Goddess take the rain away.*

You can write your own chant (rhyming or not) for your important day. End your chant with:

> *An it harm none,*
>
> *As I have spoke, so mote it be.*

Now you have charged the card. Take it home and put it up in your window. Renew the energy of the spell by repeating your chant every day until the day of the event. If the Goddess and God will it, you will have the weather you desire!

Your Magickal Alphabet

You may feel a strong connection with runes or with Pictish swirl or with hiero-glyphics, but if you don't, don't dismay! If you're really drawn to the sound or appear-ance of German, Portuguese, or another language, use it as your magickal language. You can also create your own magickal alphabet, using parts of various languages or making it up completely. The power of any instrument of magick comes from within you.

Whatever language you use, when inscribing a magickal tool or object, focus your attention on your intent while writing or inscribing, sending your energy into the writing and empowering the object for your magickal work. The magickal alphabet or symbol can take longer than your spoken language to write, giving you more time to meditate on your intent and giving your spell an extra magickal boost. Feel free to mix your languages and symbols when creating spells—if it feels right to you, it is right!

The Least You Need to Know

- You can enhance your spells by using magickal alphabets and symbols.
- Theban script can be used for creating spells and writing in your Book of Shadows.
- Magickal symbols include rune stones, which have been used for divination for centuries.

- You can create your own magickal alphabet or symbols.
- The magickal power of alphabets and symbols comes from the effect they have on you.

Part 4

Practical Magick

Magick you use in everyday life is called *practical magick*. You can work magick for health, abundance, prosperity, and love—and that's just for starters. Getting a magickal head start in these everyday areas will leave you with energy left for deeper work on your path. In this part, we'll provide some specific correspondence tables for each of these areas, and loads of ideas for spells, as well! We'll also offer guidelines for creating your own spells for practical magick. It's very commonly worked magick, and, well, it's *practical*, too.

Chapter 15

Love, Romance, and Handfasting

In This Chapter

- ◆ Love spells and magickal ethics
- ◆ Colors, stones, herbs and botanicals, and other magickal correspondences for love
- ◆ Spells to attract love or rekindle romance
- ◆ Getting hitched with a handfasting ceremony
- ◆ When you need to end a love relationship

Love, love, love. If you are like most people, you spend a lot of time thinking and wondering about love. You also probably spend a lot of time worrying about it and worrying about the state of your love life. Love spells are some of the most popular types of spells, and they have been since time immemorial.

In this chapter, we'll give you some love spells that you can try for yourself. We'll also give you a lot of suggestions for how to adapt these spells to your own particular circumstances and to your own specific desires. Before you know it, you'll be creating love spells on your own, and, with the help of your magick, you just may end up finding the love of your life!

Magickal Ethics Concerning Love

When working love spells you'll want to be particularly mindful of your magickal ethics. It is not okay to force someone to fall in love with you. If you do magick to create such an effect, you will be taking away the other person's free will. In addition, you probably will not find the relationship satisfying. In the end, you would know that he or she was just with you because of your spell. Wouldn't you rather draw the object of your affection to you by virtue of who you are?

You can work magick to make yourself more attractive. Love spells, when it comes right down to it, work on you and not on the other person. Spells involving love can help to make you feel more worthy of attention, sexy, interesting, and lovable.

Before you work a love spell, be forewarned: They do work! In olden times, love spells were inexpensive and easy to come by. Magickians and potion makers charged little to cast a love spell. The true cost came when a person wanted such a spell removed. Once human emotions are engaged, changing their course is very difficult. So, be sure of what you want, choose your words carefully, and remember your magickal ethics!

> **Making Magick**
>
> Legend has it that a certain doctor in the sixteenth century tried to cast a love spell on a young lady who had caught his eye. In preparing his spell, he asked one of her relatives to procure some of her hair. The wily relation gave the doctor some hairs from a cow, which the doctor then used in his spell. The next day, the cow appeared at his house and refused to leave his side.

Magickal Correspondences for Love

In Chapters 10, 11, and 12, you read a lot about magickal correspondences. Feel free to mix and match materials in your love spells to correspond with your magickal intent. If, for example, you are working a spell to attract love and you are looking for a lusty and passionate union, you might want to include clove, cinnamon, and the color red in your working.

On the other hand, if you are looking for a peaceful, serene, and stable relationship, you would probably want to use a different combination of ingredients in your spell. Perhaps the color pink, rose quartz, and apple will best conform to this intent and serve as the center of your spell.

The following tables give you a quick sketch of some of the correspondences you'll want to keep in mind when preparing your tailor-made love spells. Some of the ingredients you see may have been introduced to you in Part 3, but here the magickal associations you find may be a little more specific to the subject of love. Remember that there are many other magickal ingredients you can employ as well. Use these suggestions as jump-off points. Allow them to spark your creativity, imagination, and abilities to love. As ever, follow your *own* heart when choosing your magickal ingredients and also consider what resonates with your personal experiences and the purpose of your love spell.

Love Spell Colors

Color	Magickal Qualities
Orange	Energizing effects, attractiveness
Pink	Romantic love
Red	Physical passion
White	Receptivity

Love Spell Stones

Stone	Magickal Qualities
Beryl	Joy-filled partnerships
Carnelian	Venus energies
Diamond	Aids troubled unions, attracts blessings
Emerald	Healthy relationships
Garnet	Commitment, fidelity
Red coral	Attracting love and romance
Rose quartz	Self love, healing emotional injuries, romantic feelings
Ruby	Healing a broken heart

Love Spell Herbs and Botanicals

Herb/Botanical	Magickal Qualities
Acacia	General enhancement
Aloe	Luck
Amaranth	Healing heartbreak
Apple	Love, sweetness, healing
Bachelor's button	Attraction, love
Basil	Harmony, love
Barley	Healthy relationships/love, protection
Cardamom	Hospitality, fresh breath, royalty
Cinnamon	Love, lust, sensuality
Cloves	Faithfulness, purity, strength
Cyclamen	Physical love, fertility, healing heartache
Daffodil	Fertility, love, luck
Daisy	Love
Dill	Love, lust, protection
Fig	Fertility, love
Gardenia	Love, lust, healing
Ginger	Love, power
Ginseng	Beauty, healing, love, lust
Lavender	Harmony, love, prosperity, stability
Lemon balm	Healing, love
Lemongrass	Lust, healing
Magnolia	Fidelity
Nutmeg	Fidelity, healing, love, luck
Oak	Fertility, healing, strength
Orris	Long-lasting love, protection
Patchouli	Fertility, sensuality
Poppy	Fertility, love, luck, sleep
Raspberry	Love, protection of the home
Rose	Love, beauty, fertility, luck
Rye	Fidelity, love
Strawberry	Love, luck
Thyme	Healing, love, peace

Herb/Botanical	Magickal Qualities
Valerian	Love, sleep, peace
Vervain	Chastity, love, peace
Vetch	Fidelity

Seemingly ordinary clove-studded apples, those perennial autumn craft projects, may make a nice physical starting point for one of your spells. And they can always serve as sweet-scented gifts.

Be prudent and cautious when working with herbs and botanicals. Never ingest an herb or botanical unless you know for absolute certain it is edible. You also may want to wear gloves when working with plants. Better safe and hive-free than sorry!

Love Spell Runes

Rune	Magickal Qualities
Beorc	Women, Mother Earth, protection, nurturing, fertility
Ing	Power, fertility, happy conclusion, success
Mann	Relationships, cooperation, learning, communication
Othel	Family, grounding, money, tradition, care of the elderly
Wynn	Happiness, especially in love; success, control

Of course, there are other runes that you may want to consider for your specific situation and the working you intend to do. You also may want to use other alphabets or symbols in designing your spell (see Chapter 14 for more on the runes and magickal alphabets). For example, when doing candle magick, you may want to carve your astrological sign and the sign of your beloved on the candle. Remember that the Tarot suit of Cups represents love, and feel free to use Tarot cards in your spellwork.

In addition to the material components of your spell and all of their magickal nuances, you'll want to keep in mind the timing of your magick. Friday, of course, is associated with Venus, the Goddess of Love. So, depending on your magickal intent, you may want to use this day of the week (and a Venus planetary hour) to work your love spells.

Spellcasting

Try using a pointed crystal, such as a piece of rose quartz, for carving symbols on your candles when preparing a love spell. The crystal will further reinforce your magickal intent.

Love Spell Timing

Phase of the Moon	Magickal Effect
New Moon	Draw love to you
Waxing to Full Moon	Make love grow, reach fulfillment
Waning Moon	Banish a former loved one, do away with heartbreak

Moon's Astrological Sign

Cancer, Pisces, Libra, Taurus, Scorpio

Time of Day

Sunrise to noon

> **Making Magick**
>
> A witch we know tells this story: An acquaintance asked to borrow a futon mattress I wasn't using. "Cool," I thought. "I kinda like this guy." I anointed the mattress and focused an image of myself hovering over it, so the man in question would think of me often. I hoped he would ask me out. A few weeks later, he returned the futon. "I thought about you every time I got into bed," he said. "See that stain? I spilled grape juice and couldn't get it out. Every time I lay down, I worried about how I was going to tell you. I'm so sorry." So the spell worked—sort of.

Come Hither, Love

Try one of these spells to draw love (or a loved one) to you. Feel free to adapt these spells to your own situation. Tailor the spells to your intent by adding components, or use these spells to inspire you and fire up your own spell-writing creativity.

Love Talisman

For this spell you will need a piece of carnelian—a stone with strong Venus energy—some paper, a pen, and pink or red embroidery thread. On a small strip of the paper, write down all the qualities you would like your future lover to have. You may want to spend some time, even a few days, on this list. One woman we know made her list and left out a crucial detail—that the man she would become involved with be single!

When you are satisfied with your list, wrap it around the piece of carnelian. To hold the paper in place, wrap it with the embroidery thread. As you do this, say:

The perfect love

I draw to me.

As I have written,

so mote it be.

Then tie the thread securely. Note that the words of the spell do not spell out the exact person you want to attract. This spell purposely does not name the "special someone" so as not to impinge on that person's free will. So you may attract the individual you had in mind, but you may draw someone else—someone even more well-suited!—to you.

You'll want to work this love talisman on the Waxing or Full Moon. If you can, do your spellwork between sunrise and noon. Place your talisman somewhere where you will walk by it several times a day. You could place it in a small basket and hang it in your home or office. If you feel so inclined, you could place it in a small bag and wear it on your person or keep it in your pocket. It's nice, however, to keep your talisman where you can see it. Every time your eyes fall on it, you will be reminded of your intent and that will help you stay focused and keep your magick strong.

Love-Drawing Oil

Here's a love potion you can whip up and use for anointing candles or yourself. If you do decide that you want to apply this love-drawing oil to your skin, make sure that you aren't sensitive to any of the ingredients beforehand. You also may want to place this love oil in an essential oil burner or diffuser to create a warm and loving mood.

This potion will help make you more attractive to your love interest (current or future!). Mix up this oil three days before the Full Moon. You'll want to use unscented, sweet almond oil as your carrier oil for this potion. Dilute your essential oils with the almond oil. Then combine equal parts orange, ylang-ylang, and carnation oil. Add just a drop or two of cinnamon oil.

> **CAUTION**
>
> **For Protection**
>
> Remember to wear gloves when mixing your essential oils and never apply an essential oil that has not been diluted with a carrier oil to your skin. Undiluted essential oils can burn.

Store the mixture in a bottle or container in a cool dark place. On the day of the Full Moon, when you prepare for the ritual, take the bottle of oil out and place it on your altar. During the ritual, focus your intent of making yourself attractive and drawing a love relationship into your life. To help you do this, chant the following words:

With this oil I call in love.

As below, so above.

As above, so below.

Lord and Lady make it so.

When you feel you have raised enough energy, grab the bottle of oil and infuse it with your magickal intent.

A Magickal Love Snack

Share this snack with the object of your affection, and it may just help ignite your relationship.

Get out your favorite recipe for snicker doodle cookies. Or mix up a sugar cookie recipe and plan to add cinnamon to it. You also may want to include a little cardamom. While you add these spices to the cookie dough, concentrate on your magickal intent and infuse the dough with it. Visualize your love relationship in as much detail as you can. Give your imaginings as much texture and color as you can. Really allow yourself to feel what it would be like to be in that relationship. If it helps you, recite the words to your favorite love poem or write one of your own. Once you and the cookie dough have felt and absorbed those loving feelings, form your cookies. If you are so inclined, cut the cookies into special shapes. Depending upon your intent, you can make the shapes as naughty or as nice as you want.

Before you serve your cookies, whip up a little love cocktail to go with them. Pour some pomegranate juice into two cups or wine glasses. If you wish, add three drops of red wine to the juice. As you add the drops, concentrate on your magickal intent. See and feel it happening.

Relight the Fire

This spell can help you to bring romance back into a love relationship that already exists. You will need gardenia oil, carnation oil, a pink candle, a white candle, and a length of red ribbon or embroidery thread.

If your essential oils are not diluted with a carrier oil already, dilute them first. You'll probably want to use a light, unscented oil, such as sweet almond. Mix two parts gardenia oil to one part carnation oil.

Anoint both candles with your oil mixture. As you do this, infuse the candles with your magickal intent. Say:

> *Candle of pink,*
>
> *candle of white,*
>
> *let our love*
>
> *again grow bright.*

Think of your intent and imagine it coming to pass as you prepare the candles. When you feel ready, tie the candles together with the ribbon or thread. Light them both and feel your magick being sent out.

Alternately, you could use the oil mixture in your bath or as a massage oil. If you use the mixture for one of those purposes, you may want to infuse it with your magickal intent when you mix the oils together. In that case, make up a chant to help you focus your intent and send it into the oil.

Making Magick

A young witch we know tried to help a devastated friend whose long-term girlfriend had just dumped him. She put together a love spell in a heart-shaped box. She presented the box to him and told him it would work only if it was opened, to give him free choice. Soon he was juggling three girlfriends. None of them knew about the others. He was really happy and very grateful for the magick. On his birthday, he invited one of the gals to his party. All three showed up, and a huge scene ensued in which he got hit in the face with his own cake. All three women dumped him. After that, he cursed the witch profusely every time he saw her. Meddlers beware!

A Commitment to Love

A handfasting, as you probably know, is a Wiccan marriage ceremony. Handfastings are held for couples and recognize relationships between men and women, between two women, and between two men. A handfasting can be a legal marriage, but it does not have to be. A handfasting can also be a temporary commitment. This type of handfasting is an agreement between both partners to stay together for a year and a day. After that time period, they can renew their commitment contract, re-establish a new and different contract, or agree to part. This sort of arrangement gives the individuals who have been handfasted a lot of choices. Because their contract comes up for renewal, it also can remind both partners to treat each other well. Some witches define a handfasting as a marriage in which a couple is joined for as long as their love lasts.

Other witches get handfasted with the idea that their commitment is for perpetuity. In other words, it will last for this lifetime, and the partnership will continue in future lifetimes. The thinking behind this is that if you are handfasted in one life, you are more likely to run into each other in future lives.

A major part of the handfasting ceremony consists of literally and symbolically tying the knot. (You can see this done with a single scarf in the Mel Gibson movie *Braveheart*.) For simple handfasting, one not intended to extend beyond a year and a day, you can both say that you will stay together and tie a knot in a cord that is held between you. The cord should be three feet long and made of soft material. Often witches use pink, representing love and tender feelings, and silver, representing the Goddess, for their handfasting cords. Other witches choose colors to represent the four Elements. Ideally, this tying of the knot should be done on the Full Moon. You will also want to write your own vows to be spoken on such an occasion. After the cord is tied, it should be stored securely in a mutually agreed-upon place. At each Full Moon, take it and display it where both parties will see it. After the year and a day is up, you can reconsider the relationship. Should you decide to make a more long-term commitment you can use the same cord for your more formal handfasting ceremony.

Making Magick

At Aurora's legal handfasting, the same handfasting cords were used as she and her husband had used a year and a day earlier when performing their own ceremony. After four friends had each knotted a ribbon around the couple's hands with a special blessing from the Element they represented, the entire knot was carefully slipped off and placed in a special box, where it lives to this day on their home altar. This "love knot" or "marriage knot" becomes a very powerful spell that serves to remind the couple of their vows and the support they have from their community.

During a formal handfasting ritual, you work a spell when you tie your cord. Relatives or loved ones and friends participate in your union, giving their special blessing as they tie the ribbon on the couple's clasped hands. Jumping over a broom together is also often part of the ceremony, as a symbol that the couple are crossing a threshold and entering domestic life together.

After the ceremony, you will need a pretty stone box to store your cord in. You will also need the flowers that decorated your altar during the ceremony or the bouquet that you carried. Hang the flowers up to dry. This will probably take a few weeks or a month. After the flowers are dry, place them in the stone box. Add your knotted handfasting cord to the box. On small pieces of paper, write or draw symbols that represent your vows. Add these to the box. Add some of the incense used at the ceremony along with some *vervain*.

Seal the box closed with rubber cement or epoxy so that your vows will be securely locked in. Display the box in your home. The box is a magickal mechanism set up by you to reinforce your intention of commitment. Everything you put into the box brings up the good feelings associated with your relationship. The box also serves to send out the message of your commitment. And through the box you are reminded on a subconscious level of your love.

> **Words of Power**
>
> **Vervain** (*Verbena officinalis*, also called verbena) is a flowering perennial native to Europe, Asia, and Africa. The name comes from a Latin word meaning sacred leaves, twigs, or boughs of olive, myrtle, or laurel, and the plant has been used for its aphrodisiac and healing qualities for centuries. Vervain was sacred to the Druids and the Romans.

Saying Good-bye

Here's a spell to help you move on once a relationship has ended. If you have had a handfasting with your loved one, part of saying good-bye to that relationship is unbinding the cord that you used in your ceremony. Any binding spell can be undone by an unbinding spell in which the materials that were tied are untied.

Of course, before you do a "good-bye" spell, make sure that you have done the groundwork first. You have to talk to the person in question and be clear that you are breaking up. Ultimately, the spell will work on you. It will help you get over the relationship and psychically get into the idea of the split.

This spell will help you get closure after a particularly bad break-up. You will need a sheet of toilet paper and a marking pen. Write your partner's name on one end of the sheet. Write your name on the other end. Then draw a line down the middle of the paper, separating your two names. Focus your intent, and tear the sheet in half along the line.

Gently fold up your half and bury it nearby. Or put it away someplace special where you can keep it for a full cycle of the Moon. If you bury it, imagine it (yourself, your emotions) as a plant, placed in the earth to heal and grow.

Now for the freeing part! Take the half with your partner's name on it and flush it down the toilet. While you do this visualize your partner moving away from you (though not literally down the drain). Imagine him or her floating downstream in a boat, moving gently on in life. See the negativity you are holding onto from the relationship going down the drain, where it won't affect you or your former partner.

Because this spell is a banishing spell, it is best done during the Waning Moon or the dark of the Moon, just before the New Moon.

If the toilet-flushing spell seems a bit too much for your situation, you may want to try this gentler spell. Start a bonfire in a safe outdoor place, or an indoor fire in your fireplace or wood stove. Gather things that make you think of the relationship you are ready to part with. You don't have to get rid of everything a former lover gave you—that's up to you. If you don't have anything that is okay to burn (make sure it's not plastic or toxic in some way), write on a piece of paper: "My relationship as lovers with [name of person] is through." Any expensive gifts such as rings or furniture you might want to simply give back to the person who gave them. Once you have what you are going to burn, sit in front of the fire and chant:

> *Transforming power of fire, transform this relationship.*
>
> *We are now friends, not lovers. The ties that bind are cut.*

Toss the items you have chosen into the fire and watch them burn as you focus your intent. Tend the fire carefully and be sure to put it out completely when the items have been consumed; you don't want to keep the fire burning! Now your relationship can transform smoothly and amicably.

The Least You Need to Know

- Making someone fall in love with you through magick is unethical because it takes away the other person's free will.
- Successful love spells work on *you*.
- You can use or create spells to help you attract love.
- You can work magick to help you rekindle the magick in your existing relationship.
- Magick can help to bind you together in a love union.
- You can use spellcraft to help you end a love relationship and move on.

Chapter 16

Abundance

In This Chapter

- ◆ Defining abundance in its many forms
- ◆ Colors, stones, herbs and botanicals, and other magickal correspondences for abundance
- ◆ Spells to increase your abundance at home
- ◆ Drawing prosperity to you
- ◆ Abundance of the spirit

Abundance seems to be a topic that is on everyone's mind. We feel our abundance, or lack of it, underpinning many of our daily activities. As a culture we are preoccupied with money and our personal assets. We chase money, study it, worry about it, spend it, and try to save it. Not surprisingly, abundance spells are at the top of the list of popular spells.

In this chapter, we'll give you a variety of different types of abundance spells. We'll also give you suggestions for adapting these spells to your own particular circumstances and to your own unique definition of abundance. Soon you'll be constructing abundance spells on your own, and, with the help of your magick, you just may end up finding your own pot of gold.

What Does Abundance Mean to You?

In the olden days, people defined abundance in terms of their flocks and their crops. In other words, a healthy herd of cattle, goats, or sheep, plus the ability to grow plants equaled riches. That definition may hold true for you. In the modern world, your sense of abundance may be tied to your home, family, and children, or your plants, garden, or pets. Or it may be a matter of your checkbook. Or you may see abundance as more of a soul issue. However you see it, you can use the spells in this chapter to attract money, financial gain, prosperity, and even a sense of spiritual abundance.

Before you practice magick to increase your abundance, you'll probably want to give some serious thought to what it is that you really want. Is it more money? Or more time? More fun? Or more meaningful relationships, both on this Earth plane and on the spiritual realm? All of these facets of life can contribute to your feelings of abundance. Spend some time pondering these issues before you start spellcasting. Be sure that you have done your work on the mundane plane first, and be prepared, because you may just get what you ask for!

Magickal Correspondences for Abundance

You can probably think of a lot of symbols of abundance. The cornucopia, for example, has long represented the bounty of nature and successful harvests. Your cauldron or chalice, as symbols of the Goddess, are also symbols of Mother Nature's abundance. Any cave, crevice, or nook can be used to represent the Goddess and her bounty. Anything that can serve as a vessel, no matter how small, can be used as a symbol of abundance. You could place a thimble, open side up, on your windowsill and let it symbolically represent the fertile ground of your life. Plant small representations of what you want to grow in your thimble and see your desires come to pass.

Spellcasting

In terms of your magick, remember that like attracts like. So, for example, a penny will attract more money. Anything that is shaped like a coin can also be used to draw more coins to you. This is why money plants (Lunaria, also known as honesty) are so popular and are thought of as plants of prosperity.

So that you can adapt the spells in this chapter to your own circumstances, we've provided you a listing of some of the most common materials used in abundance spells. You can tailor the materials in your abundance spell to correspond with your precise magickal intent. If, for example, you were creating a spell to attract money, you might want to include basil, a piece of aventurine, and the color green in your spellworking. If the abundance that you want to attract takes the form of a lush garden, you may want to focus instead on the richness of the soil. In such a case, your spell might include seeds, Earth, and the color brown in addition to green. Review the following tables and use them the next time you feel the need to increase your own abundance.

Abundance Spell Colors

Color	Magickal Qualities
Gold	Vitality, strength, success, action, courage, the God
Green	Abundance, growth, prosperity, fertility, luck, healing
Silver	The Goddess, truth, intuition, receptivity, stability, balance
Brown	Stability, sensuality, endurance, animals, grounding, Earth

Abundance Spell Stones

Stone	Magickal Qualities
Aventurine	Money, material success
Bloodstone	Confidence, success in court
Jade	Long life, money
Lapis lazuli	Triumph over adversity
Malachite	Successful business
Rhodonite	Wisdom, confidence
Turquoise	Harmony that fosters abundance

Abundance Spell Herbs and Botanicals

Herb/Botanical	Magickal Qualities
Almond	Love, luck, money
Anise	Luck, protection
Apple	Love
Basil	Harmony, love, prosperity, success
Borage	Courage, intuitive power
Cardamom	Love

continues

Abundance Spell Herbs and Botanicals (continued)

Herb/Botanical	Magickal Qualities
Chamomile	Harmony, love, prosperity
Chestnut	Love
Cinnamon	Healing, love, prosperity, success
Cinquefoil	Love, luck, prosperity
Clover	Fidelity, prosperity, success
Comfrey	Healing, protection
Dandelion	Divination
Dragon's blood	Love, strength
Elderberry	Healing, love, prosperity
Eucalyptus	Healing
Fig tree	Fertility, love
Ginger	Love, power, success
Heliotrope	Healing, prosperity
Jasmine	Dreams, prosperity
Lavender	Harmony, love, prosperity
Moneywort	Healing, money
Myrrh	Healing, purification
Oak	Fertility, luck, prosperity, strength
Oats	Money, prosperity
Pea	Love, money
Pine	Fertility, prosperity
Pineapple	Luck, money
Rose	Beauty, fertility, love, luck
Sage	Prosperity, strength, wisdom
Sandalwood	Mental acuity, protection
Snapdragon	Prosperity
Sunflower	Fertility, friendship, prosperity
Tonka	Friendship, love, prosperity
Vervain/verbena	Love, luck, prosperity
Vetivert	Love, prosperity
Walnut	Fertility, healing
Wheat	Fertility, prosperity

Abundance Spell Runes

Rune	Magickal Qualities
Feoh	Energy, power, wealth, good fortune
Nied	Need, obstructions, success in the future
Jara	Cyclical return, harvesting, success in legal actions, birth, new beginnings
Geofu	Giving and receiving gifts
Peorth	Success in gambling or investments, finding the lost or the hidden
Othel	Family, grounding, money, tradition, care of the elderly

You may want to consider other runes that correspond with your specific situation. You also may want to use other images in designing your spell, such as astrological or alchemical symbols (see Chapter 14 for more on the runes and magickal alphabets). And don't forget about good old dollars and cents—$ and ¢. Following the magickal principle of "like attracts like," you could also use images of coins, dollar bills, diamonds, or the proverbial pot of gold (could be chocolate coins!) in your abundance spells. And don't forget about the Tarot; the suit of Pentacles, as you may recall, represents the Element of Earth, money, and abundance.

Abundance Spell Timing

Phase of the Moon	Magickal Effect
Waxing to Full Moon	Attract money, material, or what have you

Moon's Astrological Sign

The Earth signs: Taurus, Virgo, Capricorn

The Air signs: Gemini, Libra, Aquarius

Time of Day

Morning to midday

Abundance Begins at Home

This section is all about spells that will increase abundance and feelings of plenty in your home. We thought it made sense to start where you live. Some of the spells that you create can be given as gifts.

Tarot Welcome

Here's an easy spell you can work to help increase your abundance. You'll probably want to get an inexpensive set of Tarot cards for this little spell.

> **Spellcasting**
>
> If you don't have Tarot cards, you can substitute regular playing cards. Just remember that Cups are equivalent to Hearts, Wands to Clubs, Swords to Spades, and Pentacles to Diamonds.

Draw out the Ace of Pentacles and the Ace of Cups. Pentacles, of course, represent money, and you can think of Cups, in this case, as being an emblem for the abundance of your relationships.

Place the cards under a doormat inside your front door. As you do so, think of your intent—to increase your feelings of abundance. Every time you walk over your doormat, think of your intent. Imagine that the cards are helping you by drawing good things (and people!) through your front door.

Wheat Is Wealth

In agricultural societies the amount of wheat, rice, or corn you have stored could very well determine your ability to survive the winter. Grain is still an important commodity, foodstuff, and symbol. For this spell, you'll need some wheat berries, a form of grain that should be readily available at your local health-food shop.

First, sew a little pocket out of green cloth, or use a cotton or muslin tea bag. (You can purchase these at health-food and tea shops. They are reusable and work well for sachets like this one, as well as herbal bath infusions and teas!) Set your bag aside.

Mix enough wheat berries to fill your bag with a few drops of cinnamon oil. Stir the wheat berries so that they get coated with the oil. As you stir, see and feel what you want to have happen. Imagine your magick coming to pass. Add some dried chopped ginger root.

Stuff the mixture into your bag to form a sachet. Seal up the bag. Then roll it around between your hands to mix the botanicals together and to help them begin to release their aroma.

Toss the sachet in your linen closet. It's nice if you place it in between your folded towels. Your towels will smell nice, and after your bath, when you breathe in the sachet's scent, you will be reminded of your intent—to bring fulfillment and abundance into your life.

And Golden Sheaves of Grain

For this spell you will need some straw or some sheaves of wheat. If the straw is very dry and does not bend easily, soak it in a basin of warm water. Add a drop or two of heliotrope oil to the water.

When the straw is soft, take some gold embroidery thread and braid the pieces together. The gold thread will represent the success, vitality, and courage that you want in your life. If the straw/wheat you used was soft, anoint it with some oil.

Hang this pretty decoration on the wall of your home to attract bounty, or give this golden sheaf as a gift.

You can adapt this recipe to attract various kinds of abundance. If you like, use green embroidery thread for money, brown for a fertile garden, yellow for an abundance of words. Consult your correspondence tables and see what resonates for you. Feel free to mix and match colors, and you can always add orange to raise the energy of your working.

Earth Jar

This spell is for both protection and abundance. The jar itself makes a great gift, particularly for a house warming.

You will need one large jar, such as a mayonnaise jar. You will also need a small jar that will fit inside the large one. A baby food jar is perfect for this purpose.

Decorate the lids of both jars by gluing cloth or felt to them. You want to obscure any printing that is on the lids. You may want to use green material, or use any other color that says abundance and protection to you. If you can find some, glue a few feathers to the top of the baby food jar.

Place about three inches of dirt in the large jar. Add a layer of sand on top of the dirt. The sand should be about two inches deep.

Add water to the baby food jar. Then place a quartz crystal inside it. If you feel so inclined, place another stone in the baby food jar along with the quartz crystal. Consult your tables of magickal correspondences and see which stone feels right to you. You may want to pick a green one to represent prosperity, such as jade. The quartz will tend to intensify the drawing power of the other stone.

Put the lid on the baby food jar and close it tight. Place the baby food jar inside the large jar on top of the layer of sand. Surround the baby food jar with a layer of shells.

On top of the baby food jar, add three chips of *Dragon's blood* either whole or ground into a powder. Or add another type of incense depending on your preferences and your intent. Feel free to add your own little touches based on your abundance correspondence lists.

Words of Power

Dragon's blood is a type of resin that comes from the fruit of a tropical Asian tree. In past times, it was an important ingredient in varnish. Today it is mainly used as incense. Mixed with water and/or essential oils you can use Dragon's blood as a magickal ink.

Now you are ready to seal the jar. Take the jar to an area where you feel there is good air and good energy. Use the lid to scoop air into the jar.

Then seal the jar, as you do so say:

> *Earth and Air and Fire and Water,*
>
> *extend your blessings to those*
>
> *who hold this jar in their care.*

If you are going to give the jar as a gift, keep it in a dark box until it is ready to go to the home where it will live.

Making Magick

One witch we know received an Earth jar as a gift. She placed it in her home and used it as a doorstop. Some time later, the jar exploded! This strange event made her wonder about the intentions of the gift giver. So, be clear about your magickal intent and be careful not to do workings when you are stressed or angry. If you do, those feelings may well get bound up in your spell.

Money, Come to Me!

This spell will help to beautify you while it works its money-drawing magick. When used on the hands, the scrub you will make in this spell will attract wealth and good fortune to you. Used on the feet, the scrub will set you on the correct path to bring abundance into your life.

Pretty Hands, Pretty Feet

You will need half a cup of sea salt, two teaspoons of dried vervain, two teaspoons of dried vetivert, some frankincense oil, and some heliotrope oil.

Mix the salt and dried herbs together. Add four drops of frankincense oil. Add one drop of heliotrope oil. Mix it all together.

To use on your hands and attract wealth to you, wet your hands first. Then rub them with the scrub. As you rub, repeat the following:

> *Salt and herbs of Earth and Fire,*
>
> *Bring to me what I desire:*
>
> *Life of bounty*
>
> *to fulfill,*
>
> *hear my words,*
>
> *work my will.*

To find your own path of abundance, use this scrub on your feet. Wet both your hands and feet, then rub your feet with the scrub. Repeat these words as you rub:

> *Smooth the feet that they may know*
>
> *The path to tread, the way to go,*
>
> *Where fortune and good life are found,*
>
> *Upon this path I now am bound.*

When you are done, rinse off, dry yourself, enjoy your tingly new skin, and feel your abundance flow.

> **CAUTION**
>
> **For Protection** _____
>
> Although you may be tempted, do not use your Pretty Hands, Pretty Feet scrub on your face. It's designed for use on your tougher skin and may leave more delicate tissues dried out or irritated.

Money Drawing Oil (or Money-Come)

Say you have decided that what you really want is money—cold hard cash—and not some vague sense of bounty or the good life. You can use one of these spells to help attract money to you. The following essential oil blend can help you do that, and it smells nice, too. You can use four drops to equal one part, if you'd like. It depends on how much oil you want to make.

During the Waxing Moon, mix together:

- ◆ 4 parts frankincense oil
- ◆ 2 parts heliotrope oil
- ◆ 1 part orange oil
- ◆ ½ part cinnamon oil

Into this oil mixture add a pinch of powdered ginger and a crumbled bay leaf. Tear or cut up a dollar bill into tiny pieces and add it to the oil.

Use this essential oil blend to anoint your checkbook, wallet, your hands, your pockets, and whatever symbolizes your money-making ability. As you apply the oil, say:

> *By the Lady and the Law,*
>
> *An it harm none, money draw.*
>
> *An it harm none, by my will,*
>
> *Money come, my purse to fill.*

You can use Money-Come for a variety of different spells as well. If you like to carry small tangible reminders of your magick, try this spell: Anoint a horse chestnut on the night of the Full Moon and carry it on your person for a complete Moon cycle. You should even keep it under your pillow while you sleep.

Spellcasting

When you mix up your Money-Come oil, feel free to extend it with unscented almond oil. This will make the mixture less perfumey, and doing so can save you money on your essential oil budget, too. Almond, of course, is a money and fortune plant, as well as a drawer of sex and love. What a tree!

Here's yet another use for this versatile oil blend that has an application in the home: Apply the oil to cotton balls and place them around your home. To pull money into your household, stuff the anointed cotton into out-of-the-way nooks and crannies. (Remember that nooks and crannies can be seen as representations of the Goddess.) Imagine your abundance growing in all the hollows of your home.

Your Abundant Year

On your next birthday, why not make yourself a prosperity cake? The tradition of blowing out the candles on a birthday cake and making a wish is a type of prosperity spell, so why not make the rest of your cake match up with your intent?

The flour in your cake, of course, is made of wheat, which is a symbol of abundance and prosperity. Pineapples, too, have long been associated with plenty and the good life. Are you thinking what we're thinking? Pineapple Upside Down Cake!

As you mix your batter, concentrate on your magickal intent and allow it to infuse your cake. When it is ready to serve, place a green candle in the cake's center for yourself and wish for abundance in your new year.

Prosperity Pesto

Using this spell, you could turn your birthday dinner into a celebration of bounty. So why not make this year your year of abundance and prosperity?

Get out your favorite pesto recipe. Remember that basil is one of the major herbs of abundance. And it's green and tasty, too! To increase the value of your prosperity, add just a pinch of powdered bay leaf. If you like, grind the bay leaf yourself with your mortar and pestle. Concentrate on your intent while you do this.

As you add the pine nuts—another symbol of plenty—continue to focus on your magickal intent. You can also use almonds—another bounty bringer—in your recipe. Infuse your sauce with your magickal intent.

Boil up some water, cook your pasta, and enjoy the fruits of your labor!

For Protection

Before you use it in a recipe, make sure that the plant that you refer to as bay is really the same as the culinary herb known as bay leaf. A lot of plants take the common name bay. The scientific name for bay leaf is *Laurus nobilis*. And don't confuse it with any of the laurels, which are poisonous.

Leaf-Boat Spell

Here's a fun and quick spell that you can do with children. You need to have access to a body of flowing water for this one. So if you live near a stream, brook, or river, you are in luck. If you don't, you can always plan a little prosperity field trip.

You will need a marking pen and a few oak or maple leaves. Write or draw symbols of what you want on the leaves. Use words or runes or anything that has meaning to you. Imagine the thing that you want to pull in, whether it be cash or a bountiful flower garden or a general sense of contentment.

Imagine that your leaves have become little wish boats that will carry your desires out where they can manifest.

Place your leaves in the flowing water and say:

> *On this water my wishes float*
>
> *Heed the symbols on my boat*
>
> *As I have said it*
>
> *As I have sent it*
>
> *So mote it be.*

And feel your magick come to pass.

Maple-Almond Toss

Here is another spell that requires a body of water. This time you want still water, such as that of a lake or a pond. This spell, too, can be fun to do with kids.

You will need a maple leaf, some green embroidery thread, an almond, and a small rock. If you feel so inclined, write or draw symbols of what you want on the leaf. Then make a little package by wrapping the almond and the rock with the leaf. Wind the embroidery thread around your leaf package.

Take your maple-almond bundle to a body of still water. Toss it out into the pond. In this case, your throwing action literally casts your spell. When your bundle splashes down, watch the ripples in the water and say:

> As these ripples go forth,
>
> my intention goes forth.
>
> The message is sent.

Then walk away from the pond and forget about it. Allow the magickal energy you have put out with this spell to do its work.

Abundance of Spirit

Perhaps the abundance that you seek is more one of spirit than of material. Feelings of joy and of connection may certainly be a part of your definition of abundance. If you feel the need for greater spiritual connection (and don't we all, now and then?) try the following spell.

You will want to work this spell on the Full Moon or on the New Moon. It's best to be precise with your timing for this spell. The Moon should be neither Waxing nor Waning.

You'll also want to cast this spell in a magick circle. Your magick circle will protect you and ensure that the spiritual beings that you reach are benevolent ones. Read this spell over a few times and get all your equipment together before you raise your circle.

You will need mugwort oil. Mugwort is often used as an aid for moving into other realms. It also helps to promote prophetic dreams. You will also need some sage oil. Sage has strong protective qualities and also draws abundance.

You will also need three types of incense—cinnamon, bay laurel, and sandalwood. Mix these together and place them in your incense burner.

Mix a few drops of the mugwort and sage oils together. When you are ready to work this spell and are safe within your circle, anoint your temples with the oil mixture.

Light the incense. It will make quite a lot of smoke. When you have the incense burning, if you are inside, crack open a window. With your hand or a feather, wave the smoke out the window. (If you are outside, you will not need to worry about where the smoke is going.) Imagine that it is carrying your intent out and up to the Goddess. As the smoke wafts out, say:

> *As above, so below.*
>
> *In the goddess it is so.*
>
> *Winds of change for better blow.*

Think on her. Feel the abundance of her nature and know that you are a part of that nature and a part of her.

The Least You Need to Know

- Be sure of what you want before you begin work on an abundance spell. The clearer your intent, the stronger your magick will be.

- Remember, when developing your own abundance spell, that like attracts like. For example, coins or money can be used to draw more coins or money to you.

- You can turn ordinary recipes for cake or even pasta sauce into magickal mechanisms. It all depends on your intent.

- Prosperity spells can be both helpful and fun. Some are even appropriate for children.

- You can use a spell (or write your own!) to help increase your sense of connection to the Lord and Lady.

Chapter 17

Success

In This Chapter

- Colors, stones, herbs and botanicals, and other magickal correspondences for success
- Spells for job seekers
- Spells for success in the workplace
- Protect yourself
- Bad vibes, be gone!

In this chapter, we're going to be taking care of business. Here you will find spells for all things related to the workplace—from dealing with co-workers to attracting the "right" work to nurturing your personal success. As in earlier chapters, we'll give you suggestions for how to adapt spells to your own particular circumstances and to your own specific brand of success.

After you have gained some experience (and had some magickal success!), you'll want to start creating success spells on your own. To that end, we've also given you all the information you need to do it yourself. So let's begin your magickal journey along the road to success.

Magickal Correspondences for Success

Many of the stones, herbs, and symbols that you'll find in this chapter also correspond to abundance, which we discussed in Chapter 16. There is a great deal of overlap between the two concepts. Some may argue that abundance is the end result of success. Others say that an inability to feel your own abundance and to appreciate all the gifts of the Goddess will impede or even prevent you from attaining success. Which came first, abundance or success? We think that they work hand in hand. And so, too, will many of their magickally corresponding items. In all our research, we have also found that "success" tends to closely correlate with wisdom and harmony. Many of the same stones and plants magickally correspond and serve these dual purposes, as well.

As you review the following tables, remember that you can always use the color white in your spells as a substitute for another color. This is a good point to keep in mind when you find yourself frustrated by a lack of turquoise candles or another spell necessity in a hard-to-find color.

Success Spell Colors

Color	Magickal Qualities
Gold	Vitality, strength, success, action, courage, winning, the God
Green	Abundance, growth, prosperity, fertility, luck, healing
Orange	Courage, pride, success, energy, ambition, enthusiasm, opportunity
Purple	Success in business, self-esteem, higher-minded wealth, growth, spiritual insight
Brown	Stability, sensuality, endurance, animals, grounding
Turquoise	Discipline, self-knowledge, creativity, honor
Violet	Success, self-improvement, intuition
Yellow	Communication, joy, vitality, study, intelligence, creativity, charm

Success Spell Stones

Stone	Magickal Qualities
Alexandrite	Luck, joy, transformation
Amazonite	Success, self-expression, joy

Stone	Magickal Qualities
Aventurine	Money, material success, luck
Bloodstone	Confidence, business and legal affairs
Chrysoprase	Luck, prosperity, friendship
Lapis lazuli	Triumph over adversity
Malachite	Successful business, energy
Rhodonite	Wisdom, confidence
Tiger's eye	Luck, common sense, courage, prosperity
Turquoise	Harmony that fosters abundance

Success Spell Herbs and Botanicals

Herb/Botanical	Magickal Qualities
Almond	Love, luck, money
Anise	Luck, protection
Apple	Love, healing
Basil	Love, prosperity, success
Borage	Courage, intuitive power
Cardamom	Love
Carnation	Strength, vitality
Chamomile	Harmony, love, prosperity
Cedar	Healing, money, purification
Chestnut	Love
Cinnamon	Healing, prosperity, success
Cinquefoil	Love, luck, prosperity
Clover	Prosperity, success
Comfrey	Healing, protection (travel)
Dandelion	Divination, wishes
Dragon's blood	Love, strength
Elderberry	Healing, love, prosperity
Eucalyptus	Healing
Fig tree	Fertility, love
Ginger	Love, power, success

continues

Success Spell Herbs and Botanicals (continued)

Herb/Botanical	Magickal Qualities
Heliotrope	Healing, prosperity
Jasmine	Dreams, prosperity
Lavender	Harmony, love, prosperity
Lemon balm	Healing, love, success
Moneywort	Healing, money
Myrrh	Healing, purification
Oak	Fertility, luck prosperity, strength
Oats	Money, prosperity
Pine	Fertility, prosperity
Sage	Prosperity, strength, wisdom
Sandalwood	Mental acuity, protection
Snapdragon	Prosperity
Sunflower	Fertility, friendship, prosperity
Tonka	Friendship, love, prosperity
Verbena/Vervain	Love, luck, prosperity
Vetivert	Love, prosperity
Wheat	Fertility, prosperity

Success Spell Runes

Rune	Magickal Qualities
Feoh	Energy, power, wealth, good fortune
Ur	Quick change, strength, determination
Hagall	Change due to outside forces, frustration
Nied	Need, obstructions, success in the future
Ansur	Communication, wisdom, learning, social magnetism
Jara	Cyclical return, harvesting, success in legal actions, birth, new beginnings
Eolh	Protection, success, friendship
Ing	Power, fertility, success
Tir	Facing difficulties, victory, bravery, health

Don't forget about astrological symbols. And consider, too, all the images and symbols that mean success to you. What about the corner office that you wish were yours or those designer shoes you saw last week? (In some cultures, shoes are considered to be emblems of success and abundance.) When it comes to success, you can also use the "like attracts like" principle. And you may want to consider the Tarot's Ace of Pentacles for new business ventures and the Wheel of Fortune from Tarot's Major Arcana.

Success Spell Timing

Phase of the Moon	Magickal Effect
Waxing to Full Moon	Attract money, material, or luck
Waning	Banish negativity, bad luck, obstacles
Moon's Astrological Sign	
The Earth signs: Taurus, Virgo, Capricorn	
The Air signs: Gemini, Libra, Aquarius	
Time of Day	
Morning to midday for attracting	
Midday to night for banishing	

Seek and Ye Shall Find

You've heard the adage that looking for a job is a full-time job, and this can be true. So why not help yourself along with magick? Yes, you still have to write cover letters, send out your resume, fill out applications, and make all those phone calls. Do all the mundane work and then … cast your spell. Or work the magick as preparation for going out to pick up the applications, but make sure the paperwork gets done!

Job-Drawing Almond

When looking for a paying job, carry an almond in your pocket. Before setting out to pound the pavement or before that big interview, say:

> *Nut of the generous almond tree,*
>
> *fortune and livelihood draw to me.*

If you get nervous going into an interview, feel the almond in your pocket and be confident of your own success.

Perfect Job Call

Dissatisfaction on the job or a sense that you just aren't doing the right thing can hamper your success big time. These days, with all the seeming choices available to us, lack of clarity about career direction is rampant. Sometimes that perfect job can seem downright mythical or at least super-elusive. The right job for you is out there, though, and this 15-day spell can help you find it.

Spellcasting

When using water in your spells, you'll want it to be chlorine-free. To dechlorinate tap water, pour some into a basin or other open container and allow it to sit out overnight.

For this spell you will need …

- ◆ A clear bowl.
- ◆ 15 translucent green marbles.
- ◆ Spring water, rain water, well water, or any other water that does not have chlorine in it.

To prepare, think seriously about what you want in a job. What sort of qualities and attributes do you want in your job and in your workplace? How do you want to be treated? Which of your skills do you want to use? Write down your answers and come up with a list of 15 job characteristics.

We made a list to help get you started. Your list might look something like this:

1. A friendly workplace
2. Good pay
3. Fun colleagues
4. Informal office culture
5. Respect
6. Compassionate leadership
7. Fairness
8. A sense of right livelihood
9. Incandescent lighting
10. A short commute

11. Flextime options

12. 401(k) plan

13. A quiet workplace

14. Windows

15. A cheerful environment

On the first night of the Waxing Moon, fill the clear bowl with water and gather your marbles. On each night of the Waxing Moon, take a marble, hold it to your forehead, and say:

> *It is the right time,*
>
> *It is the right place,*
>
> *to bring me to* _____.

Fill in the blank with one of your desired job attributes. If the previous list of attributes were yours, on the first night you would fill in the blank with "a friendly workplace." Then drop the marble onto the clear bowl of water.

On the second night of the Waxing Moon, you would move down your list, say the first two lines of the previous chant, and then fill in "good pay." Then you would add the second marble to the bowl.

On the fifteenth night, after you have dropped your last marble into the bowl, stand in the moonlight (if it is visible) and use the water from the bowl to refresh your hands and face. Feel that you are washing yourself in your desires and intentions. As you do this, say:

> *I am calling this to me.*

Repeat this phrase three times.

Take the water outside and pour it over a plant. If you don't have access to outside space, pour the water on one of your house plants. Because the water is infused with your magick, you don't want to pour it down the drain. That would be like pouring your intentions down the drain and flushing away all the magickal energy you have built up over the course of 15 days. The plant you choose to gift with this magickally infused water will be happy, and, as your magick comes to pass, you will be, too. You could place the marbles on your altar, give them to your children (if they are old enough to play with marbles, you don't want to introduce a choking hazard), or bury the marbles outside.

Success on the Job

If you already have a job or have just landed one, you'll want to take a look at the spells in this section. They start off with workings that you do at home and then move into ones best done at your place of work.

Starting on the Right Foot

If you are about to start a new job, this spell can help you set off on the right foot. Do this spell at home before your first day at the new workplace.

You will need a basin, some whole-wheat flour, some corn meal, and a few drops of frankincense oil. In the basin, mix all the ingredients together. Then use the mixture as a dry foot scrub. Give your feet a good rub-down. The essential oil should help to soften them up.

> **CAUTION**
>
> **For Protection**
>
> If you work magick in your place of work or even at home, with the intention of influencing your place of work, think your spellwork through very carefully. Be aware of the effects any changes induced by your magick might have on your co-workers. Practice magick ethically and don't work magick for others without their consent.

When you are done rubbing, take the scrub outdoors. Find a quiet place and use the scrub to draw a small pentagram on the ground.

Stand on your pentagram. Raise your arms to the heavens and feel that you are an antenna for the divine as you say:

My path is divine.

My work is divine.

In all things,

I am successful.

So mote it be.

You may want to spend a few moments meditating after you have cast this spell. You also may want to consider working this spell as part of a ritual or within your magick circle. Depending upon the outdoor space you have used, you may want to clean up your pentagram after you are done spellcasting.

Candle of Success

Gold, of course, is the color of success. Unfortunately, gold candles are hard to find. For this spell you will need a taper candle and some gold wire. You can use a white candle or any other color that corresponds with your magickal intent. If, for instance, you wanted to work a spell for success in the field of communication, you would use a yellow candle.

Because this spell is designed to draw success to you, start it on the Full Moon. Ideally, you'll want to work with this candle spell for an entire month. This can be especially nice to do your first month at a new job or when you have just returned from vacation or other time away.

To cast your spell, beginning at the top, wrap the gold wire around your candle. Spiral it around and down. With each loop of your spiral, say:

> *Spiral round, spiral round,*
>
> *As you burn, success is found.*

Then light the candle for a certain amount of time every night. The amount of time you allow the candle to burn will depend upon your schedule and on how large the candle is. Remember, you want your candle to last all month.

> **CAUTION**
>
> **For Protection** _____
>
> To safeguard your success, never leave success candles burning unattended. If you do, you may see your dreams—and everything else—go up in smoke!

Down on the Farm

Go to a toy store and buy a little plastic farm animal (if you have children, perhaps you can borrow one). Choose a cow, goat, sheep, or pig. Remember that our agricultural ancestors (and farmers today, too) saw their flocks as a crucial measure of their own success. So in this respect, this spell relies on the principle of "like attracts like."

Place your toy farm animal on your desk, work surface, or on your computer. Anoint the animal with a small amount of heliotrope oil. As you do this, say:

> *This was a symbol of successful farming.*
>
> *This was a symbol of plentiful harvest.*
>
> *This is my symbol of joyful work.*
>
> *This is my symbol of abundant rewards.*

Tape your farm animal to your desk. Or, if you feel self-conscious, put it in your desk drawer or locker and take a peek at it often.

Cordial Colleagues Talisman

Good relations with your co-workers can make all the difference between job heaven and job hell. This spell will help you to develop harmonious relations with everyone else at your workplace.

You will need two sticks between 2 and 3 inches in length. One stick will represent you, and the other is anyone who crosses your path on a given day. You will also need some green, rose, purple, and dark blue embroidery thread.

Hold the sticks together so that they form an X, a sign of partnership and harmony. With the embroidery thread, tie the sticks to each other. Use each color as you tie. When you knot each thread, leave a little tail hanging down.

Hang this talisman in your workplace. You can dangle it from the ceiling or a light fixture, or if you want to be more discreet, hang it from the underside of your desk.

Fertile Mind

Fertility is a particular type of success. And a fertile mind can be crucial if you want to get ahead in sales or any other form of business. The ability to generate ideas at the workplace and while under pressure can be greatly enhanced with a little magick.

An egg, which is an ancient symbol of fertility, can work wonders in the workplace. So why not get a small stone egg at your local lapidary or metaphysical shop? Use color correspondence tables to choose the color and stone that is right for your situation.

Keep the egg in your desk or around your work space. Touch it every day. Allow it to ease your tension and let your ideas flow.

If your workplace is fairly informal, take off your shoes, put your egg on the floor, and roll it around under your feet. This action will help to relax you and allow your good ideas to come bubbling up. It also will call to your subconscious mind that you are working toward your own success. And it feels good, too!

Working Vehicles Bundle

For those who work in their cars or travel a lot for work, this spell will help to bring both safety and success.

You will need a 6-inch stick of sage and one of cedar. You will also need a leaf of comfrey. Comfrey represents safe journeys, cedar supports business, and sage cleanses away negative energy.

Tie the herbs together with a silver ribbon. Place them in your glove compartment or in your briefcase or suitcase. Let the herbs confer blessings for your successful journey. They will aid you in bringing profit from your journey. This is a great magickal talisman for traveling salespeople and those about to embark on business trips.

If you can't find the herbs in stick or leaf form, you can buy them in smaller, more-processed pieces at an herb shop or health-food store. In this case, make a sachet out of them by putting them in a little pouch. Cotton tea bags are great for this purpose. Tie your pouch up with silver ribbon or string and add a green stone or crystal if you feel so moved. If you are going to be selling or making a business pitch, add a coin to the bag as well, and carry it with you on your person or in your purse or briefcase.

On-the-Job Protection and Negativity Zappers

Emotions can run high at work, and when that happens, things can start going wrong. We've all had times when we've felt our energy has become unbalanced. The spells in this section can help protect you and clear away bad vibes.

Square G Spell

To safeguard your computer, aid you in dealing with electromagnetic fields, and thus protect your success in business, make yourself a square G emblem. The square G symbol affects the results of divining rods and can help your computer run smoothly. The square G seems to act as a hook, which pulls off excess energy. If you often have problems with electronic devices, batteries, or watches, the square G may be able to help stabilize your energy and preserve the smooth functioning of your gadgets.

A square G is just the letter G, but drawn all at right angles. The easiest way to make one is to draw three sides of a square, keeping the open side on the right. Starting from the bottom, draw a line halfway up the remaining side. Then make the lip of the G, by drawing a line in to the square's center.

Make your square G as simple or as fancy as you want. You could draw it on a sticky note and stick it to your desk or computer monitor. Or you could draw your G on good paper, using a magickal ink. When creating your square G, say:

> *Stable will my energies be.*
>
> *Keep the gremlins away from me.*
>
> *Electromagnetic balance is mine,*
>
> *as I draw this final line.*

Every time you enter your work area and especially before you sit down to use your computer, hold your hands over your square G drawing. You may want to rub your hands together as if washing them. Allow your emblem to cleanse your hands of excess energies.

Vacuum the Office Air

Stress and bad tempers can ruin your day. They can also drag you down and knock you off the path to success. If it has gotten tense in your office or workplace and people are stressed out, try this simple spell. You'll want to do this either late or early—when no one else is around.

All you'll need is some myrrh oil, which will act as a purifier—a psychic vacuum. Anoint the main door and doorway to your workplace with the oil. While you do this say:

> *This door is a negativity magnet.*
>
> *Inside is holy space.*
>
> *Only good enters in.*
>
> *Only good goes forth from this portal.*

The door will then suck the negativity off people as they enter the room. The atmosphere will become mellower and more conducive to everyone's success.

Clean and Clear Spell

This is a 10-second purification ritual for you to do in private. It can allow you to shake off any feelings of negativity or psychic assault. Such an ability can be particularly important to your success in high-stress situations, especially if you deal with the public. Before you start this little ritual remind yourself that the negativity is *their* stuff and not yours.

Tap your feet on the ground as if you were knocking dirt off your shoes. Make the horned sign with your forefinger and pinkie. (To do this pull your middle and ring fingers into your palm and extend your other two fingers.) Starting on one side at your feet, use your hand in this position to scoop up the negative energy clinging to your person. Then flick the energy away from you. Move all the way up your body. Then switch hands and do the other side.

This action lends you the strength of the Horned God in dealing with the situation, giving you bit of a divine boost. He's a good deity to have around when you are in need of a bit of protection.

Finally, take a few cleansing breaths. Feel that the negativity is gone.

Making Magick

One witch we know who works as a nurse and has a lot of face time with the public practices this clean and clear spell every day. When she gets off work, she goes to her car and pulls off all the negative energy from the day. This way she goes home clearer and lighter. Her kids like her better, she finds she sleeps more soundly, and she gets up ready to zip back to work and start a new day.

The Least You Need to Know

- Because they are related ideas, success and abundance share many of the same magickal correspondences.

- Success also shares many correspondences with wisdom and harmony.

- Spellcasting can help you find the job that's right for you.

- You can use spells to help improve all aspects of your work life and draw success toward you.

- You can banish negativity and the unpleasant energies of others.

18

Well-Being

In This Chapter

- ◆ Well-being is more than physical
- ◆ Colors, stones, herbs and botanicals, and other magickal correspondences for well-being
- ◆ Energy, power centers, and chakras
- ◆ Spells to cleanse and purify
- ◆ Blessings to banish stress and negativity

In this chapter, you will find spells for enhancing your well-being and techniques to help you keep yourself well. And, of course, you will find tips for how to create spells suited to your own particular circumstances and to your own issues.

In addition, as in previous chapters, we have provided tables of information on magickal correspondences. So let's take a look at what you may need to feel your best and stay that way.

Your Health: Mind, Body, and Spirit

You know that your health is not simply a matter of your body. In fact, medical science has come to acknowledge that the mind and the spirit are closely linked to the body and its overall condition. Taking care of your health, then, is also an important component of your spiritual development. Eating well, getting enough rest, and avoiding recreational drugs and overconsumption of alcohol can help to make you feel your best. That good feeling will help connect you to the natural magickal power of the Lord and the Lady.

While your health can be a spiritual issue, we don't mean to suggest that you rely solely on spiritual remedies for what ails you. If you are ill or have persistent symptoms that make you think something is wrong, first see a qualified health-care practitioner. In other words, do your work in the mundane world first, before you begin your spellwork. Your magick will work in tandem with your health-care treatment plan. In addition, you can use magick to help you relieve stress—the source of many physical problems—and to keep your mind and spirit positive and healthy.

Your Well-Being and Its Magickal Correspondences

By this point, you are probably starting to get the hang of magickal correspondences. You even may have started tailoring spells to your specific situation and magickal intent. As in earlier chapters, we're providing a few tables of correspondences. Of course, there are other components that you could use in your spells for well-being. Use your imagination, focus your intent, and make healthful magick.

Well-Being Spell Colors

Color	Magickal Qualities
Black	Absorbing negative energy, banishing, protection, binding
Blue	Tranquility, protection, change, truth
Brown	Grounding, stability, concentration
Gold	Vitality, strength, the God
Gray	Absorbing negativity, vision
Orange	Energizing effects, courage
Pink	Spiritual healing, romantic love
White	Cleansing, protection, healing, receptivity
Yellow	Vitality, joy

Well-Being Spell Stones

Stone	Magickal Qualities
Azurite	Psychic energy, healing, concentration, transformation
Beryl	Love, healing, energy, protection
Calcite	Grounding, purification, calming of fear
Citrine	Protection, energy, guards against nightmares
Garnet	Energy, strength, healing, protection
Hematite	Calming, healing, strength, intuition
Jade	Healing, protection, prosperity
Obsidian	Protection, grounding, absorbs negative energy
Peridot	Protection, prosperity, health
Rose Quartz	Self-love, emotional healing, romantic feelings
Sodalite	Healing, wisdom, neutralizes stress
Topaz	Healing, dieting, protection, emotional balance

Well-Being Spell Herbs and Botanicals

Herb/Botanical	Magickal Qualities
Amaranth	Healing, protection
Angelica	Healing, protection
Balm of Gilead	Healing, protection
Bay leaf	Healing, protection, strength
Burdock	Healing, protection, purification
Carnation	Protection, strength, vitality
Cinnamon	Healing, protection
Comfrey	Healing
Cotton	Healing, protection
Cowslip	Healing
Dragon's blood	Protection, purification, stress relief
Elderberry	Healing, protection, purification
Eucalyptus	Healing, protection
Fennel	Healing, protection, purification
Frankincense	Protection, banishes negativity, stress relief

continues

Well-Being Spell Herbs and Botanicals (continued)

Herb/Botanical	Magickal Qualities
Garlic	Healing, love, protection
Geranium	Fertility, healing, protection
Hawthorn	Fertility, protection
Heliotrope	Healing, purification
Horehound	Protection, healing, banishes negativity
Hyssop	Protection, purification
Ivy	Healing, protection
Larkspur	Healing, protection
Lavender	Harmony, protection
Mint	Healing, protection
Mugwort	Healing, protection, strength
Mulberry	Protection, strength
Myrrh	Healing, protection, purification
Nasturtium	Healing
Oak	Fertility, healing, protection, strength
Olive	Fertility, healing, protection
Onion	Healing, protection
Passionflower	Balance, calm, peace
Pennyroyal	Protection, strength
Pine	Healing, protection
Rosemary	Healing, protection, purification
Sage	Healing, protection, stress relief, wisdom
Sandalwood	Healing, mental acuity, protection
Spearmint	Healing, mental acuity
St. John's wort	Healing, protection, strength
Tansy	Healing
Thistle	Healing, protection, strength
Thyme	Healing, peace, strength
Tobacco	banishes negativity, healing, purification
Verbena/vervain	Healing, protection, purification
Willow	Healing, protection
Witch hazel	Protection, healing of heartbreak

Well-Being Spell Runes

Rune	Magickal Qualities
Feoh	Energy, power, wealth, good fortune
Thorn	Fate, protection, overcoming obstacles
Yr	Remover of obstacles, protection, access to spirit world
Eolh	Protection, friendship, success
Sigel	The life force, health, vitality, luck
Tir	Facing difficulties, victory, bravery, return to health
Eoh	Change, adjustment, improvement

Well-Being Spell Timing

Phase of the Moon	Magickal Effect
Anytime, but Waxing to Full are best	Purifying or cleansing
Waning	Banishing

Moon's Astrological Sign

Cancer, Libra, or Pisces for emotional healing

Leo for strength

Time of Day

Sunrise to noon

Energy and Your Body

There are a number of energy centers in the body. You have probably located some of these vortexes intuitively. Eastern traditions describe seven main energy centers or chakras. The chakras, which are located along your spine, are pictured as swirling balls of energy. You can open and balance each chakra and its energy by meditating. You can also use spellcraft to hone, refine, and harness the energies in your body.

The Chakras

Number	Name	Location	Rulership
First	Root or base	Base of spine	Survival, basic physical needs
Second	Sacral or spleen	Just below navel	Sexuality, sensuality, emotions
Third	Solar plexus	Below the sternum	The will
Fourth	Heart	Center of chest	Giving and receiving love
Fifth	Throat	Base of throat	Communication
Sixth	Third eye	Middle of forehead	Psychic vision
Seventh	Crown	Top of head	Connection to spiritual world and the All

Your chakras are energy centers in your body through which the life force flows and contributes to your aura.

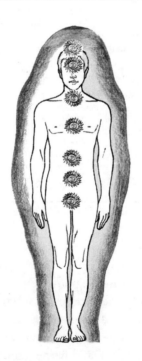

Here's an exercise you can do with a friend or with your children to help you get in touch with your chakras, or power centers, and their energies. You will need a large roll of butcher paper, some crayons, a bunch of old magazines, scissors, and a glue stick.

Unroll a length of butcher paper as long as your entire body and lie down on it. Have your friend trace the outline of your whole body.

Get up from the paper and spend a few moments contemplating your outline. On the image of your body, draw your energy centers. You may want to draw them as spirals, balls, or a clump of dots. Allow your intuition to guide you. Use whatever color feels right to you. Perhaps you know that the heart chakra is traditionally associated with the color green. But maybe your heart center feels more like gray. If that is the case, use the gray crayon and consider your color selection to be an important indicator of your psychic health. (Perhaps some heart-healing work is in order!) Now, move "outside the lines" and consider the quality and nature of the energy force that emanates from your body. What color is your aura? What shape? How far does it extend from the surface of your skin? What texture does it have? Draw your aura.

After you are done drawing your energy centers and aura, give your friend a turn, and draw his or her outline so your friend can fill in his or her energy centers and aura. Together, flip through the magazines. Again, let intuition be your guide. Pull out any images that feel healing or energizing to you. Look for ideals of your own health and well-being. You and your friend can help each other find images. When you have developed a good stack of images, you can both start a collage on and around the outline of your body.

When you are done creating your collages, you and your friend might spend some time talking about them and why you chose the images and colors you did. Later, you may want to write in your journal about what you have seen. Take a digital photograph or Polaroid snapshot of your collage and paste it into your Book of Shadows. Ask yourself what small change you can make today to bring you one step closer to your ideal of well-being. Repeat this exercise every few months and meditate on the changes you perceive in your chakra and aura energies from Solstice to Solstice.

> **Spellcasting**
>
> Amazonite is known to awaken the heart and throat chakras. Amethyst works on the crown chakra. Garnets are known to aid in opening and balancing the root and crown chakras. Aquamarine is an aid in balancing all seven chakras. So, when working with chakra energy, don't forget your gemstones and the aid they can bring you.

Creating Your Well-Being

One pattern in using magick to enhance well-being that seems to work is this—first perform a purification or a cleansing of negative energies. Follow that with a blessing to bring in positive energy. If you have a specific problem, such as stress, that you would like to do away with, use a banishing spell to make that stress go away. Feel free to mix and match techniques and, as always, you can adapt any of these spells to more precisely conform to your magickal intent based on your personal preferences and situation. To keep free of stress and negativity, cleanse and purify regularly. Think of this action as a psychic bath or tooth brushing, and make it a part of your daily hygiene routine.

Smudging: A Cleansing Technique

To purify an area, burn one of the following: sage, cedar, sandalwood, or myrrh. Cleansing your space with these plants in herb or incense form will help you feel calm and clear.

With your hands, waft the smoke toward your body or use a feather to direct the purifying vapors up and down your body. This is a good practice to maintain when you come home from a stressful workday. This ritual will help you let go of stress and will cleanse the spiritual impurities that have built up around you over the day. The smoke will also purify the energy of your home, and it smells nice, too.

Black Rock Spell

Get yourself a large, black rock—the bigger the better. Place it just inside the door to your home. Whenever you enter, reach out and touch the rock. Let it act as a negativity vacuum. When you touch it, feel the stone slurping up the bad stuff and say:

> Soak it up that I am free
>
> from the negative things I've brought with me.

This simply grounds the negative energy. Don't think of it as "giving" it to the rock. The rock simply sends the negative energy into the earth and neutralizes it.

Making Magick

A witch we used to know kept an apple doll by his front door. The doll served as a negativity purge for all who entered his house. He called her "Sickie." Upon entering the house, you picked up the doll, patted her on the head, and laid her respectfully on the table saying, "Sickie is dead." Then you could walk into the house free of any bad vibes or negative energies, because they were now grounded and neutralized.

Onion of Protection

To keep the energy in your space serene and healthful you may need a device to neutralize the effects of unpleasant company. Here's an easy and decorative solution.

Grow an onion in a pot. If you want, decorate the pot with runes. Or draw banishing symbols, such as widdershins (counterclockwise) spirals, on it. If you can get your onion to flower, all the better!

When you are expecting an unpleasant or difficult guest, place your onion by your door. It will absorb your guest's bad vibes and leave your space clean and clear.

Good Energy Mobile

Make a mobile out of crystals. Hang it in a window where the sun shines through it. The crystals and the light will raise the vibrational energy of your space and help keep you feeling energetic, spiritually uplifted, and, well, *good!*

Remember to cleanse the crystals with mugwort periodically because the crystals will soak in the energies around them—both good and bad. Mugwort, which is associated with the Air Element, is traditionally used for purifying crystals.

Out with the Old

A large part of personal well-being lies in your adaptability to change. Flexibility is key. Think of the strength of a tree that sways and bends in the wind, but does not break. If the tree did not bend, it would probably be pulled up—roots and all. Know that change is happening all the time—each year is a new beginning, each month is a new beginning, each moment, too, is a new beginning. Here's a cleansing spell to do at the end of the year (here we refer to the mundane calendar year) to help you let go and be ready for the new.

You will need your calendar from the year that just passed, a chunk of Dragon's blood incense, some charcoal, an incense burner, and a lighter.

Roll the incense across each page of your calendar. Allow it to absorb all the negativity, bad vibes, and unfortunate occurrences from the year.

Place the negatively loaded incense on the charcoal in your incense burner and light it. Let the sweet smell and the heat of the flame cleanse the negativity and consume it.

Egg Toss

This spell can help you get rid of stress, annoyances, aches and pains, or any other negative energy you have stored in your body. You will need an egg and access to outdoor space.

If you have aches and pains, gently roll the egg on the part of your body that is bothering you. Let it absorb any negative energy, stress, or upset.

If your feelings of discomfort are more generalized, roll the egg all over your body. And don't forget your head. Let it soak up anything that is bothering you.

> **CAUTION**
> **For Protection**
>
> If you are ill, see a doctor or other qualified health practitioner. Do not rely on magick alone to make you well. Remember, first do your work in the mundane world. Then work your magick.

Take your loaded egg outside and look for a tree. Focus on the egg and all that it is carrying as you look. When you find a suitable tree (one on your *own* property or in a forest or field—avoid neighbors' yards and public parks!), throw the egg against the tree. Then walk away without looking back.

Alternatively, you could roll a black stone egg over your body to absorb the negative. When you are done, cleanse the stone egg in saltwater.

Throw It Away

This is a magickal technique that you can use on a daily basis to keep you free and clear.

Every day find a small rock to carry in your pocket with you wherever you go. When a negative thought or feeling comes to you, touch the rock and let the feeling ground away from you and flow into the rock.

At the end of the day, dispose of the rock and all its accumulated energy by tossing it into a pond, river, stream, or down the storm sewer.

> **Words of Power**
>
> An **infusion** is a liquid that has been created by steeping or soaking herbs without boiling them. A **simple,** a term that comes from herbalism, is an infusion made from one single herb.

Well-Being Potions

Witches have long held knowledge of healing herbs. Herbs can help you stay centered, grounded, and feeling your best. An *infusion* or tea made of one type of herb is known as a *simple*. We first looked at using herbal teas in Chapter 12; here are some additional suggestions.

To help you feel centered, grounded, and stable in times of stress, try a simple infusion made from roots or bark. Common teas derived from these sources include licorice, ginger, and dandelion. If you think about it, it makes sense that a tea made from roots would help to make you feel more rooted and connected to the earth. So, too, barks such as sassafras and cinnamon are also a product of the earth and of trees, some of nature's most long-lived beings.

If you are feeling stressed-out or bogged-down, create a simple from cinnamon. Heat some water just to the boiling point. Turn off the heat and add a few cinnamon sticks. Allow the cinnamon to steep. As the potion steeps, the scent will cleanse the atmosphere and help you feel stable and secure.

Find a quiet place to drink your infusion. Imagine all the negativity, worry, and stress dropping away from you.

Blessings of the Mother

Teas and infusions made from flowers can help improve your mood. And we all know how a bad mood can impact your sense of well-being.

When you are feeling down or blue, consider chamomile, hibiscus, jasmine, calendula, and echinacea to raise yourself up. In addition, flower teas contain no sugar or artificial sweeteners. The more aromatic your flower tea drink, the better. You can use your sense of smell to help absorb the essence of the flower and all of its goodness.

Making a tea drink on regular basis when you are feeling low-spirited is a great and simple way to help yourself feel better and a move toward true well-being.

Other flower potions you'll want to be aware of are flower essences, in which the essence, or spirit, of the flower is preserved in purified water. Alcohol is often added as a preservative. You can buy these flower essence remedies at herbal shops or health-food stores, or make your own. To do this, fill a jar with purified water. This could be tap water that you have allowed to stand overnight to remove the chlorine, or bottled water if you prefer that for drinking. Make sure that you use flowers that are edible and ask them first if they will give of their spirit to help you. Put the flowers in the jar with the water and place them outside in the sunlight for one day. The sun and the flowers together do their magick. At the end of the day, strain out the plant

CAUTION **For Protection**

We know you know this, but we're going to say it again: Never ever ingest an herb unless you know for absolute certain that it is edible. If you have any doubt, don't do it. If you suffer from allergies or asthma, please be particularly careful with any unfamiliar plant.

material and the water remaining is the flower essence. If you wish to add a preservative you can dilute the pure water with brandy or vodka. You will only be using a few drops at a time, so there will never be much alcohol entering your body at once. Keep this essence in a sealed jar away from heat and light. Take a few drops of flower remedy in a small amount of water (or directly under your tongue) whenever you need a lift.

Blessed with Healing Waters

For this spell you are going to mix up some energized salt that you will then dissolve in water. You can also use these salts as part of your ritual bath.

You will need a cup of sea salt, a quarter of an ounce of myrrh oil, or a blend of myrrh and hemp oils. Mix the salt and oil together. Keep the mixture in a dark, airtight container. There are many other herbs that you can add to your salts to energize them, depending upon your magickal intent and your personal preferences. Consult your correspondence tables for help in selecting additions.

Light a blue, light green, or white candle.

Put a pinch of your energized salts in a small bowl of water. If you feel so inclined, you can place stones or crystals in the water, too. If you do this, you may want to add a drop of mullein oil to the water to purify the crystals and help you receive their benefits. Ground and center yourself. Use the water in the bowl to anoint your third eye area. When you anoint your forehead with the water, say:

> *Let me be inspired by the divine.*

Then anoint your temples with the water in the bowl and say:

> *May my dreams be useful and give me peace.*

Finally, anoint your heart chakra. As you do so, say:

> *May all of my workings, may all that I love be washed in divine spirit. So mote it be.*

If you like, stand barefoot in your bathtub. Pour the remaining water from the bowl over your feet and say:

> *May I walk a blessed path. So mote it be.*

Alternatively, when working this spell, you could use any other words of self-blessing that resonate for you.

Golden Vitality

Why not write your own spell to increase your energy? You'll want to use colors, such as gold, yellow, and orange, which are sacred to the Sun. Select an incense or essential oil that corresponds to the sun, such as *heliotrope*.

The stones garnet and citrine can help to lend you the vitality you need to get through difficult times. Obtain a few of these stones and make a necklace out of them. Inside your magick circle, anoint your necklace with heliotrope oil and dedicate it to the craft. Wear your necklace often and you will feel the warmth and power of the Sun all around you.

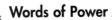

Words of Power

Heliotrope is a lovely, sweet-smelling, purple flower that gets its name from its tendency to turn toward the Sun. *Helio*, of course, is Greek for Sun.

Banish Stress

For your stress headache, you may want to take a pain reliever or try meditating. For the source of your headache, try this spell.

With a piece of string, moving widdershins (counterclockwise), lay out a spiral. Use string made from natural materials, not plastic or synthetics. As you stand in the center of the widdershins spiral, meditate on an object, place, or person that symbolizes the source of your stress. Close your eyes, breathe deeply through each of your chakra energy centers and focus on what you have seen in the spiral.

Turn yourself widdershins a few times and say:

> *Spiral down and 'round today*
>
> *Spiral, take this pain away.*

Fold the outside edges of your string spiral inward and scoop the whole thing up. Toss the string into a body of water. Allow the water to wash away the negative stress and cleanse your spirit and circumstance. (Remember, the string must be from a natural source, which will decompose in the environment without doing harm.) Do this on the Waning Moon to get rid of the source of your headache, as well as the headache itself.

To inspire positive mental energy, thought, and feeling, repeat this spell by laying the string in a deosil (clockwise) spiral to draw positive, healthful energy. As you stand in the deosil spiral and turn yourself deosil, meditate on drawing positive energy to you through the string and say:

Spiral up and 'round today

Spiral, bring health and good thoughts my way.

On the New Moon, take your string and bury it in the earth where it can absorb all of the earth's good nurturing growth energy.

Another String Spell

Wind a piece of string around your finger in a widdershins spiral. Allow the string to represent whatever it is that is bothering you. Make sure it is a symptom ("my head-ache" or "my tense back") and not a person. As you wind the string say:

By this cord _____ is bound.

Fill in the blank with your trouble of the moment. Then slide the spiral of string off your finger, take it outside, and bury it. As you do this, say:

Loose this _____ to the ground.

And again fill in the blank with your trouble of the moment.

The Least You Need to Know

- ◆ You can use spells and magickal techniques to help you deal with stress. Stress is known to cause many physical ailments.

- ◆ Spells and magickal techniques can help you dissipate or banish negative energies. Negative energy can make you feel bad and may eventually lead to disease.

- ◆ If you are ill or worried about your health, please see a doctor or other qualified medical practitioner.

- ◆ Herbal teas can help you feel good—physically, emotionally, and spiritually.

Part 5

For All Occasions

We think there's magick appropriate for just about *every* occasion. You may want to spread some positive energy around, or cleanse and prepare yourself for working magick with a ritual bath. We'll give you a lot of ritual bath spells in this part, as well as spells for deflecting negative energy. We'll talk about the circumstances under which you might want to break a spell (yours or someone else's) or use a binding spell, and we'll also learn more about the use of magick for protection.

Chapter 19

Blessings and Invocations

In This Chapter

- ◆ Spells and amulets for self-empowerment
- ◆ Blessing people and pets
- ◆ Infusing a place with positive energy
- ◆ Blessing special objects and situations
- ◆ Traditional greetings and leave-takings
- ◆ A call to the Gods: invocations

Blessing people, places, situations, and things is the most basic kind of magick there is and probably the kinds of spells witches do the most. You, too, can work magick to empower yourself and send positive energy into the world.

You can create a spell of blessing for yourself, for a new child, for a loved one, or even for a pet. And you can turn your greetings and leave-takings into blessings, as well. We'll show you how to do such blessings in this chapter.

Self-Empowerment

Empowering yourself, whether before walking into a situation where you might need to draw on all your power or just as a daily affirmation, can be done simply or as a complete dedication ritual. We recommend you do a daily blessing for yourself each morning and evening—it's a great way to open and close your day!

Here's a blessing you can do first thing in the morning. It doesn't take long to do this, so if you think you don't have time, think again. Give yourself an extra 10 or 15 minutes in the morning for this blessing and see if it doesn't change your attitude. Cathy (who's not a Wiccan, but works with the natural energies in spellwork) does this most mornings, and it leaves her feeling centered and powerful—ready to start living in the chaos of her day!

Choose a candle for its color significance: white for peace, blue for hope and tranquility, pink for harmony and nurturing. (Cathy likes to work with a blue candle, though sometimes she chooses green—abundance, growth—when she needs a boost.) Light your candle and sit in front of it quietly, meditatively. Focus on the candle or close your eyes if you like, and feel the energy and power flow within you. When you feel ready, chant:

> *Goddess, in this morning new,*
>
> *Let me find my power through you.*
>
> *Lift me, fill me, let me see,*
>
> *My life is joyous, calm, and free.*
>
> *Give me peace, my strength assure,*
>
> *I stand this day a being pure.*

When you feel it is time, extinguish the candle and begin your day with a peaceful countenance and a clear mind.

You can boost this spell a bit by anointing the candle with oils for peace or cleansing—whatever you need to get your day flowing more smoothly (*not* coffee!), or carving a rune or other symbol into the candle with the same purpose in mind, before you burn the candle. Jasmine or tuberose oils are good for peace; Cathy sometimes carves the rune Beorc into her candle, but often will simply use a plain candle, which seems to work well for her. Do what works for you, what feels right, and what you have the time for. This should become a treasured morning ritual, not another morning chore.

If you need a quick morning blessing, or can't spare the time for candles and meditation, simply go to your altar and chant:

As I will so mote it be,

Today I shall be strong and free.

Change the chant to work in those qualities you feel you most need that day.

If you have the time, or you feel you really need to stop and refocus yourself, you can work this blessing at other times of the day as well, perhaps on your lunch break. You can memorize one of the previous chants (you probably will after a few days)—or write your own—and say it to yourself while sitting in your office or riding the train into work or home as a quick reminder of your power and place in the world. You can also rework the spell as one you say before meals or before you go to bed at night, so that you end your day in as centered a place as you began it.

A more complex self-empowerment spell might involve casting a sacred magick circle, calling up all the quarters, ancestors, and deities of your choice, and asking them for help in feeling your power in whatever area or way you feel it is needed. This can be more time-consuming and may not be practical for you on a daily basis, but you might want to try incorporating it into your magickal spellworkings on a monthly basis.

You might also want to make a self-empowerment amulet that you carry with you. Start with a pouch made of a purple or red fabric. Choose a color you like, or choose one based on its correspondences; psychic power and strength are good ones. Next, get together the items you will place inside the pouch. You may want to include some herbs (marigold, mugwort, or thyme) or stones (aquamarine, garnet, or quartz); a small object with which you feel emotionally connected and strengthened would be good here as well (a ring or a key, perhaps). Place the items in your pouch and tie the pouch closed with a cord of silver or gold.

Now bless the amulet in a magick circle, asking for the strength and blessing of each of the four Elements:

> *Element of Fire, hear me this hour,*
>
> *Share with me your strength, your power.*
>
> *Bless this amulet to strengthen me,*
>
> *As I will, so mote it be.*
>
> (Repeat for each Element.)

Carry your amulet with you as a reminder of your inner strength.

Making Magick

Preparing for an important job interview, Aurora created a "houndstooth" amulet (fabric for power in the workplace, often used for suits!) with appropriate herbs and stones. She sewed a feather to represent Thoth (the Egyptian scribe god) on the outside, kept the amulet in her purse, and felt confident. She got the job!

Sending Out Positive Energy Through Blessings

There may be times when you'd like to be able to send positive energy to another person. You may know someone who is ill or in need of support, either emotionally or physically, or perhaps you simply want to send good vibes to someone you know and care for on a special day or any day. Always have the person's permission, of course, and then go to work with some of these spells, sending positive energy their way.

Blessing Children

This spell is frequently done in a ceremony shortly after a child is born and is often combined with a baby shower at which useful gifts are given. Aurora has seen this spell worked with the child in a tub of warm water strewn with flower petals—roses and lavender are good choices for their beauty, scents, and correspondences. Everyone attending the ceremony takes a turn coming forward and giving his or her blessing or wish to the child while scooping some water over the child with his or her hands. Take precautions for the infant's safety and comfort when doing the blessing this way: The water should be shallow and the infant should be held by an adult (or perhaps both parents). Check that the temperature is warm enough to be comfortable, but not too hot.

Alternatively, you can do a blessing for a child by placing a small potted tree in the center of a room, and again, each person takes a turn coming forward, saying their blessing or wish for the child, and pouring a bit of water from their drinking cup onto the tree. The tree can later be planted for the child outside, in their yard or elsewhere. It's optimal if the child can visit the tree as it and he or she grows, but this isn't always possible in today's mobile culture. Plant the tree in fertile ground and envision it growing as the child does. Some people save the placenta after the birth of their child and bury it under a tree—that symbolic act could become a part of this blessing. You can choose the type of tree based on its

For Protection

As the guardian of your children, you can work magick on their behalf without their knowledge or consent while they are too young to give it. For other peoples' children, however, you should always have the permission of the child's parent and/or the child before working magick.

Spellcasting

The Celtic Tree Calendar is based on the lunar year and includes 13 months, each named for a tree. The Celtic Tree year begins after Winter Solstice (Yule). The calendar was reintroduced by Robert Graves in *The White Goddess* (Noonday/FSG, 1948). See Appendix B for more information about lunar calendars.

correspondences (see the following table) as well as the climate in your region, should you decide to plant it outside.

Trees and Their Magickal Correspondences

Tree	Correspondences
Alder	Beauty, protection
Almond	Divination, love, luck, money, prosperity, wisdom
Apple	Happiness, healing, love, prosperity, vitality
Ash	Healing, protection, purification, wisdom
Aspen	Healing, intuitive power
Beech	Prosperity, stability
Birch	Healing, new beginnings, protection, purification
Blackthorn	Unexpected change
Cedar	Healing, longevity, prosperity, purification, strength
Cherry	Love, new beginnings
Chestnut	Love
Cottonwood	Healing, love, protection
Cypress	Immortality, mourning
Dogwood	Communication, protection, social abilities, stability
Elder	Cycle of life, protection
Elm	Love, protection, purification, wisdom
Fig	Fertility, love, strength
Fir	Fertility, flexibility, immortality, rebirth
Hawthorn	Creativity, divination, fertility, hope, protection
Hazel	Fertility, luck, wisdom
Hemlock	Empowerment
Holly	Courage, protection, strength
Juniper	Protection
Laurel	Ambition, immortality, victory
Lemon	Divination, healing
Linden	Love, luck, protection
Maple	Divination, love, prosperity
Mulberry	Protection, strength, wisdom

continues

Trees and Their Magickal Correspondences (continued)

Tree	Correspondences
Oak	Courage, healing, independence, prosperity, strength, wisdom
Olive	Healing, money, peace, prosperity, protection, security
Orange	Generosity, love
Palm	Strength, success
Peach	Divination, love
Pear	Comfort, luck, prosperity
Pine	Creativity, fertility, healing, hope, prosperity, purification
Poplar	Courage, prosperity
Sequoia	Longevity, wisdom
Sycamore	Communication, growth, love, peace
Walnut	Fertility, healing, mental acuity, protection
Willow	Childbirth, freedom, healing
Yew	Transformation

To choose a tree for a child's blessing, you can look at tree correspondences (such as in the previous table) or you might try a divination: Write tree names on slips of paper and place them face down on a flat surface. Have one of the child's parents or a chosen representative—or the child if he or she is old enough—meditate on the child's spirit and select one of the slips of paper. The tree selected will represent the child's spirit at his or her blessing.

Another blessing for a new baby is to give the child the stone they (through their mother) had pulled out of the pouch during their prebirth stone divination (see Chapter 11). The stone could be given as is, or perhaps made into a rattle or wand for the child to use at an appropriate age and have as a reminder of his or her path in this life.

If you want to do blessings for older children, you might try involving them in the process. Work some kitchen magick with them! Bake some honey cookies with them and chant together as you work, asking the Goddess to bless them and keep their natural energy alive and well:

> *Blessings on this lovely child,*
>
> *Protect her (him) well, and keep her (him) wild.*

Serve the honey cookies together as a blessing at a celebration for the child—a blessing or a birthday or other celebration—and share the blessing with everyone present. The following simple recipe for honey cookies can be modified to suit your taste and your pantry!

Honey Cookies

- ◆ 1 cup butter or margarine (2 sticks)
- ◆ ½ cup sugar
- ◆ 4 TB. honey
- ◆ ½ tsp. baking soda
- ◆ 2½ cups flour

Cream together butter or margarine, sugar, and honey. Add baking soda to honey mixture. Slowly add the flour and mix well. Chill dough in refrigerator or freezer for about two hours. Roll out dough and cut cookies (if you wish to follow Wiccan tradition, shape them into small crescent moons!), adding sprinkles or other decorations if you like. Bake on a greased cookie sheet for 20 to 25 minutes at 300 degrees until golden. Makes approximately four dozen cookies.

> **Spellcasting**
>
> For any blessing that you create, you might write it out like a letter or a poem on nice paper. You can then present the blessing to the person (if it's for a person) or place it in your Book of Shadows. If you choose to give the blessing as a gift, roll it up and tie it with a ribbon of suitable color.

Blessing Others

Now for some spells of blessing for other adults in your life. Remember, if you don't have the person's permission to work magick for him or her, you aren't practicing ethical magick.

Perhaps you have a friend who is going on a trip and you'd like to give your blessing to her. This can be done by simply sharing your intention verbally and physically: Give her a hug and say, "May your travels be enlightening, may your journey be safe." You could also give her a blessed stone or talisman. For a stone, simply select the stone based on its correspondences (citrine, hematite, mica, or quartz) or your feeling about what you should give the person. A good choice may also be a found stone. Within a magick circle, ask for the blessing of the four Elements on the stone and ask the Elements to bless the person for whom you are creating this talisman:

> *Element of Earth, bless this stone,*
>
> *Empower it to carry your blessing home*
>
> *To its recipient [person's name], make her strong,*
>
> *Bless her and keep her all the days long.*
>
> (Repeat for each of the Elements.)

Now take the blessed stone and give it to the person you want to bless. You can place the stone in a cloth pouch, if you like (choose your cloth based on your preference or the recipient's or on color correspondences).

You can *write* a blessing for someone as well. Think of this as a magickal letter or poem to the person. We've included a sample here. You can do one like this, in rhyme and free verse, or entirely in prose, as a letter would appear.

> *May Earth bless you wherever you go,*
>
> *May the blessings of Air always you know.*
>
> *May Fire bless you in many ways,*
>
> *May the blessings of Water color each of your days.*
>
> *Lord and Lady walk beside you on your path,*
>
> *Your spirit shall soar as you take your place,*
>
> *Your gift shall show through in all your actions,*
>
> *The blessings of all on your every step.*

Blessing Animals

We know that there are many people who love their animal friends at least as much as they do their human friends. If you're one of us, you might want to bless your animal friends. Though we often call animals our pets, they are generally much wiser spirits than we humans, and as such they can make their own choices about magick. You can talk to your pet about working magick on his or her behalf, and though you're not certain to get an answer you will readily understand, you can't force magick on an animal either. If you're trying to work a blessing for an animal and the animal will not cooperate—he won't sit still or come into the room where you want him to be—take this as a sign of the animal's refusal of your magickal help, and don't press your magick onto him. That said, here's a blessing you might try for your animal friends.

Create an herbal rub for the animal's coat. You might select herbs representative of the act of blessing and strengthening (chamomile or thyme) or choose one herb to represent each of the four Elements, based on their Yin/Yang energy: thyme for Water, sage for Air, birch leaves or alfalfa for Earth, fennel for Fire. Just make sure the herbs you choose are nontoxic and that the solution you create will not be abrasive to the animal's fur or skin! (For example, full-strength essential oils will burn human skin, so they surely will also damage your pet's delicate skin as well! When in doubt, consult a holistic veterinarian in your area before using an herbal rub for your pet.) Steep the herbs in water, and when the liquid has cooled, brush it on the animal's coat like a wash, chanting as you brush:

Diana, bless this animal fully well,

In your love and strength to dwell.

We chose Diana for this chant because she is the Goddess associated with dogs. You might choose another deity based on an animal correspondence—Bast for a cat, for example; or Epona for a horse—or on your personal connection with the deity. You could also speak simply to the Goddess or God. Make this a calming, meditative time for you, the animal, and the deity.

You could also create a small talisman of some sort, using a crystal or a small pouch with herbs (again, make sure they are nontoxic and nonabrasive) that you attach to the animal's collar. You could also incorporate flea-repelling qualities of the herbs for this or the wash; try eucalyptus or pennyroyal for this purpose. (Be very careful with pennyroyal; it is toxic when ingested.)

Blessing Places

Throughout your life, you'll likely live in and visit very many places. Sometimes you may want to bless a place, infusing it with positive energy. You can use smudge, incense, or ritual "sweeping" for this purpose. A house blessing is a good example. You might do this for your own home. We're imagining it as a gift for someone else (whose permission you have to bring them a house blessing!).

Bring to the new homeowner/dweller a plant or some food. We like bringing food; part of the magick is then sharing it with the recipient!

CAUTION — For Protection

Don't confuse blessing a space with creating a sacred space. While you are bringing positive energy into the space when you bless it, you are not focusing your energy on making it a crossroads between this world and the spirit world. As always, it's all in the intention.

Bread you have baked is a good choice, or perhaps those honey cookies we used in the earlier child's blessing. Share the food with the homeowner/dweller while burning some incense to cleanse the home (perhaps myrrh).

You can also bless a place by simply sending out your intention, using your finger while moving around the space in a deosil (clockwise) direction and chanting:

> *All negativity be gone, only love may stay.*

Blessing Objects and Situations

There may be special objects you wish to fill with positive energy or situations that would benefit from such a boost—can you think of one that wouldn't? Here's how to get the positive energy flowing their way.

In the case of objects—perhaps you are an artist and you want to bless your brushes, or you want to bless your wedding rings before your wedding—you can take the object to your altar if you have the time and bless it with all four Elements: by Earth, by Fire, by Water, by Air (holding the object over your pentacle or a plant, your candle, your bowl or cup of water, and your incense).

If the object is too large to bring to your altar—your car, perhaps?—you can bless it with smudge or incense, or sprinkle a blessing herb on it (try sage, lavender, or sandalwood), chanting as you do so:

> *Blessed be this _____,*
>
> *May its energy be pure.*

You can also do this to bless an object when you're away from your altar or haven't time for the full blessing from the four Elements. Keep one of the purifying herbs in your medicine pouch, so you'll have it at the ready, should you need to bless an object on the fly.

You have undoubtedly been in difficult, uncomfortable situations, and it's possible that a surge of positive energy could turn things around—it certainly wouldn't *hurt*. Light a candle and call some positive energy or the blessing of a personal deity or spirit guide into the situation, whether it's a disagreement, a miscommunication, or something else. The candle will serve to focus the individuals and make them better listeners. The blessings of the spirit world will come into the situation or the conversation. Let the positive energy work to bring everyone involved to a more peaceful state of being, and then be ready to approach the situation again from a new vantage point.

If you find yourself in a physical place and suddenly *feel* uncomfortable, this situation might be ameliorated by quickly casting a magick circle around yourself and your surroundings with the deosil (clockwise, to raise positive energy) motion of your finger, mentally envisioning a protective circle coming up and surrounding you with protection. When you're in this safe place, take deep breaths, and if you feel the need, ask for the blessing and aid of the Goddess or another deity. Don't forget to take your circle down when you are ready, retracing the circle in a widdershins (counterclockwise, to disperse the energy) direction with your finger.

Greetings and Leave-Takings

The traditional leave-taking among Wiccans is "Merry meet, and merry part, and merry meet again." The simple phrase "Merry meet" can be used for a greeting, and "Blessed Be" is used for both greeting and leave-taking. These are simple ways of sharing a blessing with those you meet and those you leave behind.

A fabulous way to greet friends and welcome them into your home is to invite them in to tea. Prepare a special tea of blessing for the occasion. This might be something you make yourself, using the herbal correspondences as a guide, though you can also purchase a tea at the grocery or health-food store that includes some of the essential herbs and may be tastier and quicker to prepare than your home brew. While you steep the tea, whether it's homemade or store-bought, focus on your intention of welcoming and blessing your guests. This is another good occasion for sharing food you have prepared, if you have the time to work a little more kitchen magick!

CAUTION

For Protection

While you can call for a deity's help in any situation, a formal invocation should only be done within the protection of a magick circle. This creates the setting where you and the deity can coexist without you getting blasted by excess energy, and without excess energy getting loose where you might have trouble containing it later. It's like inviting someone over for a formal dinner: You want to make sure the dining room is ready.

Invocations

Just as you can create blessings for just about any purpose, you should also create your own invocations. These are your special calls to the power of the Gods. Invocations are used in many different circumstances, and while you can use those you find here and elsewhere, you will soon find that what comes to mind as you are going along will suit your purpose best. Remember that your invocation isn't just a song or poem to the Goddesses and Gods, it's a method of calling a spirit into a magick circle—politely and pleasantly asking them to come. While it is a way of honoring the spirits and asking for their help, your invocation should also make it clear whom you are calling and for what purpose.

> ### Making Magick
>
> One of Aurora's spiritual teachers, Sobonfu Somé, said that if she found anyone writing an invocation down on a piece of paper, she would tear it up and burn it! Invocations should come from the heart and should also involve your soul and spirit, while focusing on the purpose of the ritual. Talk to the spirit you are invoking as you would an elder that you respect, speaking what your heart has to say at the moment. You *can* write it down, but it needn't be rehearsed.

Here are a few sample invocations that we might use in a magick circle. Cernunnos is often called as the consort to the Goddess, and Diana might be called (as we mentioned earlier) to help with blessing animals.

Invocation to Cernunnos:

> *I call to Cernunnos, you who rule over the wildwood and the wild creatures there! Great God, Cernunnos, we have need of your wildness; come, bring your lessons of the forest, lessons of the hunt. Come, Cernunnos. Welcome, Cernunnos!*

Invocation to Diana:

> *Silver Lady of the Silver Moon! I call to you, Diana of the hounds! By your shining orb and your hunting dogs, come! Bless this animal before me, as you yourself are blessed by your connection with all dogs.*

In *The Spiral Dance* by Starhawk (see Appendix B), you will find many invocations to the Goddess, the God, and to both powers. The invocations vary by context—the occasion of the invocation—and Starhawk recommends the use of music and chanting for group invocations. Look to this resource for inspiration when creating your own invocations.

The Least You Need to Know

- ◆ Blessings are a commonly used type of spell.
- ◆ You can bless people, places, things, and even situations.

◆ A blessing for a child or baby can be done communally at a baby shower or other celebration.

◆ You can carry purifying herbs with you for blessing objects on-the-go.

◆ Greetings and leave-takings are also ways of sharing a blessing with others.

◆ You can create your own invocations for use in your magick circle.

Chapter 20

Ritual Baths

In This Chapter

- ◆ What a ritual bath can do for you
- ◆ Recipes for purifying baths
- ◆ Short on time? Take a purifying shower
- ◆ Recipes for enhancing baths
- ◆ Ritual baths especially for children

A ritual bath will cleanse your body and your mind. It will relax and focus you, preparing your mind and purifying your body for magickal work. While it's not necessary to take a ritual bath every time you work magick, it can really help get your mind on a more magickal plane (we include some quicker versions of the ritual bath, if you're pressed for time).

You can also make your ritual bath a spell in itself, working an enhancing bath spell to increase just about anything—your beauty, prosperity, or intuitive power. In this chapter, we'll talk about various notions, potions, and powders, giving formulas and spells for ritual baths of all natures and purpose.

Cleansing Both Body and Mind

We mentioned ritual baths back in Chapter 6 as a step in your dedication ritual (that was a purifying bath). Here we'll go into greater detail about ritual baths, and we'll give you the recipes for baths for many purposes.

There are two types of ritual baths: purification and enhancement. A purifying bath is the type you do prior to a ceremony or important magickal working. Enhancing baths are for everything else: abundance, healing, or prosperity. In general, enhancing baths are best done during the Waxing to Full Moon. Purifying baths can be done before any working; the timing of the working is most important.

One thing about ritual baths: This type of magick is all about *you*. You can't do a ritual bath to enhance your mother's prosperity, though you can help her prepare such a bath for herself. When you prepare a ritual bath for yourself, the magick you work will be for you alone.

Preparing Your Bath

The main purpose of a ritual bath is to alter your consciousness and help shift your mind into a magickal place. The preparations for the bath are very important, as this is time for you to focus your mind on the task at hand. You will need to spend some time moving your bathroom from the realm of the mundane to the magickal. You'll enjoy your bath more if the tub is clean, so you might want to take care of that task beforehand. We suggest candles and incense for use with many of the ritual baths. These not only assist with the magickal intent of the bath but, as you know, they also help to move your mind from the mundane and can do the same to transform your bathroom. You can dress the candles with corresponding oils and herbs if you like, to give the spell of the bath an extra boost.

For Protection

Be extremely careful when burning candles in the bathroom. Place them on a solid, steady surface and make sure they are in something that catches the wax if they drip. Always be sure to extinguish them when you leave the bathroom.

Bath spaces were common in many ancient temples, and we want you to create a temple in your own bathroom. The use of candles, incense, herbs, stones, and oils will engage all of your senses (and include all four Elements: Air is represented by the incense and the scents from the bath, Fire by the lit candles and the heat of the bath, Water by the bath itself, and Earth by the herbs, oils, and stones used in the bath) in the magick of the bath.

Preparing Yourself

Once you have the bath set up, your candles lit, your herbs or oils at the ready, and your bathwater running (hot but not *too* hot), look into your bathroom mirror in the candlelight and smile at yourself. Before you get into the bathtub, touch your forehead (your third eye) and chant an affirmation:

> *I am creating change in myself.*
>
> *I am changed.*

Or try this one for a ritual bath to enhance your relationships:

> *I am creating health in my relationships.*
>
> *I have healthy relationships.*

The important thing about this affirmation is, again, to change your mindset and get yourself ready for magick. You can create one for whatever your intention, using this model. The language is an important step in visualizing the change you are making in yourself with the ritual bath: You start by saying you are *creating* change, and follow by saying you *are* changed.

Ritual Baths for Purification

The ritual bath for purification is the one you will do prior to important magickal workings and ceremonies, such as your dedication ceremony. You can perform this ritual bath before working any magick, if you would like to do so (and you have the time). This bath purifies you spiritually and physically. It will help you relax, focus, and make the shift in consciousness necessary for working magick. Ideally, you will take the bath just prior to entering your magick circle; this is not always practical, however, and if you are traveling to meet others, try to keep your mind centered in the time between your bath and working magick.

Begin by laying out the robe or clothing you will wear after your bath for the ceremony, ritual, or magick. Now start some incense burning in your bathroom—try sandalwood. Light three candles for the Maiden, Mother, and Crone aspects of the Goddess: red, black, and white. Or use whatever color of candle you feel represents your intention for the work you are doing. Run your bathwater and pour a small handful of sea salt into the water. Put some purifying and meditative essential oils in your bathwater: perhaps sandalwood, orange, or myrrh, or a pleasing combination of these and/or other oils. If you wish to use herbs in your bath, basil, chamomile, dragon's blood, and sage are all good choices. Finally, place three quartz crystals in the water, as they will enhance your intuitive abilities.

Before getting into the bath, do a self-blessing, anointing your *power points*: crown, forehead, throat or mouth, heart, solar plexus, navel, and lower abdomen. Dip your hand in the bathwater before each anointing, then chant:

Words of Power

Power points are another name for chakras, the seven energy points in the body.

Blessed is my body,

Blessed is my spirit.

Blessed is my world,

Blessed are my works.

Now you're ready to get into the tub. Relax and meditate during your bath. Feel the negative energy and tension slip away from your body as you grow stronger and your senses become more aware. As you soak, chant again:

Bathe my body and my soul,

Wash me clean and make me whole.

Spellcasting

You may not wish to invest in a lot of oils and herbs for use in the bath. The one ingredient you should have on hand is sea salt, which purifies and cleanses.

You can envision this bath as opening you up to allow in the messages of the spirit, which is what you will be doing in your ritual. Stay in the bath as long as you like, and when you are prepared, physically, mentally, and spiritually, step out and get ready to work magick.

Ritual Showers!

That's right, you *can* take a ritual shower for purification, if need be. We don't want you to think that you have to have the time for a ritual bath every time you have serious magick to work, though if you have the time, a bath will definitely be more relaxing. While it's a bit off the official Wiccan path, we encourage you to take a ritual shower when you don't have the time for a bath.

Do a self-blessing while you're in the shower. Meditate on the sound of the falling water and listen for the voice of the Goddess. Say to her, *"Let me be a conduit of your wisdom."*

When you get out of the shower, anoint your forehead and feet (or all of your power points) with a purifying, healing oil such as cinnamon, heliotrope, or orange. Now you're ready to work magick.

If you think about it, the shower you take every morning is also a ritual shower for enhancement: enhancing your beauty, cleanliness, and fortitude for the day!

Making Magick

Here is a purifying option that works well when you are working magick with a group of people, each of whom may have already had their ritual bath. This is especially nice if you're working magick outside. Fill a shallow basin with water and add a bit of sea salt to it. Place the basin near where you will work magick, and before entering the magick circle, each (barefoot) participant steps through the water in the basin. Inside the circle, one participant greets them: *"Blessed are you, child of the Goddess. Blessed are your feet that carry you on this path."*

Ritual Baths for Enhancement

Here we include the recipes for magickal baths to enhance prosperity, healing, intuitive power, and more.

Psychic Healing

If you have been exposed to some negative energy and you feel a need to remove this energy from your body, set up the following bath during a Waning Moon (good for banishing!): Light white and/or light blue candles in the bathroom. Run your bath and place a black stone in the tub (such as obsidian). This stone will absorb the negative energy. Create a bath oil using lavender oil and add a teaspoon of purifying sea salt to the bath water. Climb in, relax, focus on the stone, and visualize the negative energy streaming from your body into the stone.

Chant quietly to yourself:

Wash away, wash away, negative energy,

From this negativity I will now be free.

Wash away, wash away, purify me,

My body is cleansed, so mote it be.

After your bath, remove the stone. If possible, take it to a body of water (a lake, a river, or the ocean) and throw it in! You want to send the negative energy away from you—if you can't throw the stone in a body of water, you might wrap it in a white cloth and ask a friend to dispose of it for you. The friend can then bury it or throw it in the garbage. You don't need to know where it is, and you won't likely cross its path again.

Improving a Relationship

This is a ritual bath to enhance your attractiveness and charisma, and to help you attract affectionate relationships (romantic relationships or friendships). Light a pink candle in the bathroom. Place a few drops of rose oil in your bath; or to make a bath oil, place the rose oil in a carrier oil and then put this in your bath. Place carnelian and rose quartz stones in the bathtub. Float a handful of rose petals in the water.

> **Spellcasting**
>
> If you need to, you can substitute Epsom salts for sea salt in your ritual baths. Note that only sea salt purifies and cleanses; Epsom salts will simply cleanse.

Climb into the tub and steep yourself in the water. Relax and enjoy the scents and sensations until you feel that you are done.

Enhancing Intuitive Power

We recommend that you do psychic work in a magick circle. You can cast one around the perimeter of your bathroom for this ritual bath, which you can do anytime, though you might want to try it prior to working magick. To prepare for the bath, have one black and one white candle burning, perhaps on either side of the tub or sink. Burn cinnamon incense in the bathroom while your bath is running and place a few drops of patchouli or jasmine oil in the bath. You can also place some sage plant in the water or use some dried sage in a cotton bag. Once you're in the bath, relax and focus, then chant:

> *With this water I do call,*
>
> *My connection to the All.*
>
> *And wisdom of the realms divine,*
>
> *I call to me, and make thee mine.*

When you're ready, get out of the tub.

As a quick alternative to a bath for this ritual, you might want to do a rinse: With the same candles lit on either side of the bathroom sink, run water in the sink and place a few drops of cinnamon oil in the water. Rinse your face and hands with the refreshing water. Push your hair back from your face with your wet hands, and as you do so, look at your face in the mirror. Say, *"I am a magickal being."* Watch your face change in the candlelight. Say, *"I am connected, I am divine."*

Circle your fingers around three times in the sink, watching the water ripple. As you feel yourself becoming magickal, say the previous chant (for the bath). Leave the bathroom when you're ready.

A New Venture

This simple bath is a good one to try when you're starting a new project or dedicating yourself to a new course of study. It will raise your sense of personal power.

Use a few drops of patchouli oil in the bath or burn some patchouli incense. Create an herbal bath using mugwort and sage and place three quartz crystals in the bath. Climb in and soak!

Protection

To make a ritual bath for protection, light one or more black or blue candles in your bathroom. Choose herbs for their protective correspondence (eucalyptus, lavender, lilac, peony, or rosemary), place them in a cotton bag, and put the bag in your bathwater. You might burn some myrrh incense and add a few drops of hyacinth, lilac, or neroli oil to the water.

Climb in and relax, focusing on the warmth of the water. Feel the water enveloping your body. Feel secure in the water, then chant:

> *Element of water, protect me.*
>
> *Keep me well and let me be.*

For Protection

You may decide to play soothing music while in the bath, and if you do, please be certain that the equipment you use to play the music is on a stable surface away from the bathtub and any standing water to avoid the risk of shock or electrocution. And *never* touch any electrical appliance while you are in the water or still wet.

Spellcasting

Many occult stores (and stores on the Internet—see Appendix B) offer prepackaged bath oils and bath salts for various purposes, from prosperity to health. We offer recipes for making your own, which can be less expensive but more time-consuming. If you do a lot of baths for a particular purpose, you might want to purchase bath salts to have on hand for this.

Make me strong and I will know,

Your power inside of me will grow.

When you're ready, climb out of the bath, strong and protected.

Prosperity

While preparing this bath to enhance your prosperity, light some sandalwood incense or peel an orange—it's a refreshing and cleansing scent, and you can eat the orange while you're in the tub! Light a green candle and put a few drops of an oil for prosperity in your bathwater: patchouli or basil, perhaps. Also add a few drops of green food coloring to the water and have a green bath! While you're preparing the bath, focus on your intention of enhancing your prosperity. Place a stone such as jade or aventurine in the tub, or substitute a coin for the stone.

Anoint your forehead (the third eye) with the bathwater before you climb in and chant:

I am creating prosperity.

I am working toward abundance.

I am living an abundant life.

Now get into the bath and luxuriate in the richness of the bath and of your life. Feel the abundance flow into you. When you are ready, get out of the bath and reap the rewards of your abundant life!

Spellcasting

When using dried herbs in the bath, you might want to place the herbs in a cotton cloth, like a cotton tea bag, or tie them in an old nylon stocking before placing them in your bathwater. Having loose herbs float in the water can be annoying—you may end your bath feeling less than clean, with herbs stuck to your body and hair—and using a cloth bag will cut your cleanup time immensely! You can also boil the herbs in water on your stovetop and then strain out the herbs. Add the remaining herbal infusion to your bathwater.

Attraction

This bath will help you attract what you want—we'll use the example of good relationships. Before you prepare your bath, prepare some crossed sticks: Take two small sticks and clean them (you will float these in your bath, so rinse them off first!), and then cross them and tie them together in the shape of an X. Make two or three of these and place them in the bathwater. You can look at a correspondence table for trees (see Chapter 19), and if you have them at your disposal, almond or olive might be good choices. Otherwise, use what you have in your yard or your local park—pick up a few sticks from the ground.

Orange is a color associated with drawing things to you, be it material gain, people, or something else. So for this bath, we want you to use food coloring again and change the color of your bath. Put one or two drops of orange food coloring in the bathwater. You might also burn some incense, light an orange or pink candle, and put a few drops of essential oil in your bathwater (try tangerine or violet).

Now you are ready to get into your bath. While soaking, chant to yourself:

> *I am attracting good friends into my life,*
>
> *My relationships are harmonious, without strife.*
>
> *I am the kind of person who calls these people to me,*
>
> *I have healthy relationships and live my life fully.*

When you're feeling empowered and are ready, you can get out of the bath.

Be careful when using essential oils in your bath. A few drops go a long way—your water will be very smelly if you use too much oil. When undiluted, essential oils can burn the skin, so don't apply the oil directly to your skin. If you use essential oils, wear gloves when working with them to protect your skin. We recommend using a carrier oil. Unscented almond oil and hemp oil make good carrier oils for your essential oils in the making of bath oils.

Forgiveness

This ritual bath will help you to forgive yourself—perhaps you've done something you wish you hadn't (or haven't done something you should). Use this bath to release your guilt and free yourself from the pain of this situation. This is a very restful and soothing bath.

Light a light blue candle in your bathroom and make an herbal bath using rosemary and sage (place dried herbs in a cotton bag or use up to 6 inches of a live plant). Put 1 teaspoon of sea salt in the water. Place an aquamarine stone in your bath and chant:

> *With this bath I wash away*
>
> *The trials and worries of this day.*

Goddess cleanse and purify me,

Forgive me now and wash me clean.

Climb in and have a relaxing soak. This bath is great for healing the injury of arguments.

Ritual Baths for Children

You can work magick for your own children; why not try a magical bath? We used green food coloring in our ritual bath to enhance prosperity, above, and food coloring can be great fun for children. You can use herbs and oils as well, though you have to be more careful with children and make sure there's nothing floating in the bath a small child might try to eat.

Calming

To calm your children before bedtime, try a few drops of blue food coloring in the bath water (more or less to get the color you or your child prefer). Add a few drops of lavender oil to the bathwater for its soothing scent.

Energizing and Affirming

There may be times when you want to energize and boost the self-esteem of your child or children (after an illness, perhaps). This is a great bath for two children together, and can be fun for siblings. A note on this activity: The children should be old enough to understand that this is a special event—they cannot write on themselves whenever they want!

Start by adding a few drops of orange food coloring to the bathwater (you could also use red, if your child prefers). Add a few drops of tangerine oil to the water.

Now for the fun: If your bathroom is warm enough, get the children naked and give them a few watercolor markers (use orange to match the bathwater, or green to represent health and growth perhaps. Help the children do affirmations on their bodies, being thankful for their body parts, their strength, and their health. Ask the children to find their (left or right) hand and put a symbol on it. The symbol might be a crescent Moon for an older child; a simple circle, line, or other mark for a smaller child. If the child is old enough, choose symbols for their meaning (the crescent Moon for growth, a plant for health, etc.), and the writing of the symbols will become an affirmation for the child. For younger children, you might have to add the affirmation to your instruction (find your strong arm, your happy heart, etc.). Once they are finished, they climb into the warm bath and wash the markers away.

A variation on this activity for two children is to have them write on one another's backs, drawing symbols or words for the child on whom they are drawing and for how they feel about that child. You can guide them in this, though after they've done it a few times, they may just want to be left alone for this part. You might be amazed at what they come up with! This can take some time, and the children can do this in the bathwater, writing on each other before their backs are wet.

Making Magick

Spellcasting is both a craft and an art. Be creative when working magick, and always feel free to substitute ingredients based on the tables of magickal correspondences and what simply feels right to you.

The Least You Need to Know

◆ There are two types of ritual bath: purification and enhancement.

◆ You can take a purifying shower before working magick if you haven't the time for the full bath ritual.

◆ As with other types of spells, candles, herbs, incense, stones, and oils can be selected to boost your bath spell.

◆ Another way to boost your spell is with color correspondence, using food coloring to color your bathwater.

◆ You can create ritual baths for your children; just use commonsense precautions for their safety in the bathtub.

Chapter 21

Breaking the Spell: Purging Negative Energy

In This Chapter

◆ What is a binding spell, and is it ever okay to use it?

◆ Witch balls and other deflectors of negative energy

◆ How to break a spell—yours or someone else's

◆ Spells for prevention and protection

Binding spells are very serious, and are not generally used by most witches under *any* circumstances. Still, there may be times that call for some binding of energy and we'll talk about these in this chapter. We want to make sure you think about binding negative energy, rather than people.

We'll also tell you how to break a spell that has been worked on (or by) you, and we'll give you some spells of prevention and protection to deflect and remove any negative energy that comes your way.

Binding Spells

We can think of almost no circumstances under which it is okay to perform a *binding spell* on a person, though this is what is most often meant by binding. Why? Well, because a binding spell controls someone else's behavior, and it's not really anyone's place to do this. We very often cannot see the whole picture—binding someone may be unfair to them, and it could cause them more harm than you intended, getting you caught up in some negative karma. If you work a binding spell out of anger or fear, this energy and your act may come back to haunt you (threefold). Let's first talk about binding *energy* instead of binding *people*. Negative energy can be caught or deflected.

> **Words of Power**
>
> A **binding spell** is one you work to stop someone or something from doing something.

Here is a spell that creates an "energy trap" that you can use so that no negative energy that happens (or is sent) your way gets to you. This is a more general application of the wellness/headache spell you learned in Chapter 18.

Take some copper wire that is thin enough to coil into a small spiral and do so. Dig a hole (or several holes) in your yard. In each hole, bury a copper coil while chanting:

> *There shall be no cause to fear,*
>
> *All negativity stops right here.*
>
> *Bad energy shall here be caught,*
>
> *All ill will shall come to naught.*
>
> *By Lord and Lady and power of three,*
>
> *As I will, so mote it be.*

You may need to recharge this spell, and if you have the need for these copper negative energy containers again, you can reuse the ones you buried—as long as you remember where they are! You'll need a piece of obsidian, which is a stone that absorbs negative energy. One by one, place the obsidian on top of the buried copper coils and chant:

> *Obsidian, here I do place thee,*
>
> *To cleanse these tools of negativity.*
>
> *Again they will work to catch all negative energy,*
>
> *And from ill will, this place shall be free.*

By Lord and Lady and power of three,

As I will, so mote it be.

Now your copper coils have been cleansed and recharged and are ready to reabsorb negative energy near your home.

> **For Protection** _____
>
> This is a book primarily for those new to magick, and binding spells are really not for beginners. In fact, they are best done by a functioning community (perhaps a coven), so that the judgment of many people can help to mitigate personal emotions in discovering the best course of action. If it is clear to a community of people, for example, that one person in a partnership is being physically abusive, perhaps the community can act with a binding spell. *But binding spells should not be worked by one person, except under dire circumstances.*

When to Use a Binding Spell

We just went through this, right? The answer is *don't*. It's just not okay to do binding spells on people. You may think you know of a circumstance where it would be okay, but we doubt that (in times of war, *maybe*). Look for ways to change the situation from your perspective and work magick toward that end. If you're in an abusive relationship, for example, and there's no question that it's physically or emotionally abusive, we urge you to get help. Seek refuge with friends and family members, find assistance from government sources, and look for recourse through legal channels. If you want to work magick around the situation, work a protection spell for yourself (see later in this chapter) or do a spell to deflect negative energy, but don't do a binding spell on the other person involved. It's not an ethical thing to do, and it's not okay to ask the powers of the natural world to come in and bind the free will of another living being. It's a violation of the Wiccan Rede. So especially if you're emotionally involved with the person you're considering binding—which could really cloud your judgment—please reconsider working any binding spells on people.

That said, we'll give you a few examples of spells binding *negative behaviors*. Be sure that the behavior is one you should bind. It should be something very specific and something that affects you directly. Perhaps you have a neighbor who keeps putting toxic pesticides on your lawn (he or she can't stand your dandelions). This is behavior that directly affects you, and once you've tried to reason with your neighbor and your neighbor persists with this behavior, you might consider binding this specific behavior of your neighbor. Don't do a binding spell if you haven't already spoken to your neighbor; the binding spell should really be your last recourse.

To bind this behavior, write it down on a piece of paper. Don't be general. Write down specifically what you want to bind. Not, "I want my neighbor to stop ignoring my requests," but "My neighbor must stop putting toxic pesticides on my property." Roll this paper up and bind it with a ribbon or cord. You might choose a black cord, which works generally for banishing, or white, to bring purity and positive energy into the situation, or you might choose a color based on the situation. Because this example relates to the earth, we might choose a green or brown cord.

Now visualize the behavior being bound, chanting:

> *Halt this unwanted behavior today,*
>
> *Make it cease, without delay.*
>
> *Begin this work at my request,*
>
> *Lord and Lady do your best.*
>
> *An it harm none, we shall see,*
>
> *As I will, so mote it be.*

Keep the tied paper on your altar, so that you can take the spell apart if you need to. You may want to do this once the behavior has stopped. (See the section on disassembling or breaking spells, later in this chapter.)

You might also want to help someone bind a behavior of theirs, if they ask you to do so. If you have a friend, acquaintance, or co-worker and you know they have an addiction to alcohol, drugs, or food, don't do a binding spell to release them from this addiction unless they ask you specifically to do so. We wouldn't even ask them if they'd like help—we think they should ask you for help before you think about working magick for them. And if someone does ask for magickal help with their addiction (or other negative behavior), know that you aren't obligated to work magick on their behalf. In fact, you should make sure you really feel comfortable doing so before you agree to help, and this means considering the person, the behavior they want to change, and any other circumstances. Has this person tried to change the behavior on his or her own? Does he or she seem sincere?

CAUTION

For Protection

It's generally okay to work magick to help someone who asks for your help controlling their negative behavior, but binding spells are serious. Other spells can be worked to help people break addictions (see Chapter 18). And the person has to agree to do their share of the work—he must throw away his cigarettes or seek counseling, for example.

How serious is the negative behavior? Is it something you should do a binding spell for, or is it something he might need other magickal help with (a talisman, a self-confidence spell)? As always, be sure of your intention before working magick.

Deflecting Negative Energy

We gave you a spell to contain negative energy; now we'll do a few to *deflect* negative energy. We really like "witch balls," which are glass balls hung inside or outside the home to deflect negative energy. You can make one of these using a clear glass (or mirrored glass) holiday tree ornament. Tree ornaments are especially useful for this work because the top of the ornament has an opening, allowing you to fill the ornament. Choose a round ornament and then select materials to place inside. You might choose herbs and stones for their protective correspondences. The opening of the ornament is quite small, so your stones will have to be small as well. You might also choose some metal for the ball—metal absorbs or reflects energy. Nails or a small key would work. If your ornament is clear, you might want to place some reflective materials inside as well, perhaps tinsel or aluminum foil.

Once you have the ingredients for your witch ball, you can put it together. Do so inside a magick circle. When your ball is finished, chant:

> *Round and round and round it goes,*
>
> *Negative magick away it flows.*
>
> *Past my home and back to ground,*
>
> *No negative energy here can be found.*

Now you are ready to hang your witch ball in a window, where it will reflect any negative energy that passes by. You might also hang it outside, though a witch ball made in this way is quite breakable. You can make as many witch balls as you like and hang them in the windows of your home.

Another good general deflection spell is to sit comfortably with your eyes closed, visualizing yourself bathed in a column of white or light blue light. Visualize that this light is so pure and protective that the surface is like a mirror, reflecting any unwanted energy coming its way.

> **Making Magick**
>
> Cultures all over the world have folk-magick traditions about how to "avert the evil eye." This is basically the same as deflecting negative energy. Some of these are amulets in the shape of eyes or hands or often spheres like the witch balls described in this chapter. Blown-glass fishing floats, which can sometimes be found on beaches, are also popular for this purpose.

Good energy flows through the column easily. See the negativity bouncing off your "shield" and chant:

> *I am bathed in pure white (blue) light;*

> *All ill is deflected by the Lady's might.*

You could also create a deflective amulet to carry with you. Purchase a small mirror from a craft store and sew it onto the front of a white or silver pouch. Fill the pouch with "reflective" herbs and stones, such as a hematite stone. Charge the amulet with this chant (which could be used for any kind of amulet):

> *All negativity shall be repelled,*

> *Any unwanted energy is dispelled.*

Breaking Spells

If you are certain someone else has cursed you (and how exactly would you know— that person is not necessarily going to announce it to you), it's time to go into ritual and work some counter-magick. *Remember the Law of Three before you go any further.* The other person has made the unwise choice of working negative magick, and the laws of the universe will be handing them some hard lessons (threefold). So there is no need to "get back at them," because the Lord and Lady make sure everyone learns the karmic lessons he or she needs to learn. This may take many lifetimes for some (*most!*) people.

You *can* ritually deflect the negative energy that may be coming at you. (We say it *may* be coming at you, because someone who has chosen to do something this stupid likely bungled his or her spell.)

Spellcasting

Power is a powerful word. Just telling someone they have no power over you or a certain situation is a powerful counter-spell. That was the case in the movie *Labyrinth*: The secret the girl undergoing the initiatory journey had to discover was that the gallant older gentleman (played by David Bowie) had no power over her.

Casting Your Counter-Spell

It will be best if you can go into this ritual with something to represent the person or the spell that you are concerned about. A small representation such as a doll or a stone that you associate with the person you feel is causing the problem would work. Cast your circle, call the quarters, and call in ancestors to help and guide you and deities who you feel are appropriate for this work.

Take the representation that you will be using and present it to each Element as you would when blessing a talisman:

> *By the power of Earth, this* [stone, doll, etc.] *represents* [the person's name] *energy that s/he is sending toward me.*

(Repeat for each Element.)

Now place this representation in front of you (on the altar or in the middle of the floor, wherever you are working). With your wand, finger, or athame, circle the representation widdershins (counterclockwise) three times as you chant:

> *Any negative energy* [the person's name] *may be sending,*
>
> *The Lady and Lord do my defending.*
>
> *Negative energies be bound,*
>
> *None here will be found.*
>
> *By the power of three,*
>
> *So mote it be.*

You may also want to create a deflective protection amulet for yourself, as described later in this chapter.

Spellcasting

Add a piece of obsidian to your medicine kit and carry it with you wherever you go. This stone absorbs negative energy and is great to have available—you never know when you'll need to take care of some negative vibes in a hurry!

Breaking Your Own Spell

What if you want to break your own spell? Well, first let us say we hope this never happens to you. If it does, it may be a sign that you need to think your spells through more carefully and be certain that you really want to work magick, before doing spell-work.

Your own spells are actually easier to break than someone else's. If your spell involved an object, such as a poppet or a cord, you can break the spell by taking apart or unknotting the object within your magick circle.

Bring the object—we'll use a poppet as our example—into your magick circle and take it apart, chanting:

> *As this poppet I dismantle,*
>
> *Ground its magickal energy.*
>
> *Discharge the energy from magickal use,*

Retract the spell that was its purpose.

As I will, so mote it be.

Once you have taken the poppet apart, take the objects and ask each Element to release the magickal energy from them:

By power of Earth, these objects be

Free of magickal energy.

(Repeat for each Element.)

Now burn or bury the parts of the poppet and the spell is completely undone.

If you worked a spell that did not utilize an object, you will need to verbally retract the spell. Look back at your Book of Shadows for the particulars of the spell. You'll want to be as specific as possible, so that you break the spell you intend to break and not a different one! Here's a generic chant for such an occasion (for your spell, you should change the chant to reflect the particulars of your spell):

Energy to work my spell I sent,

I now retract thee my will to bend.

Earth absorb and ground this energy,

Let it harm none,

As I will, so mote it be.

Spellcasting

You can take a ritual bath to cleanse yourself from negative energy or for protection. Make an herbal infusion for the bath, using herbs for purification and protection, such as burdock, clove, fennel, hyssop, myrrh, parsley, rosemary, or sage. For more on ritual baths, see Chapter 20.

As a final step to break your spell, you might stand in your magick circle and go widdershins (counterclockwise to release negative energy) to each quarter, asking for the aid of each Element:

Element of Earth, ground my spell,

Element of Water, wash away the energy,

Element of Fire, burn the energy of my spell,

Element of Air, blow away the energy.

Now your spell is broken and the energy you sent out has been safely grounded.

Prevention and Protection Spells

There may be times when you feel the need to protect yourself, either from a specific person or thing or perhaps more generally. While you may not have enemies, you can't be sure that others will operate following the Wiccan Rede as you do, and you may also wish to protect yourself from negative energy in general.

There are infinite ways to do this, and every culture throughout time has had some favorites. Mirrors and witch balls use the reflection principle, reflecting negative energy just as these objects reflect light. In many cultures small mirrors are sewn onto clothes to protect the wearer.

You can create charms to hang in your house and talismans that you hang, wear, or carry. Or you might work simple energy spells to create protection around you and those you love.

A magick circle is a protective shield that you can cast around your house and strengthen whenever needed. You can also cast one around you personally with the intention that it will come with you as you move about that day.

To do this, cast the circle deosil (clockwise) around you (using your finger, wand, athame, or whatever you like to use), and saying:

> *I cast this circle round and round,*
>
> *To follow me as I walk the ground.*
>
> *Come with me where I go today,*
>
> *Protect me while I move through the fray.*

Making Magick

Aurora and another witch cast a magick circle around themselves before going into a correctional facility where they minister to Wiccan inmates. This environment is very energetically and emotionally charged. The magick circle moving with them allowed them to move freely, knowing that they had a bubble of spiritual protection around them.

When you are finished with the work of the day, dismiss the circle with a widdershins (counterclockwise) movement, saying, *"The circle is open, but unbroken. I thank you for protecting me."*

The following spell is a good one to protect your car as you travel. Close your eyes and envision your car. See yourself casting (with your athame or whatever you usually use) a magick circle around the car deosil (clockwise). See a sphere of blue protective light growing around the entire car as you cast. Now chant:

> *As I cast so is this car,*
>
> *Safe and held though I go far.*

If you feel a general need for protection, try this spell. First stop and ground yourself: Close your eyes and feel your chakras aligned, with their center core shooting deep into the earth where it grounds your energy and infuses you with the power and protection of the earth. Once you are well-grounded, envision your guardian spirit hovering directly over you, protecting you. You can call for your guardian's protection with this chant:

> *Guardian, guardian, come to my aid,*
>
> *With you on my side I shall not be afraid.*

Remember to "feed" your guardian later with food, tobacco, dancing, or whatever form of gratitude you feel is appropriate.

To create a protective talisman that you can wear, carry, or hang in your house, take a small piece of fabric in a color you associate with protection (perhaps black). You can sew it into a small pouch, or simply bundle the items in a square or circle of cloth and tie it up with cord when you're done. If you intend to wear the talisman, you might want to take the time to sew a small pouch, though if it is to be hung in a house or car, careful stitching becomes less important. If you wish to have the special protection of the specific spirit or deity you will be calling, you can sew a charm to the outside of the pouch to represent this entity, such as a small silver moon, wolf, bear, or dragon.

Have your fabric and all the ingredients you need ready when you cast your magick circle. Include stones that ground negative energy, such as obsidian and malachite. Include herbs and resins that you associate with protection as well (tobacco, bay, vervain, angelica, sage, or rosemary).

Now cast your circle and call the Elements. Call ancestors and Lord and Lady. Make an announcement of your intention, such as the following:

> *Lord and Lady, ancestors, Elementals of the four directions, I call you here to bless this protection talisman, that I will be strong and safe, and able to continue doing your work.*

Then, in your sacred space place the items in the pouch or fabric and close it up. Now hold the talisman over each Elemental representation on your altar for that blessing:

> *Blessings of Air be upon this talisman.*
>
> (Do the same for each Element.)

You now have a powerfully blessed protection talisman.

No matter how many spells you've worked to take care of the negative energy in and around your home, your car, and yourself, you still have to take every practical precaution to protect yourself. Don't let magick make you overconfident and careless! Do a safety check in your home a few times a year: Are your window locks in working order? Do you have flashlights and extra batteries around? Is the lighting outside your home adequate? What kind of locks do you have on your doors? A spell can't take care of these problems for you. Take your safety seriously, and take every precaution—magickal and mundane!

You now know how to protect yourself from anything negative that comes your way. We hope you'll only need these spells for prevention and purification and that you won't ever feel the need to bind another person. The magickal energies of the universe are powerful and positive, and if you work with them, you can become part of this great energy that is the All. This book may have been your first step on the magickal path, and we hope it is but one of many. May your magickal journey be long and fruitful!

The Least You Need to Know

- ◆ A binding spell can be worked to stop negative behavior or energy.

- ◆ You should not do a binding spell on a person, only on specific behaviors, and even this takes careful consideration of the damage your spell might do.

- ◆ Spells to absorb or deflect negative energy can be used around your home.

- ◆ You can create a spell to break another spell—yours or someone else's.

- ◆ Protection spells and amulets can be made for specific purposes or for protection in general.

Appendix A

Glossary

Air   One of the four Elements, associated with knowledge.

Akasha   The fifth Element. The energy that exists in everything; also called spirit.

All   The Lord and Lady; the energy present in everything in the universe.

altar   Surface for practicing rituals and magick; most often made from natural materials, such as wood.

amulet   A small, tangible spell; an object invested with magickal power. A rabbit's foot and a four-leaf clover are folk amulets. Amulet and talisman are often used interchangeably.

ankh   The Egyptian symbol of life.

asperging   Method for cleansing by sprinkling with saltwater or other blessed water; could be done to a person, thing, or place.

asteroids   Material left over from the creation of our solar system; more than 10,000 of them orbiting on a belt between Mars and Jupiter have been named. A number of asteroids are named after Roman goddesses (Ceres, Juno, Pallas Athene, Vesta).

astrological sign   Also signs of the zodiac; twelve signs of the calendar year based on the position of Earth on its path around the Sun.

astrology   The study of the heavens, all of its planets and stars, and their cycles as they relate to human affairs and Earthly events.

athame   A ritual knife used to direct magickal energy, cast a magick circle, and invoke the Elements. Usually represents the Element of Air, associated with knowledge.

aura   The color of a living thing's energy, created by the secondary chakras—thousands of energy centers in the body that flow into the seven primary chakras. The aura is influenced by emotions and general well-being and changes color accordingly.

binding spell   A spell worked to stop someone or something from doing something. It can also be used to bind negative behavior or energy.

birth chart   A chart showing the position of the planets at your exact time and place of birth. Your birth chart has 12 houses which correspond to 12 areas of your life. Each house is ruled by a planet or planets (depending on the position of the planets when you were born).

blessing   Spell to empower oneself and/or send positive energy into the world or to another person.

Blue Moon   The third Full Moon in a season when a season has four Full Moons rather than the traditional three (one per month).

boline   Knife with a sickle-shaped blade often used for harvesting herbs.

Book of Shadows   Notebook in which to record the specifics on spells cast, dream diaries, and personal reactions to rituals.

cakes and wine   Refers to the time at the end of a ritual when food and drink are consumed to ground and nourish the participants. A portion is always offered to the Lady and Lord. Traditionally cookies and wine were used, but this food and beverage can be anything, such as bread and water.

candles   Used specifically to work magick (candle magick) or as an element of a spell. Color correspondences are used in working candle magick, and the candle can be *dressed* with essential oils and herbs.

carrier oil   Used to dilute an essential oil. Good carrier oils include almond, jojoba, and vegetable oils.

Celtic Tree Calendar   Based on the lunar year and includes 13 months, each named for a tree. In this calendar the year begins after the Winter Solstice (Yule).

Celtic Wicca   Wiccan tradition following Celtic and Druid beliefs.

censer   A receptacle used for burning incense.

Cernunnos   The Celtic Stag God, god of nature, animals, wild places, and fertility.

chakras   Wheels of light; the seven primary energy centers of the body: lower abdomen, navel, solar plexus, heart, throat, forehead (third eye), and crown. Grounding exercises align the chakras.

chant   Spoken or sung incantation used in working spells. May or may not rhyme.

charge   Method of imbuing an object or person with a certain energy. Usually, magickal tools are charged before use. Charging can be done by laying the object out under the light of a Full Moon to receive the energy of the Goddess (or in full midday Sun to receive the energy of the God).

Charge of the Goddess   A speech often used in Wiccan rituals, this is the words of the Goddess, who entreats her followers to be joyous and free. Usually spoken by the High Priestess after drawing down the Moon.

cleanse   To purify and rid of negative energy. Performed by ritual using smudge, incense, asperging, or sweeping.

comet   Heavenly bodies made of ice and dust. Comets do not usually come very close to Earth and so appear to move slowly.

cone of power   A way of containing and "packaging" the energy channeled when creating magick or working a spell. The energy rises in the form of a cone that can then be sent elsewhere.

consecrate   To bless or dedicate to a magickal purpose. Performed by ritual.

cords   Tool for working magick; a length of string or other cord. Color correspondences are commonly used in cord magick.

coven   A group of witches who choose to practice their religion together.

crystal   A kind of stone distinguished by its structure. Crystals have been revered by people since the dawn of time.

cup (chalice)   Used in ritual and on the altar to hold wine or saltwater. Represents the Element of Water, associated with emotions, fertility, and the Goddess.

decoction   The method of extraction in preparing herbs for use in magick using boiling water.

dedicate   To promise to follow the Wiccan Rede (*"An it harm none, do what ye will"*), respect the Lord and Lady, and follow the magickal path, dedicating oneself to the greatest good for all. Any time between the New and Full Moon is a good time for dedication.

deosil Sunwise, in the Northern hemisphere, the clockwise direction. This direction raises and attracts positive energy.

Diana's bow The period in the Moon's cycle when just a sliver of the New Moon's crescent appears. Thought to be a good time for working magick related to new projects and to ask for blessings on new projects, a new home, etc.

Dianic Wicca Goddess-centered feminist Wiccan practice that evolved from the feminist movement of the 1970. Mainly a for-women-only tradition.

divination A way of opening a door of communication with the spirit world or your higher self, a method of prognostication. Runes, pendulum, and Tarot cards are commonly used tools of divination.

dragon's blood A type of resin that comes from the fruit of a tropical Asian tree. In past times, it was an important ingredient in varnish. Today it is mainly used as incense. Mixed with water and/or essential oils, you can use dragon's blood as a magickal ink.

drawing down the Moon The traditional way within a coven of invoking and drawing the Goddess into the High Priestess, who becomes the Goddess incarnate and channels the Goddess for everyone's benefit. However, this ritual can be done by anyone wishing to imbue themselves with Goddess energy.

dressing Preparing a candle for its part in a spell. May include inscribing it with words, runes, or other symbols, or adding oils or herbs.

dumb supper A ritual of connection with the honored dead, involving preparing a meal and setting the table for everyone present as well as for the honored dead. The meal is served and consumed entirely in silence, allowing the presence of whatever spirits need some sustenance to make themselves known. An ancestor altar might also be created.

Earth One of the four Elements, associated with the body, prosperity, and nature.

eclectic A modern, personally defined approach to the practice of Wicca, in which teachings are taken from various traditions.

Elementals Spirits associated with each of the four Elements. Often represented as gnomes (Earth), sylphs (Air), salamanders (Fire), and undines (Water).

Elements Four traditional components of Western magick: Earth, Air, Fire, and Water. All things are energetically composed of some balance of these four.

Esbat A Moon ritual of celebration for the Goddess, usually held on the Full Moon. Often refers to any coven meeting that is not on a Sabbat.

familiar   A specific animal whose spirit wants to work with you. The animal will be helpful to you in many ways, particularly in working magick.

Fire   One of the four Elements, associated with relationships, power, and passion.

Full Moon   The most powerful lunar phase for working magick. The power of the Goddess is at its height during the Full Moon. The energy of the Full Moon can be harnessed for three days before and after the date of the Full Moon.

Gardnerian Wicca   Wiccan tradition of Gerald Gardner and his High Priestess, Doreen Valiente, often thought of as co-creators of modern Wicca. Gardner is the author of *Witchcraft Today* (Arrow Books, Ltd., 1954), which introduced generations to the practice of Wicca.

Georgian Wicca   Wicca tradition founded by George Patterson in California in 1970.

Great Rite   The Wiccan ritual honoring the ultimate magick: sex. Often performed between a priestess and a priest who are already married or are partners in life. It is also performed in symbolic form, where the athame represents the male and the chalice represents the female.

Gregorian calendar   Standard Western calendar introduced by Pope Gregory XIII in 1582.

grimoire   A book of magickal information, including spells, chants, and facts on herbs, oils, and crystals. The word *grimoire* is derived from the French *grammaire*, meaning grammar, a work that includes the basic elements of an art or science.

grounding   The vital process of connecting your energy with Earth's energy, to allow energy to flow freely and fully for the specific purpose of a spell. Many witches use a tree visualization for this purpose.

handfasting   The Wiccan word for wedding or marriage ceremony. A handfasting can also be a temporary commitment. This type of handfasting is an agreement between both partners to stay together for a year and a day. Handfastings are held for couples and recognize relationships between men and women, between two women, and between two men. The term refers to the hands of the two people being "fasted" together.

heliotrope   A lovely, sweet-smelling purple flower that gets its name from its tendency to turn toward the Sun.

high priestess (high priest)   Head of a coven who organizes, coordinates, and leads the group. Referred to as "first among equals," the high priestess usually has greater knowledge and experience than other members of the coven.

Honorian script   Another name for Theban script, also known as the witches' alphabet. In the sixteenth century, Cornelius Agrippa (in his *Three Books of Occult Philosophy*) attributed the Theban alphabet to Honorius.

incense   Material burned to scent the air in working magick to boost the working and alter one's consciousness. Comes in many forms, including sticks, cones, and powder. Associated with the Element of Air and also, when burning, Fire.

infusion   A method of extraction in preparing herbs for use in magick using water (not boiling).

intuition   Knowledge based on insight or perception.

invocation   Method of (politely) calling a spirit into a magick circle and asking for its assistance.

karma   Spiritual cause and effect. The law of karma says that everything we do (good and bad) comes back to us.

kitchen magick   Magick worked using food and everyday items found in the household kitchen.

Lady   The Goddess, the female facet, the more creative and inclusive side of the All, which is often thought of as having three aspects: Maiden, Mother, and Crone. These aspects represent the different stages in a woman's life, aspects or personas that each person has within and manifests or calls on as needed.

Law of Three   Whatever you do will return to you threefold. Similar to karma.

Lord   The God, the male facet of the universe. Represents a more active and playful side of the All. The Lord's three life phases are Nature's Royal Prince, King, and Elder.

lunar calendar   Calendar indicating the phases of the Moon in its 29½-day cycle. Removed from the monthly view of time, this is a calendar of lunations.

lunation   The period of time averaging 29 days, 12 hours, 44 minutes, and 2.8 seconds elapsing between two successive New Moons.

lunar phase   Stage of the Moon's 29½-day cycle, from New to Waxing, Full, and Waning. Each phase is best for particular types of magick.

magick   The word for the practice in which the power of nature is harnessed toward a particular goal. Note the spelling: The *k* on the end distinguishes it from stage magic of the kind performed by people like David Copperfield.

magickal name   The name selected upon one's dedication to magick, representing the magickal self and the magickal path.

magickal record   A record of any ritual or magick one practices, including details such as the day, date, time, and place of the event, as well as the lunar phase, the elements of the ritual, and personal information on the emotional and physical health of the practitioner of the ritual or magick.

magick circle   A sacred, protected space in which one can feel safe when working magick.

maypole   A tall pole erected to dance around for a Mayday celebration (known to Wiccans as Beltane). Ribbons are tied to the top and the dancers weave a colorful pattern around the pole as they dance.

medicine pouch   Any pouch used to contain magickal items.

meteorites   The parts of a meteor that do not burn up as the meteor enters Earth's atmosphere and land on Earth.

Moon sign   The astrological sign the Moon is in. The Moon visits each sign of the Zodiac for about 2½ days each month. Just as you have a Sun sign, you also have a Moon sign, the sign the Moon was in at your birth.

mundane   Worldly; of the world, as opposed to *magickal*.

New Moon   Phase of the Moon beginning when it is not visible in the sky. Good time for starting new projects.

pentacle   Five-pointed star inside a circle, symbol of Wicca and the five Elements: Air, Fire, Water, Earth, and Akasha (spirit). When used as a tool (made out of metal or clay), it is the representative of the Element of Earth; associated with the body, prosperity, and nature; used for protection and healing rituals.

Pictish swirl   A form of writing based on ancient Pictish symbols. The Picts lived in northern Scotland as early as the third century.

planetary hours   A concept in which each of the 24 hours in a day is ruled by one of the following planets: Sun, Venus, Mercury, Moon, Saturn, Jupiter, Mars. This makes each hour best-suited for a particular type of magickal working.

poppet   Doll created to represent someone or something with a magickal purpose in mind; very useful in healing spells and in bringing about change in oneself.

power   The energy for action within everything in the world. Used in working magick.

power animal   A representative animal, a spirit helper connected with all the animals of its kind, that is called on for assistance in working magick.

power points   Chakras or energy centers of the body.

practical magick   Magick used in everyday life, such as kitchen magick. A simple way of weaving magickal energy into your life.

quarters   Each of the energies of the four cardinal directions: North, East, South, and West. "Calling the quarters" refers to calling the energies of the directions (and their associated Elements: Air, Fire, Water, and Earth) into your magick circle.

Reclaiming tradition   Wiccan tradition that emphasizes egalitarian control, environmental and feminist values, and political awareness; speaks about the difference between *power over* and *power with*. Popularized by Starhawk, author of *The Spiral Dance* (Harper & Row, 1979).

retrograde   A term used when a planet appears to be moving backward through the zodiac when viewed from Earth. This is an illusion caused by our view of the planets from Earth as they orbit the Sun.

ritual bath   For purification, a means of cleansing the body and the mind prior to performing a ritual or magick. For enhancement, a bath spell to create or enhance a property or situation, such as health or prosperity.

ritual sweeping   A method of cleansing a space by actually sweeping it or by visualizing and enacting the sweeping away of negative energy.

Roman alphabet   The alphabet that evolved from ancient Rome and is used in writing most Western European languages (as opposed to magickal alphabets such as Theban script).

runes   An ancient alphabet, sometimes called the Viking Oracle; used as a tool of divination by the Vikings since it was given to the Norse God, Odin.

Sabbats   The eight Wiccan holidays: Samhain (Halloween), Yule, Imbolc (Candlemas), Eostara, Beltane, Litha, Lughnasadh (Lammas), and Mabon.

sacred space   A place where one feels powerful and confident, and that has been cleansed and consecrated for working magick.

scrying   A term meaning *divination* by allowing your eyes to see shapes or forms in a hazy object; it allows for communication with the other side.

Seax-Wicca   Wicca tradition founded by Gerald Gardner protégé Raymond Buckland in 1973.

shaman   Priest(ess) or healer in a traditional culture.

sigil   A magickal symbol; a stamp or seal used as a magickal signature.

simple   An infusion made from one single herb.

skyclad   Clad in only the sky, or naked. Many witches (especially Gardnerians) prefer to practice magick this way.

smudge   Herbs burnt for the purifying and cleansing aspects of the smoke.

solitary witch   One who practices alone and is not a member of a coven. Also called a solitaire.

spellcraft   A form of magick practiced by many magick-workers to change themselves or the world around them. It utilizes the interconnection of all things (the All) to harness natural power to bring about a particular outcome. A spell is like a prayer, but when casting a spell, you may call on a variety of forces—gods, goddesses, Elementals, stones, herbs, helper spirits—to help achieve your goal.

Sun sign   Also called signs of the Zodiac; the astrological sign at the time of your birth, based on the position of Earth in its annual path around the Sun. There are 12 Sun signs.

Theban script   Also called Honorian script and the witches' alphabet, it is not linked to any spoken language. Gardnerian witches often use it in rituals, and many witches use it to inscribe their tools.

timing   Important aspect of planning successful spellwork, including day of week, time of day, planetary hour, Moon phase, Moon sign, and Sun sign.

tincturing   A method of preparing an herbal medicine by extracting compounds from the herb with alcohol.

vervain (*verbena officinalis*)   A flowering perennial native to Europe, Asia, and Africa. The name come from a Latin word meaning sacred leaves, twigs, or boughs of olive, myrtle, or laurel. The plant has been used for centuries for its aphrodisiac and healing qualities. Vervain was sacred to the Druids and the Romans.

visualize   To envision, or create mental pictures of something.

void of course Moon   When the Moon is between signs, having left one and not yet entered another. Not a good time to work magick or start new projects.

wand   Magickal tool made of wood and used to direct magickal energy. Usually associated with the Element of Fire and with power and passion, the wand is a phallic symbol.

Waning Moon   The Moon as it decreases in visibility from Full toward the New Moon. A good time for working banishing magick.

Water   One of the four Elements, associated with emotions, fertility, and the Goddess.

Waxing Moon   The Moon as it grows in visibility from New toward Full. A good time to work magick to grow, enhance, or increase.

Wheel of the Year   Depicts the natural cycle of life and death through all eight of the Sabbats.

white-handled knife   Knife used for cutting during a ritual (unlike the ritual purpose of the athame), often called a white-handled knife to distinguish it from the athame (which is often black-handled). Used for any kind of cutting or carving required while working magick or performing a ritual, such as cutting yarn, cords, or candle wax.

Wicca   A nature-based spiritual practice.

Wiccan Rede   *"An it harm none, do what you will."* The most basic tenet of Wicca, governing the ethics of Wicca and spellworking. The Wiccan Rede means that you can do what you will, provided no one is harmed in the process—including yourself.

widdershins   Anti-sunwise; in the Northern hemisphere, the counterclockwise direction. This motion releases and disperses energy and also releases negativity.

witchcraft   Refers to anyone working with energy, magick, healing, and ritual in any culture around the world; not necessarily *Wiccan*.

Yin and Yang   Names for the active and receptive (masculine/feminine, outward/inward, conscious/subconscious) energies in the universe, symbolizing the harmony of opposites.

Resources

Here are some resources we think you'll find useful as you delve into the study of spellcraft, magick, and Wicca. We've included a number of books and several websites, as well.

Books

Adler, Margot. *Drawing Down the Moon: Witches, Druids, Goddess-Worshippers, and other Pagans in America Today.* New York: Arkana, 1997.

Allrich, Karri Ann. *Cooking by Moonlight: A Witch's Guide to Culinary Magic.* St. Paul, MN: Llewellyn, 2003.

Beyerl, Paul. *A Compendium of Herbal Magick.* Custer, WA: Phoenix, 1998.

———. *The Master Book of Herbalism.* Blaine, WA: Phoenix, 1984.

———. *A Wiccan Bardo, Revisited: Initiation and Self Transformation.* Kirkland, WA: The Hermit's Grove, 1999.

Blamires, Steve. *Celtic Tree Mysteries.* St. Paul, MN: Llewellyn, 2002.

———. *Glamoury: Magic of the Celtic Green World.* St. Paul, MN: Llewellyn, 1995.

———. *The Irish Celtic Magical Tradition.* San Francisco: Aquarian Press, 1992.

Buckland, Raymond. *Buckland's Complete Book of Witchcraft.* St. Paul, MN: Llewellyn, 1986.

Budapest, Zsuzsanna. *The Grandmother of Time: A Woman's Book of Celebrations, Spells, and Sacred Objects for Every Month of the Year.* San Francisco: Harper, 1989.

Cabot, Laurie. *The Witch in Every Woman: Reawakening the Magical Nature of the Feminine to Heal, Protect, and Empower.* New York: Delta, 1997.

Coney, Norma. *The Complete Candlemaker: Techniques, Projects & Inspiration.* New York: Sterling, 1999.

Conway, D. J. *Wicca: The Complete Craft.* Berkeley, CA: Crossing Press, 2001.

Cruden, Loren. *Compass of the Heart.* Rochester, VT: Destiny Books, 1996.

———. *Coyote's Council Fire.* Rochester, VT: Inner Traditions, 1995.

———. *Medicine Grove, A Shamanic Herbal.* Rochester, VT: Destiny Books, 1997.

———. *The Spirit of Place: A Workbook for Sacred Alignment: Ceremonies and Visualizations for Cultivating Your Relationship with the Earth.* Rochester, VT: Inner Traditions, 1995.

Cunningham, Scott. *Cunningham's Encyclopedia of Crystal, Gem and Metal Magick.* St. Paul, MN: Llewellyn, 1988.

———. *Cunningham's Encyclopedia of Magical Herbs.* St. Paul, MN: Llewellyn, 1985.

———. *Earth, Air, Fire & Water: More Techniques of Natural Magic.* St. Paul, MN: Llewellyn, 2000.

———. *Earth Power: Techniques of Natural Magic.* St. Paul, MN: Llewellyn, 1999.

———. *Living Wicca: A Further Guide for the Solitary Practitioner.* St. Paul, MN: Llewellyn, 1993.

———. *The Magic of Food: Legends, Lore, and Spellwork.* St. Paul, MN: Llewellyn, 1990.

———. *Wicca: A Guide for the Solitary Practitioner.* St. Paul, MN: Llewellyn, 1988.

Curott, Phyllis. *Book of Shadows: A Modern Woman's Journey into the Wisdom of Witchcraft and the Magic of the Goddess.* New York: Broadway Books, 1999.

Drew, A. J. *Wicca Spellcraft for Men.* Franklin Lakes, NJ: New Page, 2001.

Dunwich, Gerina. *Herbal Magick.* Franklin Lakes, NJ: New Page, 2002.

———. *The Wicca Garden: A Modern Witch's Book of Magickal and Enchanted Herbs.* New York: Citadel, 1996.

Eisler, Riane. *The Chalice and the Blade.* San Francisco: Harper, 1988.

Farrars, Janet, and Stewart Farrars. Eight Sabbats for Witches. Blaine, WA: Phoenix, 1996.

———. *A Witches' Bible: The Complete Witches' Handbook.* Blaine, WA: Phoenix, 1996.

———. *The Witches' Goddess: The Feminine Principle of Divinity*. Blaine, WA: Phoenix, 1987.

Feldman, Gail Carr, and Katherine A. Gleason. *Releasing the Goddess Within.* Indianapolis, IN: Alpha Books, 2003.

Feldman, Gail Carr, and Eve Adamson. *Releasing the Mother Goddess.* Indianapolis, IN: Alpha Books, 2003.

Gardner, Gerald. *High Magic's Aid.* 1949. Rpt. Hinton, WV: Godolphin House, 1996.

———. *The Meaning of Witchcraft.* 1959. Rpt. St. Paul, MN: Llewellyn, 1988.

———. *Witchraft Today.* 1954. Rpt. New York: Citadel, 2004.

Gerwick-Brodeur, Madeline, and Lisa Lenard. *The Complete Idiot's Guide to Astrology, Third Edition.* Indianapolis, IN: Alpha Books, 2003.

Greer, John Michael. *Natural Magick: Potions and Powers from the Magical Garden.* St. Paul, MN: Llewellyn, 2000.

Grimassi, Raven. *Encyclopedia of Wicca and Witchcraft*. St. Paul, MN: Llewellyn, 2000.

———. *Spirit of the Witch: Religion & Spirituality in Contemporary Witchcraft*. St. Paul, MN: Llewellyn, 2003.

———. *The Wiccan Mysteries: Ancient Origins & Teachings*. St. Paul, MN: Llewellyn, 1997.

Harner, Michael. *The Way of the Shaman*. San Francisco: Harper, 1990.

Harvey, Graham, and Charlotte Hardman. P*agan Pathways, A Guide to the Ancient Earth Traditions*. London: HarperCollins, 1996.

Hugin the Bard. *A Bard's Book of Pagan Songs*. St. Paul, MN: Llewellyn, 1998.

Klein, Tzipora. *Celebrating Life Rites of Passage for All Ages*. Oak Park, IL: Delphi Press, Inc., 1992.

Knight, Sirona. *Empowering Your Life with Wicca*. Indianapolis, IN: Alpha Books, 2003.

Leek, Sybil. *The Complete Art of Witchcraft*. New York: Signet, 1971.

Leland, Charles. *Aradia: Gospel of the Witches*. Trans. by Dina and Mario Pazzaglini. 1897. Rpt. Blaine, WA: Phoenix, 1999.

Liguana, Miria, and Nina Metzner. *The Complete Idiot's Guide to Wicca Craft*. Indianapolis, IN: Alpha Books, 2004.

Lipp, Deborah. *The Elements of Ritual: Air, Fire, Water & Earth in the Wiccan Circle*. St. Paul, MN: Llewellyn, 2003.

Llewellyn's 2004 Magical Almanac. St. Paul, MN: Llewellyn, 2003.

McColman, Carl. *The Well-Read Witch*. Franklin Lakes, NJ: The Career Press, 2002.

McCoy, Edain. *Sabbats: A Witch's Approach to Living the Old Ways*. St. Paul, MN: Llewellyn, 1994.

Melody. *Love Is in the Earth: A Kaleidoscope of Crystals Update*. Wheat Ridge, CO: Earth-Love, 1995.

Miller, Arthur. *The Crucible*. 1953. Rpt. New York: Penguin Putnam, 1976.

Morrison, Dorothy. *The Craft: A Witch's Book of Shadows.* St. Paul, MN: Llewellyn, 2001.

———. *Everyday Magic: Spells and Rituals for Modern Living.* St. Paul, MN: Llewellyn 1998.

Mother Tongue Ink. *We'Moon '04: Gaia Rhythms for Womyn.* Estacada, OR: Mother Tongue Ink, 2003.

Mountainwater, Shekhinah. *Ariadne's Thread: A Workbook of Goddess Magic.* Freedom, CA: Crossing Press, 1991.

Oppenheimer, Betty, and Deborah Balmuth. *The Candlemaker's Companion: A Complete Guide to Rolling, Pouring, Dipping, and Decorating Your Own Candles.* North Adams, MA: Storey Books, 1997.

Passmore, Nancy F. W. *The '04 Lunar Calendar: Dedicated to the Goddess in Her Many Guises.* Boston: Luna Press, 2003.

Paterson, Helena, and Margaret Walty. *The Celtic Lunar Zodiac.* St. Paul, MN: Llewellyn, 1997.

Pickering, David. *Cassell's Dictionary of Witchcraft.* London: Cassell, 1996.

Poulson, Willow. *Sabbat Entertaining: Celebrating the Wiccan Holidays with Style.* New York: Citadel, 2002.

Ravenwolf, Silver. *To Light a Sacred Flame: Practical Witchcraft for the New Millennium.* St. Paul, MN: Llewellyn, 1999.

———. *To Ride a Silver Broomstick: New Generation Witchcraft.* St. Paul, MN: Llewellyn, 1993.

———. *Solitary Witch: The Ultimate Book of Shadows for the New Generation.* St. Paul, MN: Llewellyn, 2003.

———. *To Stir a Magick Cauldron: A Witch's Guide to Casting and Conjuring.* St. Paul, MN: Llewellyn, 1995.

Scott, Laura, and Mary Kay Linge. *The Complete Idiot's Guide to Divining the Future.* Indianapolis, IN: Alpha Books, 2003.

Somé, Malidoma Patrice. *The Healing Wisdom of Africa.* New York: Penguin Putnam, 1998.

———. *Of Water and the Spirit: Ritual, Magick, and Initiation in the Life of an African Shaman.* New York: Penguin Putnam, 1995.

———. *Ritual: Power, Healing, and Community.* New York: Penguin, 1997.

Somé, Sobonfu. *Falling Out of Grace.* El Sobrante, CA: North Bay Press, 2003.

———. *The Spirit of Intimacy: Ancient African Teachings in the Ways of Relationships.* New York: Quill, 2000.

———. *Welcoming Spirit Home.* Novato, CA: New World Library, 1999.

Starhawk. *The Spiral Dance: A Rebirth of the Ancient Religion of the Great Goddess.* 1979. Rpt. New York: Harper, 1989.

Starhawk, and Hilary Valentine. *The Twelve Wild Swans.* San Francisco: Harper, 2001.

Stine, Jean Marie. *Empowering Your Life with Runes.* Indianapolis, IN: Alpha Books, 2004.

Thorsson, Edred. *Futhark, a Handbook of Rune Magic.* Boston: Red Wheel/Weiser, 1988.

Tognetti, Arlene, and Lisa Lenard. *The Complete Idiot's Guide to Tarot, Second Edition.* Indianapolis, IN: Alpha Books, 2003.

Vale, V., and John Sulak. *Modern Pagans, An Investigation of Contemporary Pagan Practices.* San Francisco, CA: Re/Search Publications, 2001.

Valiente, Doreen. *Charge of the Goddess.* Brighton, UK: Hexagon, 2000.

———. *Natural Magic.* Blaine, WA: Phoenix, 1985.

———. *Rebirth of Witchcraft.* Blaine, WA: Phoenix, 1989.

———. *Witchcraft for Tomorrow.* Blaine, WA: Phoenix, 1988.

West, Kate. *The Real Witches' Kitchen.* London: Thorson's, 2002.

Wood, Jamie. *The Wicca Herbal: Recipes, Magick, and Abundance.* Berkeley, CA: Celestial Arts, 2003.

Zimmermann, Denise, and Katherine A. Gleason. *The Complete Idiot's Guide to Wicca and Witchcraft, Second Edition.* Indianapolis, IN: Alpha Books, 2003.

Websites

Coven of Cythrawl website, with Theban script download:
www.coven-of-cythrawl.com/Theban_script.htm

Culinary Teas, for reusable cotton tea bags:
www.culinaryteas.com/Tea_Accessories/1219.html

Hob's Green, Pagan site with downloadable lunar and Celtic Tree calendars:
www.hobsgreen.com

Isis Books, metaphysical store website:
www.isisbooks.com

Music by Kenny Klein: *The Fairy Queen* (with Lori Watley), *Gold of the Autumn, High Grows the Barley, Muses*; for details, see Kenny's website:
www.drak.net/kennyklein/index.html

Ladyhawk's Trasures, Wicca supplies:
www.ladyhawkstreasures.com

Lord Kyl's fonts, downloadable runes and other fonts:
fonts.lordkyl.net

My Witch Shop, ritual tools and supplies:
www.mywitchshop.com

Pentacle Press, blank Books of Shadows, metaphysical items:
www.pentaclepress.com

Reclaiming Tradition website:
www.reclaiming.org

Snake and Snake Productions, lunar phase cards and calendars:
www.snakeandsnake.com

Sobonfu Somé, for information on ritual training with:
www.sobonfu.com

Sunrise and Sunset, calendars and calculators for sunrise and sunset:
www.sunrisesunset.com and planetaryhours.com

U.S. Naval Observatory:
aa.usno.navy.mil/data/docs/RS_OneDay.html#forma

The Wiccan-Pagan Times website:
www.twpt.com

Poppet Pattern

This is a very simple pattern for a poppet. Trace this figure twice onto whatever material you decide to make your poppet out of, and then cut it out and sew the two halves together, leaving enough of the border unsewn (perhaps at the head) to fill the poppet with the herbs, stones, writing, and other materials you've decided to use for your spell. You can also fill the poppet with cotton batting or other material to plump it up, if you prefer. Adapt this pattern as you like—you can photocopy it to make it larger or smaller, for instance, and you can add yarn, hair, or other details if you feel it necessary for your spell. Choose your poppet material based on its color (and pattern) and on flammability—if you're planning to burn your poppet, don't buy polyester material! (For more on poppets, see Chapter 3.)

As you begin to sew your poppet, you might chant:

> *This poppet now I do endow*
>
> *Each stitch with magickal power.*

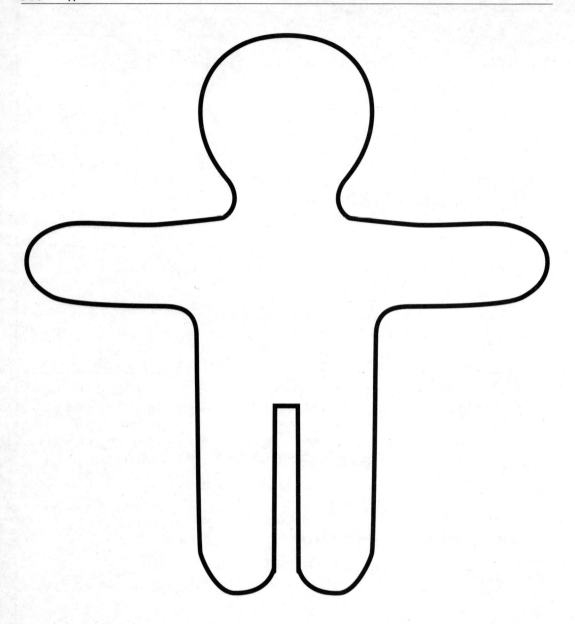

Index

D

R

X-Y-Z

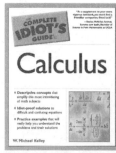